PREFACE

In the past, it was generally considered a creditable achievement if you could master one skill in the workplace. The farmer knew farming, the weaver learnt weaving, and the shoemaker definitely kept to his last. Even today, most people are fully occupied with the furtherance of their own careers and invest heavily in the training and dedication which is required. And yet suddenly everyone is being confronted with the dilemma of computer systems. They have invaded every labour, education, social and leisure environment and have critically affected the way in which actual work is carried out. It is a situation where the majority of people involved may not be fully effective, and that frequently includes the managers and controllers who are nominally responsible for the introduction or running of these systems. Consider some of the following possibilities:

Scenario 1: You head up a reasonably efficient French Department, and now the Dean has told you that the Faculty is going to computerise all of its administration. Although you know next to nothing about computer systems, he proposes to make you a member of the development monitoring team. What do you do?

Scenario 2: After a number of years in the Data Processing department, you have finally made it to the 'Senior Analyst' grade. Your first job is to set up a maintenance database for the local transport company. Unfortunately, you do not have the wholehearted cooperation of the workers' representative for the company's garage. How do you handle it?

Scenario 3: The analyst is bursting to try out his latest strategic techniques on your organisation, while all you want is some maintenance on your well-tried and accepted COBOL business packages. How do you redirect his efforts?

If any of these strikes a familiar chord, then this book is for you.

It is essentially addressed to anyone who may participate at any level in the introduction, development, testing, installation, operation and maintenance of an information system - and in today's marketplace that means just about everybody.

The emphasis is not on providing answers. Every situation and every problem is unique and will almost certainly warrant an individual response. However, it is the ability to ask the right sort of questions that is important. This applies as much to the designer as to the user, and it this ability that will maximise the chances of developing a system which matches the originating need. As a follow on, this implies that the designer or developer of the system must be able to communicate effectively with the project manager and end user. These two points lead directly to the major objectives of the book:

❏ The end-user has to become familiar with, and use the language of, the system developer. This will ensure that his or her expertise and understanding of the end requirement is fully expressed during the feasibility and development phases.

❏ The developer must recognise that system projects are about people, not objects. It is the client staff who will be using the end product, not the other way round.

In line with the above objectives, the book has been written with three types of reader in mind:

The User: This is the major class, where someone is about to participate in a system development programme, without knowing too much about information systems, computers or any of the associated skills. This is often the eventual manager or user of the system. The lack of knowledge may lead to stress and panic levels which are both unacceptable and unnecessary. The material that follows will allow someone to contribute as a useful member of the development team even though there is no prior expertise in system models, hardware or programming.

The Developer: He or she will be conversant with the models and tools used in carrying out a design. However, the formal print-outs and presentation slides which are his stock-in-trade do not necessarily include an appreciation of the human factors involved in a successful implementation of a system. This book aims to redress that situation.

The Student: Current undergraduate and graduate courses tend to concentrate on the mechanical processes related to system operation. This is where the data is extracted by technique A, collated and defined in model B, drawn on diagram C and subsequently entered into table D. All this is valid material for simulating a system, but may not, perhaps, dwell sufficiently on the real-life problems that can arise from such modelling. Again, this book will offer a perception of the wider impact of the design process.

By way of a summary, the discussion will be centred on the skills needed for successful multi-party control and technical administration of a system development program. The material covered will be related to setting up a viable framework for the project, making competent decisions at a strategic level and

Developing Information Systems

The Manager's Guide

Michael Bronzite

 SIGMA PRESS

Wilmslow, England

 ADDISON-WESLEY PUBLISHING COMPANY

Wokingham, England · Reading, Massachusetts · Menlo Park, California · New York
Don Mills, Ontario · Amsterdam · Bonn · Sydney · Singapore · Tokyo · Madrid
San Juan · Milan · Paris · Mexico City

Cover designed by Design House, Marple Bridge, Cheshire
Typeset and designed in Great Britain by Sigma Hi-Tech Services Ltd, Wilmslow,
Printed in Malta by Interprint Ltd, Valletta

First printed 1991

ISBN: 0-201-56883-7

British Library Cataloguing in Publication Data
A CIP catalogue record for this book is available from the British Library

Library of Congress Cataloguing in Publication Data available

defining the nature of the required development activities. In other words, we shall be concentrating on the development *structure*, rather the development process itself.

Apart from the first one, each chapter will be terminated by a number of questions which will utilise the material given in the body of the work. The subject matter is often subjective or judgmental and it follows that there can be no right or wrong answer or solution. There are however sensible answers and solutions, and to reach those is the real objective, both for the questions and indeed for the entire book.

As is customary in this type of book, references and quotations have been taken from various sources, and some well-known application programs have been mentioned or described. May I stress that the copyright for all quotations used in this book remains with the original owners, who have generously allowed me to quote from their material. With regard to commercial software, these have been used as examples of their class, and no recommendation or promotion is to be implied. However, for all that, I have been helped by a number of people and in particular I would like to thank Malindi Lamb of Intasoft Limited and Phillip Crabtree of Excelerator Products Software Limited. Both were unstinting in their efforts to help me.

M.B. London

Dedication:

For Ruthie

CONTENTS

THE REQUIREMENT SPECIFICATION

MANAGING THE DESIGN

1

Frame of Reference

User Department Management

A reluctance to become involved with the underlying technical concepts of computers is also exhibited by managers in control of departments which are, or will be, making use of information systems. Just as a well-defined policy environment is critical for success, so it is equally important to have the active participation of those responsible for operating the system once it is implemented.

Bibliography: Reference 1 p.9

The Causes

Middle- and upper-level managers with no background in software are often given responsibility for software development. There is an old management axiom that states "A good manager can manage any project". We should add: "if he or she is willing to apply effective methods of control, disregard mythology, and become conversant in a rapidly changing technology". The manager must communicate with all constituencies associated with software development – system requester, software developers, users, and others. Communication can break down because the special nature of software and the problems associated with its development are misunderstood.

Bibliography: Reference 3 p.24

1.1 The Objectives

All over the world, there is feverish activity. Nippon Electric Company, Saudi International Bank, Siemens, Imperial Chemical Industries, Alcatel, General Motors all have something in common. They are all either *installing,* or *upgrading,* or *replacing* information systems for use within their organisations. And virtually every other type of business, from the international consumer chains down to the local doctor and plumber, is doing exactly the same. Which suggests two things. In the first place, there must be an awful lot of demand out there, with a corresponding shortage of good consultants, designers and application engineers. Secondly, there has to be a large number of users who are probably not getting the best possible system because they do not know enough to participate in the definition process. It is a situation where system related projects can go disastrously wrong.

This book, first and foremost, is about preventing failure in the design and installation of information systems. It cannot *guarantee* success, but it will provide coherent guidelines, identify priorities and establish checklists that will make that result more probable. It has been written to help all those in the system application chain, from the consultant strategist and installation engineer to the client manager and end user. In addition, the Systems Engineering, Office Automation or general MBA student will find that it provides a useful reference to a number of existing disciplines.

In general terms, it is only by having all the parties knowledgeable and involved, by ensuring that the system designer, end user and project coordinator are all talking on the same wavelength that one can start to think of a 'successful' system enterprise. This is not a book about computer system design – there is a more than adequate coverage on that topic in every local bookshop and library. It is a book primarily concerned with laying down an effective *framework* for system design and development. It will allow people round a table, with differing disciplines, to understand and use common terms and prioritise objectives in a constructive manner. It will also concentrate on how to achieve smooth interworking between all the different groups, how to communicate effectively and how to respond constructively in a crisis situation. In short, how to form an effective project team for systems engineering, how to coordinate and manage it, and how to provide a programme for the satisfactory operation of that team. The qualifications needed to read the book are the usual ones for the participation in development programmes: common sense and an open mind.

This first chapter is used to justify and explain the ground-plan for the rest of the book. After reviewing a stereotyped 'project failure', the basic priorities relating to any project are identified. This, in turn, is followed by an introduction to the topic of project 'balance' which serves to identify and harmonise the different objectives of all the people working on the project. The chapter ends by reviewing the scope of the book and introduces the model projects that will be used to illustrate the points raised in the text. However, before we go into all this detail, let's take a quick look at the state of system engineering today.

The current situation is roughly analogous to the great stockings or 'nylons' market of the late forties in Europe. After a period of intense shortages, the 'client' base created an unlimited demand pressure and any street peddler with his suitcase full of 'Evening Rapture' or 'Svelte' was in a commanding position. No talk then of quality control or how long before the product defects occurred. No talk then, and not too much now in today's world of system application. However, today there is one additional mystery. It is regrettable but understandable if an ex-TV mechanic fails to design and install a reliable multi-user system. On the other hand, it is decidedly more surprising when the professionals, the experienced well-trained national and international consultant organisations also end up with egg all over their faces – and some very disgruntled clients. It doesn't happen every time, but it does happen all too frequently – and the quotations at the beginning of all the chapters after this one give some measure of the magnitude of the problem. These journalists' reports tend to suggest that we have not yet reached the promised land in the field of modern system design. Even with the use of technically experienced personnel, advanced hardware technology and the latest structured design philosophy – the difficulties have still not gone away. Delays stretch through years, costs overrun by tens and hundreds of millions of pounds (or dollars or swiss francs) and client frustration reaches the level of consulting a legal advisor for possible redress in the courts. No, we are not quite at the promised land yet.

In reality, there is only one question of any importance. Let us assume that you are about to be involved in a new system which is going to be developed (whether your interest is as a consultant or designer or client is not really important). The only bottom-line query is: how do you ensure that this will *not* be one of those disaster projects where the time and cost overruns are matched only by the lack of client satisfaction and the poor performance of the resulting package?

This is the question that is to be addressed in the chapters that follow.

1.2   The Conventional Project

The brief scenario in this section is intended to capture the possible limitations and misuse of a standard life cycle approach. The formal description of a life cycle is given in Chapter three, but what follows is an example of the classical disaster project. Hopefully, it will be recognised as a parody, rather than a reality comparable to some past experience.

Initial Conditions

Company ABC, the well known manufacturer of sludge, decides to install an advanced data handling system and calls on the consultants XYZ, among others, to quote for the task. The ABC management knows little about computers, while XYZ knows nothing about sludge. The only clear fact is that the contract will go to the lowest bidder.

Feasibility Study

XYZ wins the contract and sets out to define the operational requirements of the new system. By virtue of cost and time constraints, two new graduates are assigned to the task and told to report back in three weeks with a product specification. The staff at ABC are sensibly hostile as they fear potential redundancies while the management cannot provide inputs as they do not know what they want. On the contrary, they are waiting to be told what to do by the 'experts'.

Design Phase

The XYZ Managing Director's nephew has the import agency for 'TableStore', a new experimental relational database system under development in Syria. For purely technical reasons, the ABC project is universally judged an ideal candidate for this system and translation of the handbooks from Arabic is organised. At the same time, two other new graduates (the first two are now system analysts in a rival organisation) set about creating a logical design from the Requirement Specification. It doesn't seem necessary or cost effective to waste the time of ABC personnel with joint meetings, so progress is rapid. The small hitch, when the translation agency is found to have retired to Portugal with his friend, is overcome with the nephew offering to do the job himself. The resulting handbooks are not particularly legible but they are available. The very competitive IBM clone from the 'IMB' organisation in Manila is selected for the hardware since the three year comprehensive guarantee was thought to offer high security. A problem arose with the new 'Tab' query language, but this is found to be because the database was originally configured to work only with the Unix operating system. A conversion team is put on the job and a necessary rescheduling exercise carried out. Shortly after, ABC are somewhat surprised to hear that the cost estimates have now quadrupled and that handover would be about one year late. However, what can they do – they are in the hands of the experts?

Installation

The product documentation is written by two new graduates (the previous pair having left to become independent consultants) based on whatever they could find in the project files. The Product Specifications have the resulting advantage of brevity. The ABC management are relieved that their new system is finally ready and allocate one whole weekend to switch over from their existing system to the new one. In fact the handover would have been completed by the following Wednesday, but for the realisation that the accompanying free operating system 'IMB-DOS' is not exactly the same as 'MS-DOS'. But it only takes two weeks overall. The real pity was that ABC had not realised that system tests are only carried out after installation (as XYZ explain, for cost-effective reasons). The three months without either the old or the new system did not bankrupt the company – but it was a close run thing.

Maintenance

With a new found wisdom, ABC appoint a manager for information systems. Within a few days of the appointment he is able to report that the new system is not being used properly (the staff cannot understand the documentation), it does not relate to the operations of ABC and in any case it appears to have a number of serious faults associated with it. In addition, the hardware overheats and replacement parts from Manila have yet to arrive. In effect, the system is unworkable. His recommendations of a) immediately dropping the system and b) not using XYZ again are reluctantly accepted by senior management. On the other side, XYZ will not complain. After all, as their brochure subsequently points out, the state-of-the-art system developed for ABC had proved to have very low maintenance costs throughout its entire use with that company.

What Should be Expected?

It is unlikely that the totality of mistakes shown above has ever happened in real life (even though some individual parts of the story may be familiar). Nevertheless, as a cautionary tale of how the elements of a project life cycle can be misapplied, there are a number of conclusions that ought to be drawn. In particular, a well-run project leading to a satisfactory system application will usually require:

❑ Competence by all parties

❑ Involvement of all parties

❑ Shared responsibility at every stage of the project

❑ Top-down planning to meet overall objectives

❑ Product selection based on value, not price

❑ Defined and agreed deliverables

❑ Good communications and sound crisis management

There are others, but these are the main points and most of these topics will be discussed later on in the book. If we look for the key common denominator in this list, virtually all the above objectives will tend to be covered if the interacting parties are considered to be competent, i.e. trained, experienced and motivated.

Now let's move on to the more critical situation where the parties *are* taken to be competent. Consider, for the moment, any major international consultancy company. Think about their personnel selection mechanism. The shortlist, the structured interviews, motivation testing, qualification requirements, references for character and work experience. There really seems to be no way that an unsuitable or inexperienced person can join the staff. And then think of the promotion process – the track record, the face fitting, the competition ... What I am suggesting at some length is that, if anyone can afford one of these groups and if they send a team comprising a project manager and system analysts down to the local site, then it is reasonable to assume that this team will be adequately professional. In other words, they should not be compared to the system team of XYZ in our parody of a few pages back. Similarly, whoever is using these specialists, say, an international merchant bank, then the odds are that it will have its own data processing department, staffed by a similar process, and again not to be compared with ABC. Under these circumstances, it is surely fair to suppose that everyone can relax since none of the faults highlighted above can possibly happen.

And yet project failures continue to occur.

Of course, it may be assumed that most projects are eventually installed with a reasonable degree of mutual satisfaction – but, whether the this assumption is valid or not, there are certainly some rogues that do go spectacularly wrong. And it is this assertion, that project failure can still result from a partnership between serious professional organisations using the latest techniques, that is central to the nature and scope of the book. Is there any support for this hypothesis? The following extracts are taken from the Bibliography references:

Ref. 6   p.3   (A strong advocate of structured design)

'Projects which exceed their projected development costs and their projected development timescales are very often the norm. In addition, many of these systems do not provide the facilities the user required.'

Ref. 7   p.ix   (A strong opponent of structured design)

'It is disheartening and frustrating that despite all the grandiose proclamations of problem solution and noble efforts of users, analysts, and developers that requirements definition remains a highly imperfect process. ... Users complaints of "unworkable", "not what I wanted", or "incomplete" remain a recurring and common user reaction to delivered applications.'

Ref. 24 p.xi (Project Manager's viewpoint)

'Time and again when acting as a consultant, or in a trouble-shooting role, or when in general contact with numerous computer installations, I came up against the same difficulties and mistakes in the way that organisations manage their DP. It seems unfortunate that so many managers must learn the hard way, struggling through similar learning processes. The aggregate money wasted by all these organisations is frightening!'

To recap the current position. As with many other human activities, there is a definite risk associated with investing time and effort in system development for commercial application. In other words, it can go badly wrong. The discussion to date has identified a number of attributes whose presence in a project will almost certainly be needed to ensure project success. However, in addition, there seems to be another missing ingredient, 'factor x', which is also required if the project is to reach an acceptable conclusion. The nature of this factor will shortly be evaluated, briefly in section 1.4 and in a more detailed manner in Chapter 4. However, before we go much further, it will be helpful to identify the key assumptions underlying this book and, further, to define just what is meant by 'success'.

1.3   The Working Basis for System Engineering

Ever since the word 'structured' became respectable, Life Cycles have been the philosophical mainstay for system engineering models. We illustrated the basic format in section 1.2 and will tread carefully through this subject in Chapter 3, but can pause now to say a few words in more general terms.

Broadly speaking, the term 'system engineering' is used here to signify the study, introduction or modification of a computer based data processing and storage system. 'System design' is more restrictive and is considered as a sub-element of system engineering. It starts from a requirement specification document which itself was the result of a feasibility study. From this document, the logical design is implemented which is then followed by the physical design. This in turn leads to post design activity i.e. test, implementation and maintenance. All these terms are described in more detail in the chapter on Development Strategies, but an outline of all this activity is given in Figure 1.1.

From this figure, three major phases can be crudely identified in any project that the combined personnel have to undertake:

❑ Feasibility Study

❑ System Design

❑ Post-Design Activity

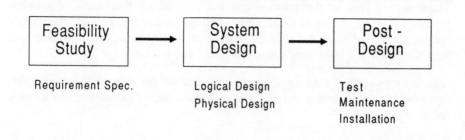

Figure 1.1: System Engineering

Most books concentrate at length on the middle portion i.e. on the various procedures, techniques and objectives of system design. This situation should be kept in mind as we review below the three maxims of system development.

The Three Maxims

To be fair, there is no theoretical underpinning or mathematical basis for the arguments in this section. However, what follows is backed by the best system arbiter there is: the cost impact of ignoring it.

MAXIM 1 *The most important work has been completed before System Design begins.*

The most crucial deliverable in the entire exercise is the one that is written right at the outset of the project. This is the Requirement Specification, the document based on client inputs that defines the objectives for the project. In the current context, the terms 'important' or 'crucial' are applied in the sense of 'cost to repair'. For this discussion, Figure 1.1 can again be used since it covers the classical representation of the entire project. Consider the injection of an error into each phase of the project and evaluate the cost of repair assuming that the system has already been handed over to the client. An error in physical design, say, will involve new physical design, new test, and new installation phases. This is clearly cheaper than an error at the logical design stage which will involve added activity to clear the error. On this basis, an error in the Requirement Specification is the most expensive type of all, and it is this which renders it 'important'. It is clear that money and time spent on minimising errors in the very first phase of a project is going to be the most effective.

MAXIM 2 *The most expensive work begins only after the System Design activity has been completed.*

The faults may get *introduced* during system design. However, they get corrected and *paid for* after handover when the budget goes under the catch-all title of

Maintenance. This is the point where the cost of all that study, discussion, planning, meeting, coding, checking, testing, documenting and training is completely overtaken by the ultimate expense of clearing those few inevitable little bugs that are found after installation. But don't take my word for it:

'The maintenance of existing software can account for over 60% of all effort expended by a development organisation. The percentage continues to rise as more software is produced.'

Ref. 3 p.322

'... 50% of DP budgets allocated to maintenance, more than 50% of programmer time consumed by ongoing maintenance, and more than $30 billion spent on maintenance annually worldwide ...'

Ref. 28 p.13

Other sources confirm this general position. Perhaps these figures will not apply in every case – it could be that some organisation uses special techniques. But for most people it looks like a good working hypothesis.

MAXIM 3 *The Other Party is also human*

This should be written in large gold lettering in every office where information systems work is being carried out. A decision is an agreement between people. An installation is a sign-off or acceptance by an individual or group of persons. Put at its simplest – when a client and the consultant fall out, the eventual satisfaction levels tend to be low regardless of physical artifacts such as price, performance or quality of documentation.

The statement may appear obvious, but the implications are far reaching. A project, any project, is inherently a complex group activity which relies on effective interaction and agreement at a multi-participant level. It is the only way to effect decisions and to progress through the programme of the project. (What causes a project break-up seems very similar to the forces at work in a personal relationship under stress. Perhaps project managers should have an individual Marriage Guidance Counsellor on their advice team). In any case, this orientation, where the coordination of the project is seen as a team activity, will have a far-reaching effect and will be covered in some depth in Chapter 4.

The Two Criteria

There is one other item in this section which will also affect the thrust and arguments put forward later in the book. This relates to the topic of 'success' and the provision of a sensible definition for this term. Given a moment's thought, it should be clear that success is a human-related quality. Machines don't care. Only humans strive to achieve – and measure the result by some arbitrary benchmark.

So 'success' could be agreed by all the parties to be: system handover on schedule with a performance level of 7.7 or better. Or it could be: containment of the documentation budget to 150,000 DM. All this means that success is related to the group activity eventually satisfying perceived group targets. At a pragmatic level, we can describe this with two time-related criteria:

CRITERION 1 *Your opposite number is prepared to recommend you to his colleagues – two weeks after handover.*

Notice how this definition cuts right across technical or budgetry performance. It is a measure, simply, of the other party's satisfaction. There is an obvious catch in that the criterion is judgmental. It assumes that the other party is a) a free agent i.e. under no extraordinary pressure from his or any other organisation and b) is competent to assess the results of the project in a meaningful way. That aside, cost and time overruns, for example, *simply do not matter in themselves*. If, in the opinion of the other party , there was a legitimate reason for them, then they will not affect his judgement. Of course, the undeniable overall objective is the gainful use of the new system for the commercial body that requested it in the first place. But legitimate delays and enhancements can so modify the original requirements, that a mechanical benchmark of success is no longer a fair test. If the above definition still seems unacceptable, turn the proposition round. How successful is the project where every formal parameter of an agreed Requirement Specification has been met, but, for whatever reason, the parties involved are now violently antagonistic to each other? The practical answer has to be: not very much. After all, a well-nigh perfect system (whatever that means) can be installed on site and made operational. However, if the client is determined not to use it and goes on emphasising all the real or imagined defects, then the usable timescale for that system is going to be very limited.

There will always be exceptions. It has always been true that there are a few people who consistently push forward the frontiers of the possible. With these rare individuals – for example engineers such as Isambard Brunel, Barnes Wallis or Steve Jobs – the output product will be of overriding value for its own sake, regardless of how many toes are trodden on. However, for the rest of us ordinary mortals, satisfying our project partners is still probably the best measure of having done all that is reasonably possible in some mutual undertaking. That is the first criterion. It is an assessment, as we discovered earlier, before the major part of the expenses are established (maxim 2) and, in effect, before the real quality of the design is shown under operating conditions. This leads to the second measure:

CRITERION 2 *Your Opposite Number is still prepared to recommend you to his colleagues – one year after handover.*

It implies that there has been good on-going cooperation in the post-delivery timeframe and that the performance, downtime, support facilities and corrective costs were all within reasonable bounds. This is a more stringent hurdle, and one might wonder just how much of the system engineering activity carried out over the last five years (and by whom?) would pass this particular test.

Naturally, this set of criteria begs the question: who cares? There are companies and consultants who will travel happily from system disaster to disaster. They survive temporarily because the demand is high or because business continues to thrive in spite of, rather than because of, all their efforts. In addition, there may be no reason for new potential partners to check the credibility of their opposite number. For all that, the bulk of new business is the result of word-of-mouth recommendations so the definitions do have some real-world significance.

In summary, the priorities and definitions laid down in this section will point the way to efficient planning of a system project. As such they have been used to formulate the main topics to be pursued in later chapters.

1.4   The Concept of Balance

It is time to discuss the nature of 'factor x' mentioned earlier. Consider again the examples given at the front of the chapter. What seems to be happening is a separation between the client and the design authority. There is a falling out between friends. (Does anyone express sentiments other that those of the warmest regard and mutual admiration – at the start of a project?) The project has to evolve in accordance with capabilities and decisions of the designers. In the same timeframe, the client retains the expectations of the original specifications. Later, the discrepancy is brought out into the open and the shock is made evident. Clearly, regular communications between the parties has much to commend it, although that cannot be the complete answer.

There is an underlying problem and it can be best illustrated by looking at the work I do for a good friend of mine, let's call him Jim. These contracts are infrequent and of a minor nature, which is probably just as well, otherwise someone might end up getting hurt. He runs a growing business, allocates a task and expects it to get done as a result. He certainly does not want to waste time with further discussions about optimised approaches or strategic considerations. Which is fine and commendable – but only up to a point! He is naturally a bottom-up sort of person – identify the problem, sort it out fast with whatever it takes (and no more), and move on. I am, conversely, top-down – identify the strata of operation that still work perfectly, work down progressively until the malfunction is identified, solve within the existing framework such that the overall system integrity is not disturbed, document, test, and only then move on. Both methods have their merit, but they are very different. The implication of all this is that, if I were ever asked to carry out an extended consultancy exercise with Jim, we would need some very frank discussion on the common style of operation, right from the beginning. If not, we would always be at loggerheads, with exasperation and frustration just round the corner.

This question of compatibility of outlook by the team members can be extended from the particular to the general. We can consider aspects of structured design as a parameter of style. Again, this subject will be covered more thoroughly in section 3.3 of the chapter on Development Strategies. However, for the moment, consider that there are two ways of treating system design: structured or non-structured (with the further possibility of some mix between the two). The former implies a high degree of order and discipline with the design requirement frozen as a snapshot in time. The latter is more flexible, relates better to the changing real world but is not easy to pin down in terms of design strategy or project schedules. Once again, it is not a matter of one method being right or wrong – they are both equally valid (or equally fraught with risk) as different possible approaches to solving the same problem.

One can visualise a single dimension or axis of style where the position along the axis indicates the degree of structure that is planned to be used for the project in question. Now, consider the participants of this project. If one member is strongly in favour of a highly structured approach and another member insists on a more flexible format then there is not going to be a lot of agreement or positive decision making on this project. We can say that the makeup of the members is 'unbalanced' for this project, in that there is strong inherent disagreement on how to proceed. In effect, we can add another dimension to the previous consideration of style, and this is illustrated in Figure 1.2.

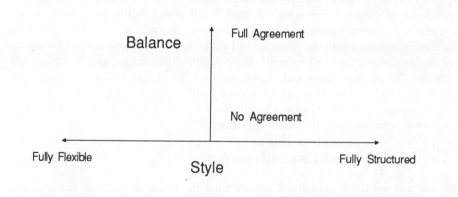

Figure 1.2: The Design Plane

A high value along the axis 'balance' implies that, whatever the methodology or approach being considered, there is a good measure of agreement between the parties on how to proceed. Conversely, poor agreement would give a correspondingly low value. This is not to say that individuals with different personal viewpoints cannot work together. What should be clear, however, is that the *modus operandi*, whatever it is, should be well defined, agreed and documented by all the parties right at the start of the project.

1.5   The Scope of the Book

So far we have identified some of the key questions that should be resolved in a programme concerned with system development. These questions have been addressed in the following major sections of the book:

Background

It is clear that a comprehensive review of the operations related to a business organisation involves both the analyst and suitable members of the organisation. Not only must all the participants be willing to give time to the project, but they must also be competent to join in the decision-making process to flesh out the programme for the project. In turn, this implies that all parties understand the main objectives and can discuss them with a common vocabulary.

To achieve this commonality of viewpoint, the first part of the book discusses the general area of system engineering along with the terms that are in standard usage for this activity. Chapter 2 gives a broad overview of the tools and techniques that are generally applied in the formulation of a Requirement Specification. They are also in common use for the subsequent work of translating that requirement into a practical system. Following on from this treatment of the more or less mechanical processes of system engineering, Chapter 3 will give a full account of the topics related to the general strategy of the development program. This, again, calls for a collective agreement on the approach to be adopted and requires a good perception of the options available along with their respective advantages and disadvantages. Finally, this section closes with a discussion of the factors that go to make good interactive balance between all the parties involved in the project. The nature of the personnel, the roles they have to fulfil and all the factors that can lead to a high degree of balance are fully discussed in Chapter 4.

The Requirement Specification

If you can get the Requirement Specification right you are well on the way to a successful system implementation. On these grounds, the next two chapters lay out the project environment that will enhance the accuracy and validity of this document. Chapter 5 is, in fact, entitled the 'environment' and it concentrates on an *ad hoc* check-list for all the items that should be should be considered when drawing up this specification. This check-list is based on the premise that factors such as emergency power-down procedures or maintenance strategies have to be considered right at the start of the design rather than half way through the programme. If they are treated as add-on modules which can be implemented after the main work is done, then the overall integrity of the system is likely to be degraded along with the problem of debugging the extra errors introduced at the late stage in the design. Chapter 6 goes on to provide a methodology for the generation of the specification. One of the problems here is the question of requirement complexity or 'solvability'. Some projects go into a cost and delivery overload because someone allowed an 'anti-gravity' clause to get into the specification. In order to work literally above the ground, you can use, for example, a plane or a balloon. They work, but are NIH (not invented here). It is much more stimulating to try to design an anti-gravity platform. It does not exist, probably not designable with current techniques, costs are unlimited and it is a real challenge as well as being enormous fun for the design staff. In the same way, an ambitious and challenging requirement for the system can provide a lot of intellectual stimulation and excitement for the design team. However, such stimulation usually comes *very* expensive, and a more disciplined approach may be less exciting but more likely to be realised within realistic schedule and cost constraints. This is the sort of problem that needs the control tools discussed in this chapter.

Managing the Design

This section is really another common sense approach to ensuring that the project remains under control of the administration team. The first part, Chapter 7, provides a basic review of parameters and procedures which will be used to meet the demands of the project programme. Chapter 8 then describes all the different strategies and methods of communication that can and should be used between interested parties for the duration of the development phase. Finally, Chapter 9 reviews the possible mechanisms that can be used to implement change control in a positive and constructive manner. In effect, this whole section is concerned with setting up a development framework that contains enough checks and balances to eliminate the possibility of a 'disaster scenario' comparable to the one described in section 1.2 above.

The Post-Design Phase

Much like taking exams or receiving an income-tax demand, the installation of a new system can be a fundamentally traumatic experience. On the other hand, there really is no particular need for a tension filled week (or month) during which Murphy's Laws run riot and your sanity is tested to beyond any reasonable limit. Planning the installation to take hardware, software and humanware frailties into account can make the transition fairly painless. In this capacity, Chapter 10 offers another check-list to ensure that all the obvious (and therefore usually overlooked) precautions can be carried out. Finally, Chapter 11 gives an airing to the subject that is the Cinderella of the whole exercise – Maintenance. By being aware of the problem areas and potential traps for the unwary, the structure of the output product can be planned right from the outset to ensure that the final system can be maintained in a cost-effective manner.

Overview

The last chapter provides a wrap-up session and goes over all the topics covered in the preceding chapters. In addition, it discusses the ideal notion of 'good design' along with the problems of practical application of the concept. The section ends with a review of the future possibilities in the field of system engineering.

1.6   The Hypothetical Models

One example is worth 10 pages of specification. In order to illustrate the principles and mechanisms defined in the following pages, they will be applied to simulations of real life situations. In this case, two examples will be addressed: a new system of data storage generated internally by the Newtown General Hospital; and the introduction of a options-generating procedure for the development of new products by the Universal Solid State corporation. In both cases, in order to keep the discussion to a reasonable length, only an outline of the real requirements will be used to highlight the processes involved. It is obvious that not everyone is concerned with hospital administration or hi-tech innovation, but, for all that, they will serve as models for most potential applications. To that end, we can provide a brief introduction to each of these cases.

First, let's take a look at the hospital model. Individual medical records databases have come into popular usage over the last few years but have often been low budget affairs which suffered from dependency on specific hardware and non-compatibility with the general hospital data processing packages. Broadly speaking, the provision of an integrated data system in a hospital-based environment still constitutes something of a daunting challenge. However, in the real world the tide is slowly turning, and for our model purposes, the surgical department of Newtown General is going to institute a database of records for handling information associated with patients while they are in the ward and theatres of the General Surgery department.

For the other situation, Universal Solid State has been having problems controlling the planning and introduction of new products for manufacture. Marketing survey results are used by a number of European subsidiaries; Design is carried out in Toronto; and Production is implemented at three factories in Korea. Bringing together all the relevant information for the regular management meetings has become a problem with a high priority rating.

At this point, both organisations have called in a team to control the proposed development projects, and have selected the All-Data consultancy group for that role. Even with the restriction that only a superficial view of the problems can be given, the simulation models will still illustrate how the principles under discussion can be applied such as to dramatically reduce the chances of project failure.

As a basis for development in subsequent chapters, it will be assumed that the decision has been made to go ahead with the projects (and how to get to that decision could be the subject of a book in its own right). In addition, it is further assumed that the management team has been called in at the initial assessment level. In both cases, it has been given the overall, if somewhat vague, brief of providing a computer based system to replace the current approach. The general assumption is that the data will be stored in tables which describe Patients, Wards and Operating Theatres on the one hand, and Marketing, Product Formats, Schedules and Documentation Configuration for the other. On the personnel side, a number of the staff in both cases have adopted the positions that a) the decision was made without consulting them, b) this will be an added burden to an already overloaded work profile and c) their job is probably under threat, anyway. We can take it from there.

1.7   Summary

The general objective of the book is to provide a ground-plan for a successful system engineering project. This chapter has outlined the disciplines needed and provided the structural basis for what is to follow. The 'disaster project' scenario reinforces the idea that a system development project must be highly structured and planned in order to avoid the more obvious traps. In particular, it identifies those qualities required to ensure success:

❑ Competence by all parties to the development

❑ Involvement by all parties

❑ Prior agreement on major policy decisions

❑ Prior agreement on all project deliverables

❑ Good communications throughout the project

In addition, we have reviewed the basic foundations of any development cycle. These will be used to help in the allocation of priorities and they are worth rephrasing here for emphasis:

Maxim 1 Getting the requirement specification right is the most cost-sensitive event of the whole project.

Maxim 2 Prepare to spend the major part of the budget after the design phase is over.

Maxim 3 The project critically involves other people and only combined team work can lead to success.

Criterion 1 If all parties are satisfied after system handover, the development programme was (probably) not a failure.

Criterion 2 If the parties are still satisfied one year after installation, then the system was definitely a success.

Following on, the concept of the 'development plane' was briefly covered. This introduces the idea that the 'style' of a project can be quantified and the related value can be used along one axis of this plane. The other axis will be a measure of the commonality of approach or acceptance of approach by all the members of the project team. Obviously, a high value along this axis will assist in achieving a good measure of project cooperation.

Consolidating all these avenues of investigation, it is clear that all parties to the project should have a sound knowledge of the general practices of system engineering; that the requirement specification should be given priority treatment compared with all other phases of the design process; that the project planning should concentrate on the effective use of all the combined resource available; and, finally, that the post-design costs must be minimised by the adoption of a suitable strategy early on in the development cycle.

These pointers have been used to structure the book, and the first area to be addressed will ensure that all parties use the same vocabulary and understand the significance of the techniques to be selected. It permits efficient, shared decision-making by providing everyone with the same background information.

One last point: with the sole exception of this chapter, the examples given at the head of each chapter are extracts from various reports printed by reputable computer newspapers over the last few years. It is possible that one or two of these quotations may contain minor errors (journalists, after all, are only human), but taken together they constitute a reliable and coherent body of data. Using this book may help to reduce the number of such reports.

2

Design Tools

£500m software waste

British users and suppliers pour £500m down the drain every year because of the poor software quality and lack of expertise.

The bulk of the waste is in error-ridden software and in user maintenance costs due to a lack of quality control at the design stage.

Computer Weekly p.1 17.3.88

MoD rejects Chots flak

The Ministry of Defence has dismissed allegations that it is wasting its time on a huge office automation project.

. . . .

Committee member Dr John Gilbert dismissed the Chots programme saying: ''I regard most of that effort as completely wasted.''

His views were supported by Horace Mitchell, chairman of the Business Equipment and Information Technology Association, who gave evidence to the select committee.

''Procedures are very long and complex and as a result what is eventually delivered is often not what the users want because requirements have changed.

Chots has already been going on for two years. It's a classic example of too much procedure obscuring what the user needs.''

Datalink p.6 9.5.88

MPs sound alarm on project's £1.2bn bill

The UK's largest civil computer project at the Department of Social Security, has gone £500 million over budget. . .

Labour's health spokesman Robin Cook said: 'It's a complete outrage. The secretary of state should be called to account.' . . .

Only last week, Peter Lloyd, parliamentary secretary for social security, described the computerisation programme, known as the Operational Strategy, as a 'magnificent achievement'.

Computing p.1 1.12.88

2.1 Introduction

The topics or mechanisms covered in this chapter are only rarely discussed in the computer press. This is not a measure of their lack of importance, but, rather, that they are so fundamental that they are virtually taken for granted. These analytical procedures that we are going to cover are mainly concerned with the formation of the *logical model* of the system. This model tends to be an abstraction of the real world in that it seeks to identify the 'what' of the system without reference to the 'how'. Thus, the *method* of data transfer between, say, departments in an organisation will not be addressed. On the other hand, the actual nature or content of the data being transferred will be fully analysed and documented. Once this model has been formalised, it is then used as a basis for the actual physical implementation that is to be installed as the final product. However, as the reports at the head of the chapter show, with or without these techniques it is still relatively easy to provide a gross overrun on schedule and budget. So it is worth keeping in mind that these techniques may take a lot of effort and a corresponding long time to implement, and this itself can cause serious problems in project implementation.

For all that, with proper use they remain powerful tools for the generation, evaluation and redesign of the logical model related to any information system. For this reason, and because of their general application, we will be spending some time in discussing their basic modes of operation. However, we had better begin with a definition of the model, since it is at the heart of everything that follows:

*The **logical model** of any information system, manual or automated, existing or planned, comprises designated data elements undergoing modification in a pre-determined fashion as they move between defined locations of the organisation.*

That doesn't completely solve the problem as it leaves open the definition of a data element. In any case, as explanations go, it may sound rather pedantic and lacking in general usefulness.

Let's start by defining the term data element and going on to establish the convention used in writing it down:

*A **data element** is any recognisable item within the information system that warrants the use of some unique label or tag to identify it. The identifier label shall comprise one or more words separated by spaces with the first letter of each word being upper case.*

Different sources will use slightly different conventions in providing a label, but the application of the data element concept will always be the same. For added clarity, in the discussion that follows, the data element will be written in *Italic text*.

We can now look at what this all means in a more informal way. An office chair, in itself, is an object – not a data element. But it will be represented in the organisation through a number of (possibly linked) data elements. Thus, this chair could turn up as a *Purchase Requisition Number* or be listed in the *Office Inventory Listing* or appear as part of the *Budget Allocation File*. These are all data elements that are connected in some way back to the original chair. In a similar way, a product marketing report will be identified by some reference number – the data element – which can then be used within a particular data system.

The 'predetermined modification' in the first definition above will consist of the way in which one date element is variously linked as it travels through the organisation. Thus, on one data path a *Patient ID Number* may be linked to a *Local Doctor ID* and an *Address*. This might be part of the *Patient Data File*. Conversely, in another modification, it could also be attached to an *Operating Theatre Number* and a *Surgeon Name*. This could, perhaps, be entered as part of the *General Surgery Listing*.

The term 'location' in the above definition also deserves a moment's consideration. There are two possible meanings. The first sense is that of physical site (i.e. Nurse Jones or, say, the Ward 217 mailbox) to which some data can be addressed. The second sense is that of a database file, say the *Patient File* table, which can be upgraded with the entry of new data. This use can be thought of as an electronic address for data. Note that from a modelling point of view, these two physically different approaches may sometimes be treated as equivalent. In that case, the differences will only reappear at the implementation stage.

Bringing all this together, we can see that the logical model is simply a convenient representation of the way data (which is used to describe real objects) is identified, joined with other data and transmitted round the organisation to particular centres or data stores.

Returning now to the topic under discussion, this chapter will provide a management overview of the more popular tools that can be applied to the field of system engineering. As considered above, their main use is in generating the logical model that makes visible all the current and planned processes that use data. In addition, they will indicate clearly the data connections or linkages that exist between different parts of the organisation under study. In yet another sense they constitute a bridge or means of communication between the analyst and the end-user. Both parties can examine the existing or proposed system by means of the diagrams generated by these techniques and can make meaningful decisions as a result of such assessments. One of the first important deliverables of such analyses and decisions is the definition of the requirement specification.

There are a number of graphic representations used for system analysis that won't be discussed here. These include Jackson Structured Design (ref. 12 p. 103), Warnier-Orr Diagrams (ref. 12 p. 107) and Decision Tables (ref. 5 p. 215). Having said that, the tools that we shall be reviewing are in common use and have proved to be very effective in recent times. These are Data Flow Diagrams (DFD), Data Dictionaries (DD) and Entity Relation Diagrams (ERD). They are relative newcomers in that they utilise analytical techniques and disciplines that have only been developed in the last 10 to 20 years. It was the continued pressure to improve the design capabilities of the analyst and to accommodate larger and more complex systems that led to their development and subsequent enhancements. Indeed, the fact that they are still being used today is a pragmatic measure of their success in meeting that objective. In addition, they also have a powerful capability as a error-checking vehicle, i.e. to highlight the presence of a built-in mistake or omission. However, for most purposes, they can be treated as simple language products, with rules of use that are optimised to provide a comprehensive description of the system.

As suggested in the first chapter, these tools may not be the complete answer for the analysis of data systems, but they are an important part of that answer. This does not imply that the end-user has to become an expert in these disciplines. However, it would be to his or her advantage if there were some familiarity with the vocabulary, methods and practices of these techniques. At the very minimum, they provide an important means of communication with the system designer.

2.2   Data Flow Diagrams (DFD)

This is a methodology for treating the system as a series of processes which modify the incoming data in some controlled manner and produce the transformed data as an output which can then be treated by other processes. The initial feasibility study is largely concerned with producing such diagrams which, in a sense, 'fix' the current data handling within the organisation. Following review and acceptance by the client, a new set of diagrams can then be generated which include all the modifications and improvements that are to be developed.

The language of Data Flow Diagrams is not complex. The four basic data elements of these diagrams are outlined in Figure 2.1. The rounded symbol portrays the process which acts on the input data and produces corresponding modified data which is either directed to another process or to a data store. The process, itself, is nearly always defined by a strong verb and an object. This effectively identifies the nature of the change going on inside the rounded box. Thus Accept Cheque or Review Budget could be legitimate process labels. But College Principal or Assess could not. Vague labels, such as Clear Problems or Process Data do not provide any real indication of the nature of the process, and their use is generally frowned upon. The arrowed lines constitute data flows and are always labelled with a relevant name which indicates the nature of the data being transferred in the direction of the arrow. The external sources and sinks of information are shown as rectangular boxes while internal data stores are represented by two parallel lines enclosing the name of the store. In this case, the nature of the data is clearly indicated in the name of the store so there is no additional need to name the arrowed line to and from these elements. There are various ways of drawing these symbols (for example: the rounded figure can be shown as a true circle in some definitions), but the differences are ones of style rather than function and are not significant.

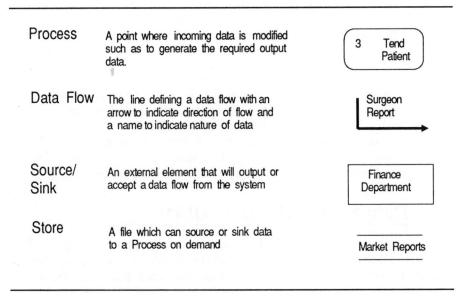

Figure 2.1: Elements of a Data Flow Diagram

A typical example is given in Figure 2.2 where the current data flow for new product start-up in Universal Solid State is outlined. We can assume that the processes under review are contained within an overall envelope which we can call *Prepare New Proposals* and which is carried out by the the Product Control Group. Note that, at this point, the latter cannot be a data element in that it is not represented anywhere on the diagram or at any other place. Then, Figure 2.2 can be explained simply in basic English terms:

❑ *Senior Management* – an external body – sends a *New Product Request* for evaluation.

❑ The initial review body will take the latest marketing information from the database *Market Reports* and examine the possibilities for a new model of an existing product or a brand new piece of equipment (*Explore Options*).

❑ The result of all this deliberation will be a reported number of possibilities (*Option List*) for further review.

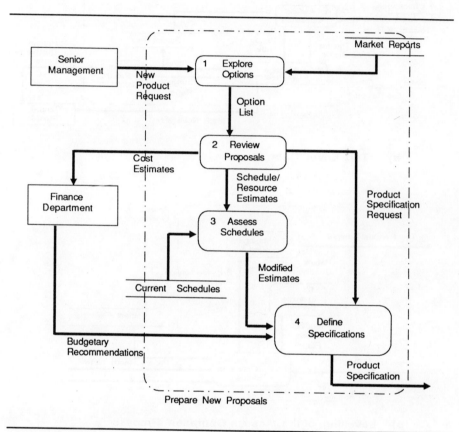

Figure 2.2: The Data Flow for the product control group

❑ The formal review will generate data – *Cost Estimates* – *that will be fed to the external Finance Department*. In addition other data will be generated, *Schedule/Resource Estimates*, and sent to Production, while a *Product Specification Request* is forwarded to the Technical Group.

❑ Production will assess the new estimates and consider them in line with existing schedules. Problems and conflicts can be screened out at this stage (*Modified Estimates*).

❑ The Technical Group will take inputs from Production, and the *Finance Department* and generate a suitable proposal for a *Product Specification*. This is then fed on to the next process.

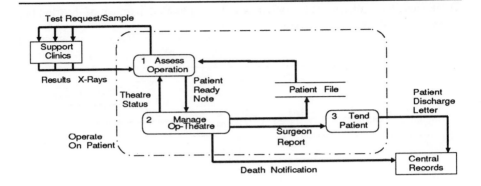

a) Top Level Data Flow

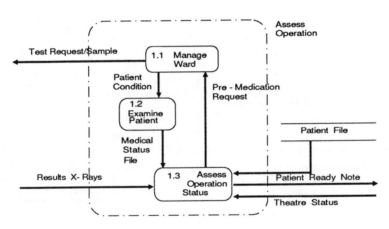

b) Levelling of the Assess Operation Process

Figure 2.3: Data Flow in the hospital

Notice that the diagram gives a clearer, graphic, image of the steps that are undertaken when selecting a new product, compared with the equivalent text-based message above. On the other hand, keep in mind that the Data Flow Diagram is simply a 'what' document: there is no indication, at this stage, of 'who' carries out any of these activities (no mention of Production or Technical Group); or 'when', or 'how long' it will all take. Further, there is no indication of sequence, that is which data flows are required before which process can be initiated.

As a second example of a Data Flow Diagram, consider the (simplified) steps taken in the Hospital to confirm that a specified operation shall take place on a particular patient who has already been admitted to the surgical ward for that purpose.

These steps are given in Figure 2.3a and in equivalent English they conform to:

❏ The ward will organise the required pre-operation samples for testing (or a request for, say, a Cardiogram) by the various *Support Clinics*, say Cardiology, and check the *Results*.

❏ Examine the data in *Patient File* and confirm that all the details there match the physical patient in the ward.

❏ Monitor the incoming *Theatre Status* note from the Surgical Administration, which establishes that the theatre is available and that all the related personnel such as Surgeon and Head Nurse are in a 'go' condition for the operation.

❏ If all indicators are positive, send a *Patient Ready Note* to the Surgical Department.

❏ After the operation, send a *Surgeon Report* to the Ward which will be considered in forming the post-operative treatment strategy. In addition, update the *Patient File* with the first results of the operation.

❏ OR, if warranted, send a *Death Notification* to the Hospital *Central Records*.

❏ Following a satisfactory convalescence, the Ward will send a *Patient Discharge Letter* to *Central Records*.

It is worth emphasising that each DFD will contain only a relatively few number of processes. This is mainly to keep the overall diagram uncluttered and easy to read. But, of course, the total number of processes in any real system will be enormous. This conflict is handled by a method of progressively expanding downward the top-most process and this is called <u>levelling</u>. The two DFDs we have discussed show the whole system as a number of processes. (The top-most diagram, which represents the complete system, consists of only one process – linked to all the external sources and sinks – and is usually given the special name of Context Diagram.) Notice that each of the processes shown in the examples is numbered: thus in Figure 2.2 the process *Review Proposals* is given the number 2, while in Figure 2.3a the *Assess Operation* process is given the number 1. There is no special priority or ordering of these numbers, it simply allows a tag or unique numerical identification for each of the processes so labelled. Now we can go down a level and look at all the sub-processes that go to make up the top-level function. In this case, Figure 2.3b shows the break-down of Process 1 – *Assess Operation* – from Figure 2.3a. The three important things to check in a lower-level drawing are:

a) The numbering is consistent:

All processes are numbered such as to indicate the top-level process from which they are derived. Thus, in the example they are 1.1, 1.2, etc., since they are all derived from the higher process 1. In a similar way the first sub-process under, say, *Tend Patient* would have the identifier 3.1.

b) All inputs and outputs balance:

All the input and output data-flows in the higher-level process are identically matched by the same inputs and outputs shown in the expanded lower-level diagram. They will carry the data-flow labels and arrows as before, but this time will not indicate the destination or source of the data-flow. This would be redundant, as they are already identified at a higher level. On the other hand, local data-flows may be indicated at the lower level and receive no mention elsewhere. Such is the case with the *Pre-medication Request* shown in Figure 2.3b. It is certainly needed where shown, but there is no reason to list it in the original diagram.

c) Levelling goes on until the lowest process reached:

Levelling can continue down through more layers of process expansion until a process cannot be broken down further. Thus, if *Examine Patient* requires more processes to fully identify all the actions involved, and it probably does, then it too can be levelled. Thus, it could include, say, process 1.2.1 *Check Blood Pressure* and 1.2.2 *Count Pulse Rate* and so on. It is clearly a matter of judgement where to stop splitting the functions. Would you split *Count Pulse Rate* into lower level processes? Probably not, but the option is always open if considered necessary. Notice the new level of numbering which is consistent with all processes above it.

As a summary of the value of the Data Flow Diagram, we can say that it is a powerful yet simple language used by the system analyst to record a clear pictorial description of the way in which data is used and modified in a system. It is not the complete picture of the system, but it does attack one important part of it – that is, the nature of the data and the way in which it moves through the organisation. It is inherently a top-down approach, which is no bad thing, and provides a straightforward means of documenting and reviewing the way in which the system works. But there is another aspect of data flow which involves the use of a more formal definition of that data.

2.3   The Data Dictionary (DD)

This is the one that causes all the work! A data dictionary is fundamental to the modern approach of analysing commercial information systems. It exists to hold the exact definition of all the labels and descriptions that are used in the data flow analysis and in other equivalent areas. It is thus a store of definitions of all the terms used. In Figure 2.2 we glibly use the name *Finance Department* as an external store. Is that the local finance department, or do we mean the centralised head office Comptroller's Office? Whatever is intended, the exact definition will have to be resident in the data dictionary. Further, every time the data flow diagram is modified, a corresponding change to the DD may well be required. The two items have to move forward in synchronism.

There are no generic rules laid down for the formulation of the dictionary. It can contain a restricted list of definitions, or, conversely, can contain a whole rag-bag of items – both temporary and permanent – associated with the system development project. If a particular approach makes sense to the members of the project team then use it, if not then change it to something more comfortable. But do make sure that this is agreed and carried out *at the start* of the development cycle, because changing the structure of the data dictionary half way through the exercise is labour intensive, prone to error and will not look good as an entry in the schedule slippage chart. In a similar way, ensure that the means of writing and upgrading the dictionary have been agreed from the beginning. It could be a manual handwritten document, a word-processed text file, a separate database file, a fully automated CASE product, or even a possible mix of some of the above. Whatever method is to be used, get it fixed and agreed right at the outset.

After all that preamble, we can take a brief look at the minimum structure of a data dictionary. This will contain an exact definition of all the data elements used in data flow diagrams (including the last entry below, which will be discussed later on in this section):

❑ **Data Flows**(e.g. Patient Ready Note)

❑ **Stores**(e.g. Patient File)

❑ **External Entities**(e.g. Finance Department)

❑ **Processes**(e.g. Assess Schedules)

❑ **Functional Primitives**(e.g. Count Pulse Rate)

Again, what is meant by 'exact definition' is open to discussion. One possible interpretation could be provided by a tabular descriptive format with the example data element taken from Figure 2.2:

DATA FLOW NAME	ALIAS	COMPOSITION	SOURCE PROCESS	DESTINATION PROCESS	REMARKS
Option List	-	Ref Number Prod Name Volume Dev Time Res Centre	Explore Options	Review Proposals	-

This could be said to uniquely define *Option List* in terms of the data items that it represents. Another possible definition model is given in Figure 2.5a which is a text-based format outlining more or less the same information. However, both of these definitions are dependent on the pre-determined physical structure of layout that has been adopted.

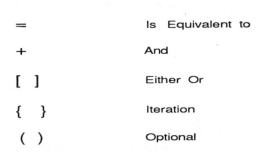

=	Is Equivalent to
+	And
[ ]	Either Or
{ }	Iteration
( )	Optional

Figure 2.4: Relational operators for the Data Dictionary

A more generic approach is to use the data elements that comprise the item under discussion along with a number of relational operators which have been defined in Figure 2.4. The meaning of these operators is largely self-explanatory but the following examples should help to underline their application:

small_family   =   mother   +
**   father   +**
**   (child)**

The convention to be adopted here is to use heavy type in giving data dictionary definitions of data elements. Each data element is written with lower case characters and all words in the label are linked with the underscore symbol.

Returning to the simple data dictionary example above, we are saying that the data element *Small Family* is equivalent to (the '=' symbol) the data elements *Mother* and *Father* (the '+' symbol) along with an optional member of the data element *Child* (the '( )' symbols). In this case, the small family (the physical object, not the data-element) is taken to have a maximum of three members with two adults included. Now take the case of the single parent family:

single_parent_family =   [mother|father]   +
**   {child}**

The vertical line is the 'choice' symbol in the 'either-or' operator of the first line. Notice here that the *Child* data element is no longer optional: if it were not there,

there would not be a single parent! In the same vein, by virtue of the data type, there cannot be the case of *Father* and *Mother* – it has to be one or the other. On the other hand there is no required limit to the number of *Child* data types and this is indicated by the 'iteration' sign i.e. one or more members. Finally, consider a person who belong to a small family:

small_family_member   =   [father|mother|(child)]

Only one selection is required here and this includes the possibility that a child is optionally present in the family.

After that digression, we can return to the more practical examples from the models. In the first place, let's go back to the data type *Option List*:

option_list	**=**	**product_ref_number**	**+**
		product_name	**+**
		production_volume	**+**
		development_time	**+**
		research_centre	

Here, the information is stripped down to the absolute minimum, but is independent of any physical layout. As another example of this elemental approach, consider again the outputs of Figure 2.3a. Imagine for the moment that a higher level Data Flow Diagram exists with a single output from the overall process *Operate On Patient* to the external entity *Central Records*. Such a data flow could have the name *Update Central Recs*, and could be defined:

update_central_recs	**=**	**[discharge_letter|death_not]**	
discharge_letter	**=**	**patient_number**	**+**
		surname	**+**
		address	**+**
		. . . .	
death_notification	**=**	**date**	**+**
		patient_number	**+**
		surgeon	**+**
		ward	**+**
		. . . .	
address	**=**	**(apart_number)**	**+**
		(apart_block_name)	**+**
		st_number	**+**
		street_name	**+**
		. . . .	

This is an example of the way in which the dictionary contains structured or hierarchical definitions: one element of the the *Update Central Recs* data flow is the item *Discharge Letter*. This is defined, in turn, by the data element *Address*.

Finally, *Address*, itself, can be examined and is broken down into its constituent elements which are simple integer or text-string data types. In principal, one could add the definition of *Street Number*, but it hardly seems worth while.

Let's go back to the basics of data dictionary formulation making the assumption that it will have a minimum structure and a text based physical layout. Then each entry will be treated in a slightly different way depending on the data element involved:

Data Flow

The example of Figure 2.5a is representative of the approach. The labels are written using the layout format defined for a data dictionary, and one can visualise the data flow information existing as a real form (paper or screen based) that is filled in and passed from department to department. Notice that the items source and date at the bottom are useful parts of the document since they will define when the document was created and by whom. This can be important in trying to keep track of the latest update to the dictionary.

Data Store

This will be a portion of a database comprising one or more tables and such a table is indicated in Figure 2.5b. The Alias entry is quite important as there may be different names for the same data element. Thus the X-Ray clinic may call the *Patient File* the *In Patient* record. This may not be desirable but it does happen in the real world. Incidentally, this can be easily displayed in the basic definition:

patient_file	**=**	**patient_number**	**+**
		surname	**+**
		. . . .	**+**
		ward_name	**+**
		date_of_entry	
	=	**in_patient**	

External Element

As it is external to the field of enquiry, only limited information is required. But there has to be some reference to it, and this is given in Figure 2.5c.

Processes

In general, a process is described in terms of the lower level processes. Thus, from Figure 2.3b:

assess_operation	**=**	**manage_ward**	**+**
		examine_patient	**+**
		assess_operation_status	

```
DATA FLOW
option _ list

ALIAS
-

COMPOSITION
product_ref_ number
product_ name
production _ volume
development _ time
research _ centre

Source      Date
```

a) Data Flow

```
DATA STORE
patient _ file

ALIAS
in _patient

COMPOSITION
patient _number
surname
first_ name
surgeon
consultant
ward_ name
date _of_ entry

Source      Date
```

b) Data Store

```
EXTERNAL ENTITY
senior_ management

ALIAS
management
headquarters

LOCATION
figure _2.2

DATA FLOWS
new_ product_ request

Source      Date
```

c) External Element

```
PROCESS
take_ pulse

PROCESS NUMBER
1.2.2

DESCRIPTION
Measure at radial artery
IF    ('baby'  AND  '130')
  OR ('child'  AND  '100')
  OR ('adult'  AND  '72')
THEN   Pulse Good
ELSE   Pulse Bad

Source      Date
```

d) Process Mini-Spec

Figure 2.5: Data Dictionary entries

and each of the right hand side terms will be equally defined in the dictionary in terms of *their* levelled components. Say:

**examine_patient   =   check_blood_pressure +
                                     count_pulse_rate   +
                                     . . . .**

Functional Primitives

At some point, the levelling mechanism will reach a process which is not worth splitting further (perhaps the data element *Check Blood Pressure* would be considered in this light). Such a process is termed a <u>functional primitive</u>. It will often consist of one input, one output, and a relatively simple data conversion between the two. This 'relatively simple conversion' becomes the subject of a <u>mini-spec</u> which provides a dictionary definition of the exact nature of the process in question. Again, there is some flexibility in considering what is meant by the term 'exact nature'. If, for example, the team on a particular project feels that each mini-spec should identify the incoming and outgoing data flows -then create the mini-spec in that format. If they will accept a more basic style, then use that approach. There are a number of ways to write a mini-spec and one example is given in Figure 2.5d which can be taken as a boolean logic outline of the process 1.2.2. In equivalent English, it might be a set of instructions on how to fill in that portion of the *Medical Status File* form (data flow from Figure 2.3b), and this could run on the following lines:

❑ Apply forefingers lightly to the patient's radial artery on the wrist of the left hand.

❑ Ensure that the pulse is readily detectable.
>   If pulse felt, then carry on
>   Else, try wrist on other arm
>> If strong pulse on right arm, carry on
>> Else look for pulse source elsewhere

❑ Count pulse-rate
>   If patient is type <u>baby</u> and pulse measured approx. 130, then tick box after PULSE
>   Else, if patient is type <u>child</u> and pulse measured approx. 100, tick box after PULSE
>   Else, if patient is type <u>adult</u> and pulse measured approx. 70, tick box after PULSE
>   Else, place cross in box after PULSE

In turn, each functional primitive is generated in a similar manner. Once they have been entered into the dictionary, then all the processes in the system will be totally defined. Along with the structured definitions of the data flows and files, they will now provide a complete definition of every element of the system. However, when the layout of the system, in terms of its data flow diagrams, is modified in any way, then the corresponding elements of the DD will have to be changed to reflect those modifications.

The Data Dictionary is primarily concerned with integrity of the design, providing exact definitions of all the terms used. In addition, it will help to control unwanted duplication of functions and processes. This means that many people, working on different parts of the same project, can access the dictionary and determine all the defined relationships and linkages for one particular element of the system. As we have seen, the format of the dictionary is open to considerable freedom of choice and that perhaps is a disadvantage, in that it lacks standardisation from project to project. On the other hand, it does mean that it can be modified to satisfy the unique needs of the group working on each particular system project.

The Data Dictionary will be found in virtually all modern system developments, but the down side is that it calls for a lot of work if it is to be generated and maintained manually.

2.4   The Entity-Relationship Diagram (ERD)

This is the last of the basic tools used by the analyst and is primarily of importance in the formation and modelling of the database files that are to be developed for the system. More formally, Entities constitute logical groups of data which are linked together by defined Relations built into the system. Up to now we have been concentrating on data flows and processes without worrying too much about the sources of these flows or where the process results might be kept. The entity is more of a static element which doesn't move or change and is represented in the data flow diagram by the element type 'data store'. Consider the *Market Reports* file of Universal (Figure 2.2). This is an entity which could possibly be described in Data Dictionary terms:

market_reports	**=**	**report_number**	**+**
		title	**+**
		author	**+**
		date_of_report	**+**
		review_product	**+**
		sample_size	**+**
		. . . .	

From this definition it is clear that the entity *Market Reports* is literally the sum of its parts, or, to use the formal term, the sum of its attributes. In fact, it is generally true that an entity will be described in terms of its attributes, and these elements translate directly to the physical world where the equivalent table in a database will contain the appropriate column headings. Notice that the records or rows of actual results entered into the table under the correct column heading is the real operational data that will reflect the state of the organisation. However, at the modelling stage, it is only the entities, their names and attributes that matter.

The entity-relationship model was first proposed by Chen in 1976, and gained general acceptance through the 80s. The way in which the model is represented on paper (or screen, for that matter) varies considerably from user to user but the underlying premises are generally well standardised. In broad terms, the main objects of interest are:

Entity: A static data element comprising a Label, a set of Attributes, and an Identifier. It is equivalent to the database data object 'table'.

Label: The name of the Entity which describes its essential nature or purpose. As for the other data elements, the label is given with upper case first letters, with words separated by spaces.

Attribute: One of the data objects which are the constituent parts of the Entity. In database terms, the attribute is equivalent to the 'column-heading'.

Identifier: The particular attribute, or minimum set of attributes, which always contains unique data. In application terms, this translates to the key or primary key column(s) of a database table.

Relation: The nature of the link between entities which may vary in *degree*. This variation is indicated alongside the connecting *link* between the entities.

Label: Again, the label comprises a set of words separated by spaces which describes the type of relationship involved.

Degree: The definition of the possible number of linkage records at each end of the relationship. This is discussed further below, and can be of the form:
> one – one
> one – many
> many – one
> many – many

As already mentioned, the graphical notation used to indicate the above elements varies over a number of styles. The notation adopted in this book is given in Figure 2.6a. Remember that the rectangular box in the ER Diagram is equivalent to a data element represented by two parallel lines (the data-store) in the corresponding DFD. The relationship examples shown in Figure 2.6a should read:

"The *Product Format* entity *Depends On* the *Market Analysis* entity".

In other words, the two entities are linked, in this case, by the relationship *Depends On*. Notice the 'm .. m' underneath the connecting link. From the listings under 'degree', this means that the link is many-many, i.e. a number of products may depend on or be affected by one or more report, and conversely, one product may depend on a number of reports.

Some more examples are given in 2.6b. Here the degree of the relation between *Fieldmarshall* and *General* is one – many, and is the same between the *General* and the *Sergeant*. Hopefully, the other examples are equally clear as to the degree.

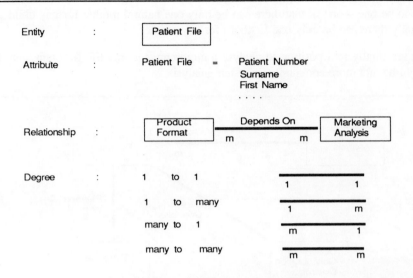

a) The Entity Diagram Notation

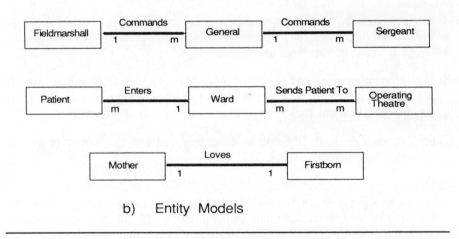

b) Entity Models

Figure 2.6: The Entity Relationship Diagram

Thus, in the second example, it is assumed that many surgical wards will send patients to one operating theatre. On the other hand, one ward may well send patients to different operating theatres. Therefore the degree is again many – many. It is different for the patient entity. While many patients may enter one ward, the reverse (in any reasonable timeframe) is simply not true – one patient cannot be entered into many wards. Thus it is a many – one relationship. The last example has to be one – one in that there can be only one natural mother for any child and equally there can be only one firstborn for any mother.

We are finally in a position to analyse a more conventional ER Diagram, one that might be met more commonly in system analysis.

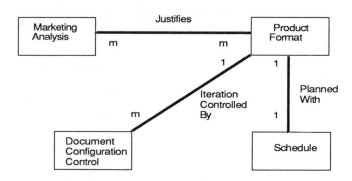

Figure 2.7: The Universal ER Diagram

Consider Figure 2.7. which represents a (very simplified) picture of how the entities concerned with new product design in Universal Solid State are interrelated. It can be expressed as follows:

❑ The information contained in one or more *Marketing Analysis* will be used to justify one *Product Format* of a new product development programme. There may be more than one such *Product Format* in the overall programme.

❑ Each *Product Format* will be planned and managed with the support of its own individual *Schedule* material.

❑ The changes introduced to each *Product Format* will be monitored by the *Document Configuration Control*. Each new modification or upgrade to the *Product Format* (i.e. each iteration of the product) will call up a new document configuration and there will be a new set for every iteration.

From this example, we can see that the ER Diagram is a reasonably straightforward way of illustrating the linkages between all the Entities that were established in the logical model. The Diagram can be drawn, or modified, and reviewed in an iterative cycle until all parties are satisfied that it truly represents the logical state of the system Entity elements. At that point, the Entities will have been defined in terms of their Attributes, Identifiers, Relationships and corresponding Degrees. This will then provide enough information for the designer to go away, work his magic spells and return with a database consisting of a set of tables that will reflect the layout given in the ER Diagrams. (This conversion is related to database design and is beyond the scope of this book, but the interested reader will find an outline of the processes involved in 'Databases and Database Systems', E. Oxborrow, Chartwell-Bratt, 1986, p61.)

In conclusion, the ER Diagram can be seen as a necessary prelude to realising a dedicated database design for any system. Again, the language constructs are not too complex, and it offers the means for group review of one important sector of the logical system.

2.5   Summary

The purpose of this chapter was to introduce some current techniques used in the formation and use of the logical model. The topics have been treated with very broad strokes (entire books have been written on each technique), but they should still enable the end-user to join with the system designer in assessing and reviewing potential system models related to his or her particular application. At the very least, it will prepare the non-technical members of the team for the sort of documentation that they will meet on such a project.

Three commonly used tools have been reviewed, and we can highlight the major points arising for each of them:

Data Flow Diagrams

Used to define the nature of data and the way it is transported round the organisation. It is an abstraction of the real world in that it only defines *what* the flows consist of and ignores *how* the data is moved.

In its simplified form, only four symbols are used: the rounded figure -the process; the rectangle which represents the external sink/source; parallel lines for the data store; and the arrowed line which constitutes the data flow itself.

Each process can be broken down into more basic elements and this technique is called levelling. Each sublevel process will, in turn, be numbered to relate it to the higher level diagram, and the inputs and outputs to the lower diagram will exactly match the inputs and outputs in the higher level process.

The entire logical model can be represented by a complete set of levelled data flow diagrams.

Data Dictionary

At the minimum, this item will hold complete definitions of all the data elements used in the DFDs and ERs. These definitions will comprise one expression containing subordinate data elements linked by relational operators.

Where a process cannot be further divided into constituent parts, it is termed a functional primitive, and is defined in the dictionary by means of a mini-spec. This mini-spec may be written in many ways, one example being a form of simplified or structured English.

Setting up and maintaining a data dictionary is labour and time consuming if carried out manually, but this is becoming less necessary as automated tools come into general use.

Entity Relationship Diagram

This tool shows how the static entities have links or relations with one another in the system. Within the ERD, entities are defined by their label or name, their attributes, the unique identifier, and the defined relation(s) to other entities. The degree of a relation indicates whether one or more instances of the entity (rows of the table) will be applied by the relation.

The entities in the ERD are equivalent to the table in the database, and the proper design of the system database will reflect the information present in the ERD.

For further reading, ref. 5 in the bibliography gives comprehensive coverage of Data Flow Diagrams and Data Dictionaries, while ref. 8 provides a brief outline of Entity Relation Models.

Questions

1. An adolescent is about to change a wheel on the car under your careful supervision (the tyre is flat and the car is parked in your driveway). Provide a data flow diagram to cover the situation.

2. Provide a context diagram and levelled set of data flow diagrams to explain how the garage might record the sale of a new tyre. The interest is in the paper work relating to the transaction and how the stock control could be handled.

3. Assume that pumping up the tyre is a functional primitive (and that you have a handpump and pressure gauge to hand). Provide a simple mini-spec to define it.

4. The tyre is obviously an Entity, as is the garage, and the customer. Provide a set of attributes for each which could be of potential use in a Spare-Parts Database. Write down the entity definitions as possible entries in a data dictionary.

5. Finally, propose a feasible Entity Relationship Diagram linking all the entities of question 4.

3

Development Strategies

SSADM shows signs of age

The government-backed design methodology SSADM is coming under fire from consultants who believe the system is not appropriate for the changing requirements of modern systems.

According to George Rzevski, of consultancy Brainin Rzevski, top-down methodologies such as SSADM are not suitable for systems such as those in production planning or dealing rooms, where requirements are not fixed.

Rzevski said: 'With this type of system there is not time to spend a year going through the top-down modelling and then design because requirements can change.'

Computing p.4 25.5.89

Putting the case for a human angle

Giving development staff a toolbox full of expensive gadgets is likely to do little for your application back-log, although it will probably keep your programmers amused for a while. Despite all the claims made for it, case is not an instant remedy. It requires new working methods, careful management and an understanding of its limitations.

Computing p.17 21.6.90

Suppliers defend their case against reports

Computer aided software engineering suppliers are angry about a report which refutes many of their claims for support and productivity gains.

The 1000-page report, by consultant Rosemary Rock-Evans, entitled 'Case Analyst Workbenches', evaluates many of the existing case tools on the market and concludes that productivity claims of over 50% claimed by vendors and developers are 'impossibly high'.

. . . .

Rock-Evens remarks are backed up by a recent survey carried out by Price Waterhouse, which said that one of the main problems data processing managers have about case is cutting through the hype.

Computing p.6 2.2.89

3.1 Introduction

High-technology projects do not just happen. At least, the successful ones do not. It takes a great deal of planning and basic decision-making to generate a system that can even start to provide the required result in the given time for the defined cost. Remember that all this structural planning has to happen right at the beginning of a project. It may be carried out by only one of the parties, for example, by insisting that the consultant follows every nuance of the end-users' procedures. Better still, it could be a shared agreement, where everyone knows and agrees on how the development programme is to be carried out. Information system projects are no exception to the general engineering need for an envelope of defined operational methods and objectives. To show how this need can be satisfied, we will outline the potential strategies and modes of operation that can be considered. Keep in mind that if you don't consider, formulate and agree on an approach that is optimum for *your* project, the effectiveness of the resulting system will almost certainly be impaired.

Let's clear up this question of why it is so important that the general approach has to be addressed right at the beginning of the project. There are two major reasons. The first one, discussed above, is that a clear cut policy – agreed and applied consistently at all levels – will ensure a coherent program. This concept of working within a well-defined framework of mutually supportive procedures will to lead to a useful product being developed within an acceptable timeframe. And the converse also generally holds true.

The second reason is that, in one sense, each of the topics covered in this chapter is a trap. By and large, once the strategic decision has been made (or not made) at the start, the situation is sensibly locked up and unchangeable. What this means is that, if a mistake is made at the outset, you are going to be stuck with the resulting problems that are generated. We will discuss the properties of CASE tools later in the chapter, but for the moment consider the following scenario. Assume that we are going to use a particular CASE package. It will offer a number of services, certain design tools (of the type discussed in the last chapter), a variety of user interfaces and a selection of defined output report formats. We have carefully explored the market and found the right product for the projected application.

Now consider the implications of changing to another competitive product – half way through the development schedule! One can visualise the types of question that might be considered. Will the new output documentation be compatible with the old? Will the existing data dictionary talk to the new one? Will added staff training be needed? And so on. This is what I mean by a trap since, for all practical purposes, the CASE tool defines the way the project will run. It follows that a mistake in the selection mechanism for a software tool will be very expensive to rectify. It even goes further that this, in that the next project will almost certainly use the same design team – which is product-trained and experienced in just this one inappropriate tool ...

In essence, this chapter will discuss those areas of strategy that support the decision-making processes during the life of the development activity. The discussion will centre on three main areas :

❏ Life cycle definitions

❏ Structured methodology versus Prototyping

❏ CASE tool selection and application

The objective, for each of these topics, will be to establish the advantages and disadvantages of going down a particular route so that sensible project-based choices can t e made for each specific case.

3.2 The Life Cycle Format

Essentially, this section is concerned with identifying and defining the various parts of the total system design activity. This is important in order to understand the overall scope of the exercise and to allocate the time and resource needed for each of these activities, in the order in which they occur.

The Basic Cycle

The System (/Software/Structured) Development Life Cycle or SDLC will be found in all the text books, where each version comprises a slightly different variation of the same open-loop sequence of items. The basic approach of this somewhat dated (but still much used) model of system design is given in Figure 3.1a. Here, each project is seen as starting with analysis and terminating with the post-installation maintenance phase.

Analysis

This general term can be taken to include all the activities up to the generation of the design specification. Thus, it includes the initial *Feasibility Study* where a candidate project is reviewed for possible inclusion in some future work programme. This will identify the potential advantage or need for a new or modified system, and provide initial estimates for costs and timescales. If approved, this is followed by the *Review* phase, where a detailed breakdown of the existing system is obtained. Finally, the details from this review are modified in the *Requirement* phase to establish the changes that are to be carried out. This is encapsulated in the generation of the Design Specification which is still largely in textual language form. For a discussion on the types and contents of documentation used in such a project, see section 4 of Chapter 6. While not always identified as such, this lead-up to the specification must be the most cost sensitive phase of the whole project, since errors injected at this point will have maximum impact in corrective costs further down the line.

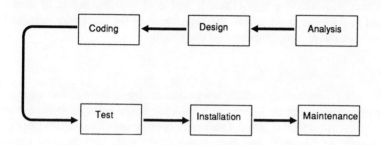

a) The 'classical' Life Cycle

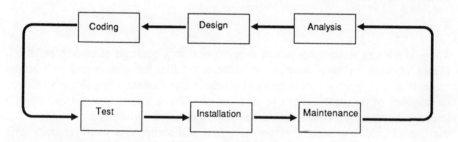

b) The 'closed-loop' Life Cycle

Figure 3.1: System Development Life Cycle (SDLC)

Design

The design phase breaks down into two main sections. The first comprises the *Logical Design* where abstract modelling of the system is carried out by means of the graphic tools discussed in the last chapter (possibly embedded in a CASE approach). This is where the data model is broken down to the functional primitive processes along with the data elements that they work with. All this information is assembled in the data dictionary. This phase is concerned primarily with the _what_ rather than the _how_ and leads to the generation of the *System* or *Product Definition* document which contains an exact definition of all the elements and their use in the system to be designed. The practical impacts of the requirements laid down during the logical design are established during the *Physical Design* phase, which is very much involved with the _how_. Thus, it will deal with the nature of actual files to be used in database applications, the appearance of the screen formats, and the layout details of the reports generated by the system.

Coding

This is the formal programming section where the computer instruction code is prepared. For example, where an Entity, with associated Attributes, is indicated in the logical design, it is translated into a Table with appropriate Column-headings in the physical design. At this stage, the formulation of the table into database terms could possibly be implemented in a third generation language like COBOL, either manually or via an automatic code generator tool. (It may cost more using a tool, but there will be a big reduction in the number of post-delivery bugs found.) Conversely, it could be created directly in a high level relational database language, e.g. using the 'create table' command of SQL. Either way, the software defining the system is generated in this part of the life cycle.

Test

There is no way to completely test every option in a package of system software. (Think about it – if there were, no military or satellite software would ever be the cause of an operational failure or abort routine.) The realistic objective is to reduce the number of post-test failures to an acceptable level. The best way is by using a structured approach through the design phase (minimum errors being introduced in the first place). A structured system program will comprise a main program (this will establish the overall direction of the system) and sub-routines (or procedures in Pascal terms) which carry out all the detailed work. The main program can be substituted by a harness where simple link statements connect the sub-routines, while for other tests the sub-routines can be replaced by dummy modules – essentially empty routines which return the program flow straight back to the main program. Following the design, there will be a test plan, agreed in advance, which will involve some or all of the following:

Specifications: Integrity checks to confirm consistent information in Diagrams and Dictionary and conformance to the Requirement Specification.

Coding: Spelling, syntax and punctuation checks on textual material.

Top Down: Apply dummy modules for lower levels which can still carry out primitive test functions.

Bottom Up: Use a test-bed harness which will allow the validation of individual designed modules.

Performance: Specify a dummy test data-pack as a suitable benchmark. This may not match the ultimate user performance, but could be valuable for comparative assessments between system variants and upgrades.

Test budgets can be a bit of a problem in that someone always has to pay for them. In the words of our friends ABC from Chapter 1:

❏ There is 'nothing' to show for the money spent

❏ It takes up valuable resource and equipment – both for the planning and for the execution and

❏ The ensuing rework of specifications, code and documentation has probably not been allowed for.

❏ In any case, probably the overall project is running so late that the only sensible thing to do is to cut down on the test activities to recover some of the lost time.

While these attitudes may not arise within your organisation, planning and obtaining agreements over the necessary budgets well in advance of actual use is still probably a good practice. (For a few well chosen words on the subject, see reference 4, p.19.)

Installation

There is nothing very state-of-the-art in getting married. It is a common enough practice, and yet it seems to offer a unique set of financial problems and interpersonal adjustments each time it occurs. This is roughly the situation every time a new system is installed. The requirements are well understood, everyone wants to make it work, and yet the frustration and headaches seem peculiar to the specific system being handed over. More will be said on this subject in Chapter 10.

Maintenance

This is another label that can mean all things to all men. At one level, it is simply a budgetary catch-phrase which captures all the expenses that occur as a result of operating (or wishing to operate) the software following installation on the client site. More technically, it can be a collective term for work associated with:

Actual maintenance: Where software bugs and hardware interlinks will need on-going correction.

Learning curve upgrades: As the end-users apply the system, so they obtain a better understanding of the system as it performs today, compared with the originally defined objectives. It would be reasonable to expect that some added fine tuning will be requested.

Application Program and Hardware evolution: With each version change both in hardware and software there will be requirements for, at minimum, new interfaces within the system. Every application software upgrade is claimed by the vendor to be compatible with the previous version. While usually true to about 99.8%, Bronzite's Rule states that part of your application always uses the other 0.2%. Thus, a new output printer or an upgraded text processor may possibly not operate with the existing system without some labour intensive modification.

Complete new System Overhaul: Merging the current Personnel package and the Finance Reporting system, for example, will involve a comprehensive overview of all of the software used in both areas. Either you bolt on existing sub-elements from package A onto package B, or you go right back to the Analysis phase and start from scratch again. There are additional functions that could be considered under Maintenance, but they will be discussed in more detail in Chapter 11. However, even the restricted list above goes some way to explaining why the cost of software maintenance has been reported to be so high.

The Closed-loop Cycle

The last section has identified why, in one sense, the format of the life cycle as shown in Figure 3.1a is not totally realistic. The simple modification to provide a continuous loop, given in Figure 3.1b, appears closer to what happens in real life. Here, maintenance reverts to its original meaning i.e. essentially debugging the software, while all the other activities given above are implemented by going round the loop again. An understanding of this closed loop approach is important in that it emphasises the on-going commitment that has to go with any new system development. What this means is that the effective system life cycle, as currently applied, is a superset of Figure 3.1b and comprises three stages :

Stage 1:   The first iteration of an information system SALES_1 will be undertaken.

Stage 2:   System SALES_1 will be added to the number of tested systems and will continue to loop, i.e. to be used and modified, for the foreseeable future. There will *never* be a time when it does not need continued funding and resource application.

Stage 3:   The only process, short of killing the organisation, that will terminate the use of system SALES_1 will be its replacement by system SALES_2 which is bigger and more expensive. Return to stage 1.

This view of system application underscores the well reported software crisis (for example, reference 3, p. 22). Since no system is ever discarded, only replaced by something bigger, the servicing of_existing systems continues to grow without constraint as new systems are added to the pile. This growth will, in turn, use an ever larger proportion of the available resources and staff. We will go into possible scenarios for controlling this activity explosion in Chapter 11, but for the moment, just remember: a system is for life.

3.3 Structured Design

This is one of those decision areas where the emotional tides appear to run deep. Either one is seen to be (firmly) in favour of structured methodology, or (totally) committed to the advantages of prototyping. We are here concerned with the philosophy of system development and this is no trivial matter as it involves the definition of the project guidelines, along with the setting up of the resulting objectives and deliverables. The conflict is primarily concerned with the different possible ways to carry out the Life Cycle activities discussed above. However, before making a commitment to either route, let's see what is involved.

Structured Methodology

This approach has developed from the early system techniques of the 60s. These became notorious for their failures (ref. 5, p.6) and, from that time, system development has had to evolve to apply a disciplined and structured set of procedures and tools along with a defined set of documents which fully describe the system to be delivered. These procedures and tools permit the life cycle activities to be carried out in a controlled and manageable sequence.

The essence of the approach is given in Figure 3.2. To begin the process, analysis is carried out on the existing working system (say, entering information, about the patients requiring surgery, on forms which are stored in central filing cabinets). This is then reduced to a logical model where data items and their flow are identified. Among other things, this would result in a data dictionary which exactly defines the current processing of incoming patient data. At this point, modifications are introduced into the logical model such as to reflect the desired improvements – the design process. Finally the new logical model is again translated back to a physical implementation for use by the client. The logical changes could include new data flows (say, copying data to Central Records which was previously only sent to the Operating Theatre) This time, the physical implementation could be an electronic data storage system installed in each ward where separate screens can be called up as input forms to be filled in by the resident sister or staff nurse (or whoever is designated to cover this task).

This sequential approach to the implementation of a system development life cycle is fundamental to the structured technique. Each particular methodology, such as SADT (SoftTech Inc.), YSM (Yourdon) or SSADM (LBMS) may use slightly different graphic symbols, reporting forms or models but their underlying objective is always the same. They all use a formal set of tools and disciplines which enable the activities outlined in a system development life cycle to be implemented in a planned and timely manner. The tools tend to be based on data-flow and entity-relation diagrams and each methodology will use its own set of reasonably comprehensive and pre-defined checklists.

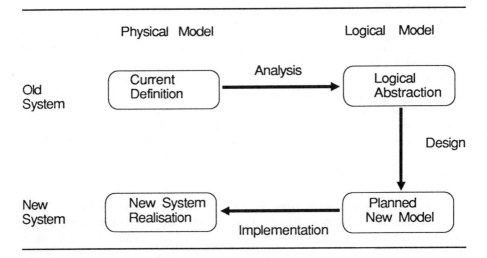

Figure 3.2: The basic structured analysis process

As an example, we can briefly review some of the key characteristics of SSADM (Structured System Analysis and Design Methodology):

❑ Primarily concerned with the Analysis and Design phases of the life cycle. (effectively the ground covered by Figure 3.2.)

❑ Standardised design rules, forms and checklists implemented for every project.

❑ Documentation sets are predefined as customer deliverables for each stage of the development.

❑ User reviews used at each stage (see options under Chapter 8).

❑ The Analysis and Design phases are split into six activities:

    Analysis: Analyse the existing system
    Definition: Define the improvements to be implemented
    Options: Establish the operating environment to be used
    Data: Complete data design (tables and columns)
    Process: Complete process design (system transactions)
    Design: Create system database and programming code

There is, of course, a lot more to SSADM than this simple outline and for a more comprehensive discussion see reference 6.

What will be the general result of using this philosophy?

Pros:

❑ Good project framework. In an ideal world, cost and time forecasting can be easily applied.

❑ Good audit, cross checking, and error identification mechanisms. This is very important in terms of system debugging which can comprise the major part of installation and testing costs.

❑ Popular commercial packages for CASE tool application and other automated techniques are readily available.

❑ Commonly accepted philosophy for system design. This means that related skills and consultant support are easy to find in the marketplace.

Cons:

❑ Requires a well ordered environment in which to work. The existing situation must be well defined and the new objectives clear. Structured development does not go well with chaos.

❑ The planning is essentially open-loop. That is, each phase of the life cycle is completed before the next phase is started. Changing the ground rules or calling up modifications to previously fixed objectives constitutes a poorly ordered environment. See above.

❑ The project control is thorough but to some extent inflexible. In line with the above comments, this may mean freezing the design objectives over a period of years, which is not realistic. (See the report at the start of the chapter.)

❑ Initial costs are high, training costs are high, and changes to design strategy within the organisation may require careful consideration.

In summary, this is a powerful, effective and readily available approach to system design which can be implemented with tools from a number of suppliers. However, the down-side has to be carefully evaluated in order to satisfy your specific requirements (and this should be fully discussed with a potential vendor who may possibly have suitable work-rounds).

Prototyping

The supporters of this relatively new approach to the Life Cycle activities will claim that it largely overcomes all the disadvantages discussed above. This is more or less true, but pure Prototyping is still not the universal panacea – and we shall see why in the discussion that follows.

The major difference between this technique and the methodologies outlined above, is that there is feedback between the designer and end-user. It may be optional (and even strongly recommended) with the structured methods, but here it is inherent in the design process itself. The basic approach is given in Figure 3.3 which shows how the definition of an arbitrary module is determined.

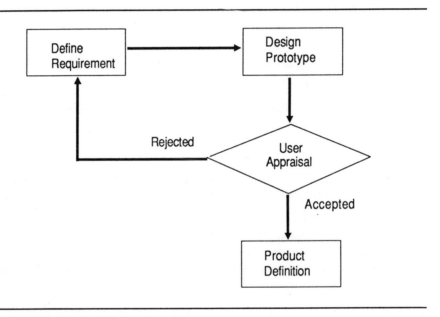

Figure 3.3: Prototyping module definition

In general terms, the designer will take the requirement specification and apply it to create an actual working model of the module under review. This means that a simplified input/output system is available for the end-users to try out on their keyboards and screens. They may input data (which will probably be of a rather restricted nature) and read results from the screens (via partially finished menus and forms). If the prototype does not provide the right system result, then the end-user makes recommendations for change; the design requirement is modified; and this leads ultimately to a new prototype to be tested. The important thing is that this loop totally involves the end-users in monitoring the development process, and that the design continues to be modified until they are fully satisfied with the *look* and *feel* of the working model. Only at that point will the details of both the system structure (logical design) and user interface (physical design) be transferred into the product definition document. Notice that the prototype itself should not be used as part of the final system.

It is not all plain sailing. Unlimited iterations or looping will still cost project-based money and this, hopefully, will concentrate the mind on what is really needed and what is merely decorative in terms of reworking an existing proposal. In fact, project management will be difficult, due to the open nature of the development plan. Again, selecting what to design into a prototype model and what can be left out, involves some skilful judgement and experience by the design leaders. Even then, some crucial element may be inadvertently omitted with serious knock-on effects at a later date. In order to generate prototype models, there will have to be a set of tools installed that will permit the fast assembly of menus, forms, and general screen based information displays. Perhaps more importantly, the design team will have to be adept in the use of these particular tools in turning round proposals and modifications into new prototype models. Finally, there will have to be a well defined procedure for keeping the details of intermediate models, since this sort of *ad hoc* system building may sometimes lead to an overall degradation in system performance or user satisfaction. At that point, it will be necessary to return to an earlier model as a starting point for additional work.

Again, it will be of value to look at the main advantages and disadvantages in selecting this approach.

Pros:

❑ Positively involves the end-users in the design process. They know (and formally approve) the nature of the delivered system.

❑ Easily tested by all other interested parties to the new system. Will help to reduce cross-departmental installation problems.

❑ Flexible in responding to change. Works well with uncertainty and risk (which is often the normal environment for system application).

❑ First deliveries for assessment generated in weeks rather than months or years.

Cons:

❑ Not constrained to top-down analysis. Therefore finished system product may not be optimised, and error checking across the system may call for special care.

❑ Schedule and costing estimates can prove difficult to model with any accuracy, since the number of prototyping iterations and the resulting time taken are not formally controlled.

❑ The models cannot be used to evaluate the performance of the finished production system. This is because a restricted model will not emulate, for example, the total number of users, or the maximum number of records being sorted in a table.

❑ Documentation, quality assurance and configuration control, though still important, can be difficult to maintain in a fast changing situation.

❑ Requires prototyping tools and experienced design staff, both for generating the
fast-turn-round prototypes and for demonstrating them to the end-users. Such
personnel may not always be available.

This can be a successful technique which provides strong links between the
designer and user. It enables system development to be applied in fluid situations
and follows a well proven engineering way of working, i.e. evolve the product
through a number of iterative trial-and-error processes. The down side tends to be
related to problems of project management along with change definition and
control and these difficulties have to be addressed responsibly by each project
team.

Mixed Methodology

It would obviously be attractive if the positive features of the two philosophies
covered above could be combined i.e. to mix the controlled project planning of the
one with the user involvement and flexibility of the other. This can be most simply
achieved by embedding one inside the other, although the advantages are
correspondingly limited. For example, the design phase of a standard SDLC
(System Design Life Cycle) could include a prototyping section devoted only to
defining the system requirements. Another possibility would be to apply structured
analysis before each prototype is defined and made. This is prototyping with the
analysis phase built in. Neither of these two really address the issue of fully
interweaving the two techniques. One way of achieving this has been labelled
Phased Design and is described in reference 10 of the Bibliography. Here, the
overall system is broken down into major separate sub-systems and each
sub-system is handled as an individual development exercise i.e. with coding to a
virtually finished product. At that point, the user will review the result, either
accepting or rejecting the total design. A broad outline of this mixed approach is
given in Figure 3.4 (based on Figure 5 of reference 10). Again, this is not a perfect
methodology since, ideally, it requires a project where the major elements of the
design can be easily isolated from each other.

Summary

This section has been concerned with identifying the options open to the designers
and users at the start of a specific system development project. We have discussed
the different possible ways to implement the Life Cycle activities and the strengths
and weaknesses of the choices involved. In this context, it is important to establish
the basic operating conditions of the planned system. Thus, at the simplest level, is
it primarily a well ordered or poorly ordered environment, is it a well structured
project or a sensibly open-ended one, and can it be broken down into reasonably

independent sections? The answers to these questions should have an important influence on the strategy to be adopted. On the other hand, it may already have been fixed as a result of decisions made for other projects within the end-user organisation. Whatever the situation, a selection will have to be made for your project – structured, prototyping or mixed. This will then identify the sort of problem areas that could be anticipated to occur within the project envelope.

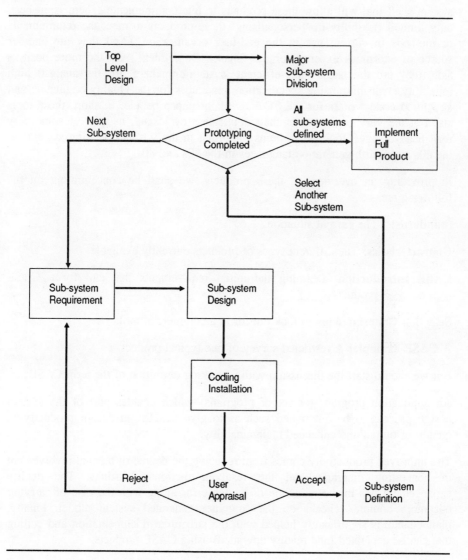

Figure 3.4: The mixed methodology

3.4   The Power Users (CASE)

The acronym CASE stands for 'Computer Aided Software Engineering' and CASE tools exert a considerable fascination in the world of system design – even with their current problems. Thus, there are no effective standards (as yet) for what a CASE tool *is*, or for what it *does*. There is no commonly agreed language or system shell that will allow these products to intercommunicate. There is, at best, only limited flexibility in 'personalising' these products to meet the requirements or methods in current use in the end-user organisation. (And they are another source of enormous expense for the Finance Department.) On the more positive side, they are the latest super-efficient 'system-crunchers' for the analyst; high reliability error-minimising specification generators for the Quality engineers; and structured code writers for the COBOL Maintenance people. In short, these tools stand at the very beginning of their application cycle and, in spite of some very real disadvantages, look set to be as important in the 90s as operating systems in the 60s and fourth generation languages in the 70s and 80s.

In providing an overview of these products, we shall be concentrating on the following areas :

Standards: The current situation.

Characteristics: The different types of products currently available.

CASE Introduction: Defining the initial requirements that call for a CASE product.

Selection Criteria: What to look out for in a commercial tool.

A CASE example: A restricted survey of one typical product.

But we should start the discussion with a working definition of the term CASE:

An application program (or set of programs) which enables part of the system design process to be automated such as to give benefits in design productivity, quality of output and enhanced maintainability.

The improved productivity comes from reducing the degree of manual involvement in generating diagrams and the resultant dictionary listings. The quality enhancement lies in the reduction of human error along with the ease of carrying out more complex checks on the computer generated system model. Finally, maintenance is significantly helped with the structured documentation and coding that can be generated (and readily upgraded) using CASE products.

Standards

Perhaps one of the key strengths of relational databases, compared to other types, is the *de facto* acceptance of the query language SQL as the standard interface. Of course, there are other good points, but having the possibility of a common interface between different commercial products has not exactly harmed their cause. In contrast, it has to be admitted that CASE tools do not yet operate to any universally recognised standard that can be applied to benchmarking (measuring the performance of like products with generic test procedures) or to input/output interfaces. In an ideal world, there would be some sort of CASE harness – possibly with a block layout similar to that illustrated in Figure 3.5. This would allow any product from any vendor to be applied in a particular design environment. In addition, there would be a standard interface to the favourite external database or word processor. This may eventually come to pass – but do not expect too much in the near future.

Is there anyone out there who cares? Well, it is certainly true that most people have an overwhelming urge to fall asleep when the question of Standards is brought up, but then most people are not responsible for the design, selection and integration of CASE tools into the system development process. In that capacity, some knowledge of the interfacing capabilities of each commercial tool will be found useful. At minimum, it will help in the comparative assessment of CASE products which could be candidates for some system design project.

The industry itself has recognised the need for interface standards and there are various standards committees at work in various parts of the globe. Just how much effort is being applied can be judged from a short survey of the current situation in the U.S and Europe:

DEF-STD-2167: Where the U.S military consider that the software system requirements are particularly stringent then the resulting product has to meet this standard. For this reason, a number of CASE vendors have supplied tools which generate documents and test plans in accordance with this standard. It is a reliable but expensive route.

CAIS: Common APSE Interface Set. (Ada Project Support Environment) Another U.S military standard under development, based on the approved language Ada.

IRDS: Information Resource Dictionary Systems. The work is being concentrated on defining the requirements of the data dictionary, which is central to any structured design approach. Both OSI and ANSI (roughly: European and U.S) working groups are currently working on competing specifications.

CDIF: CASE Data Interchange Format. This has the objective of providing a common format for the transfer of text and graphic data between different CASE packages. Ultimately under ANSI, a first draft was to be reviewed in 1990.

PCTE: Portable Common Tool Environment. The standard to define a common interface for integrating CASE tools (much like the harness discussed above). This is largely European driven – sourced by ESPRIT for a number of years and presently supported by ECMA.

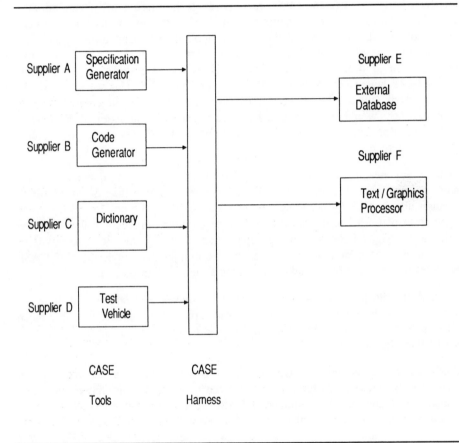

Figure 3.5: The perfect CASE interface

In summary, the last three above are all broadly established with respect to a basic framework, and will probably continue to be refined in matters of detail over the next two or three years. Commercial products will probably declare their conformance to one or more of these standards in the same timeframe and until then it would be prudent to study rather carefully the individual product interface specifications.

Characteristics

The role of the CASE tool is to automate one or more of the activities identified in the system development life cycle (see section 3.1). At this point, we can explore some of the properties that would be expected from a product being used to meet this objective:

Graphic Tool

Any product which enables *drawings* and *diagrams* to be easily designed, assembled, modified and printed is clearly going to help in producing the sort of graphic information discussed in the last chapter. Such a product will create part of the documentation required during the *design analysis* stage and most general purpose CASE tools will contain a module to provide these features.

Data Dictionary

This facility added to the graphic capability will provide a full featured design tool and specification generator. There is usually a cross-checking link between the dictionary and graphic representation in that audits can be carried out to identify items in a diagram that have not been defined in the dictionary – and vice versa. The dictionary will become the basis of the product definition and of the eventual database resulting from the design process.

Code Generator

There are products specially geared to produce program code in a specified programming language – usually COBOL, and sometimes Ada, Pascal, C or PL/1. Some packages provide an 'outline' or meta-code of the system to be developed in the required language and this is used as a model from which full code can be subsequently generated by programmers. At a more sophisticated level, there are commercial tools available which first create such an outline, and then go on to develop the actual operational code from it. An example applicable to real-time systems, and requiring a workstation platform, is the Verilog tool GEODE. This will develop executable code in C from the system definition.

User Interface Tools

These are not strictly CASE products, but can make a tangible improvement in the ease of use and general applicability. (And these are the features that usually sell the product to senior management)

❏ **Windows:** Each window comprises a region of screen within which a particular application program can run. Some windowing systems will allow applications running in a number of windows to run simultaneously, while others will only let one window be active at any one time. Even the latter could allow, for example, the gradual development of a DFD in one window while at the same time describing the results with a word processor in the other.

❏ **Menus:** A useful technique for getting away from the command line interface. The old way would be to type, for example, the somewhat terse and little-understood command instruction "type filename.doc>prn" followed by the RETURN key. This is one MS-DOS command which causes a particular file to be printed. With a menu, one might use the mouse or pointing device to select an output menu; to select from that sub-menu the object printer and finally to select 'filename.doc' from another menu of files that automatically dropped down once the output device had been chosen. Menu systems are easy to use and build up user confidence because they do not require an elephantine memory for specialised key functions. In addition, they do not generate obscure and incomprehensible syntax error messages.

❏ **Screen Painter:** Most systems ultimately define the exact nature of the data that is to be entered into, held on, or retrieved from the relevant data store. The user has little choice in this matter. However, the way that data is displayed on the screen is open to modification. Remember that the screen is often the only point of contact between the system requirements defined by the designer and the comfort or satisfaction of the end user sitting daily at the terminal. As an example of how the user may have different expectations from a screen display, consider a typical form that is to be filled in by the user ('Date of birth','Place of birth', 'Sex of child', ...). Using a screen painter, this requirement can be fashioned into a format that seems right or agreeable to the end-user. The computer will not care either way, but the American user, for example, will want to input a date with the month number before the day number in a date piece of information. On the other hand, the European user will usually want to put the day before the month. Using this tool, the screen can be readily personalised to create any particular layout structure as required.

Another important aspect of the screen painter is that it enables the appearance of a given screen form to be *quickly* generated and modified. This allows the client to be shown a model on the screen which can, as it were, be effectively shaped to provide a pleasing impression to the end-user. This fast 'while-you-wait' service is important if working with *Prototyping* which we looked at in section 3.2.

IPSE Tools

Integrated Project Support Environment (IPSE) products effectively carry out the promise of Figure 3.5 in that they offer a complete set of integrated CASE tools to carry out all the life cycle activity. However, the set is sourced from only one organisation and will not necessarily interface with any other package that you are currently using. This means that the level of commitment from the purchaser has to be reasonably high in that the product is, initially, *very* expensive, the training needs are considerable, and the degree of flexibility with other vendors or products may be limited. On the other hand, if you can live with all the above, it is an extremely powerful product. It is a sort of second generation CASE tool, and should be considered for really large projects – preferably after having gained experience with one or two 'ordinary' CASE applications.

At the boundary between individual CASE tools and the full IPSE philosophy there are ICASE or *integrated* CASE products. At this point, these tools do not fit into a universal harness as postulated above, but will interface with specified commercial products from other vendors which address another part of the system life cycle activity. This is clearly a step forward, but the choice is necessarily restricted and is still defined by the vendor rather than the purchaser.

CASE Introduction

A point sometimes overlooked is that information systems have actually been successfully developed without the use of CASE tools. No heavy outlay, no complex training programme, freedom to use existing methods – these are arguments that can always be made for the simple approach. However, the truth is that there are enormous advantages to automating the design process. On the other hand, it is equally obvious that there are some serious potential drawbacks attached and these different aspects are illustrated in Figure 3.6.

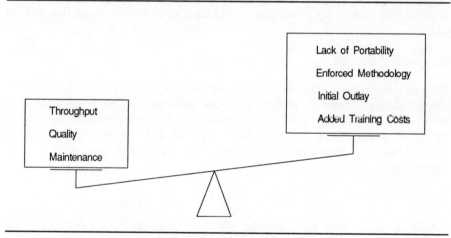

Figure 3.6: Weighing up the merits of CASE usage

For these reasons, this is an area where one should move forward with a fair degree of caution. The justification for using CASE has to be a strong one, and has to be well presented, in order to win over the budget controllers. In any case, the following points should be kept in mind:

CASE Model

Introducing CASE into the organisation for the next large project is almost certainly a recipe for disaster. The CASE techniques will be unfamiliar and the schedules will be critical and watched over by many interested parties. Any failures or misapplication of the CASE methodology will be used as the scapegoat for the failings of the rest of the project. Far better to introduce it on the basis of a long-term strategic involvement. In this way, one can start with a small pilot scheme where the working environment is sensibly benign and the learning-curve errors are containable.

Training

Again, do not fudge the training issue. Get advice on what constitutes a reasonable amount of training and what it will cost. And then budget for the full amount for every member of the design team, right from the outset. A small introductory project will call for a small team so the costs should be correspondingly acceptable.

Maintenance

It is not worth penny-pinching by cutting back on full maintenance and hot-line support. The cost tends to be roughly 10% of the initial outlay and the odds are that you will make very sound use of this service, especially in the first year of use.

In-house Support

Over and above every other factor, there are two requirements needed to get over the introductory hurdle. In the first place, the particular project manager or team leader should be strongly motivated to succeed using CASE tools. In the second, the senior management should be fully informed and supportive of the whole undertaking. Until these conditions hold true, it is not worth planning further action in this area.

Staff

Finally, a word about the personnel who have gone through this training and application period. By virtue of this added experience, their value to the organisation *and on the open labour market* will have materially increased. It would be a shame if their conditions of employment were such that they subsequently choose to move on.

Selection Criteria

If your organisation is open to proposals for a CASE approach to system design, then it is important that that the right set of CASE tools is chosen for the intended project.

Preliminaries

The first task is purely the mechanical one of information gathering, i.e. taking stock of the current products in terms of hardware, software, and long term objectives. This will generally call for some technical support in assessing the various models under review :

❏ **Hardware:** Define the current (and planned) hardware platforms that are to be utilised. As an example, consider a possible implementation for a PC based system. Are the screens to be monochrome (Hercules) or colour (EGA/VGA)? What is the available RAM capacity (Extended or Expanded)? Which types of printers (Lineprinter, Laser, Dot Matrix) are being used? Will results need to be ported to Workstations, Minis, VAX or mainframe machines?

❏ **Software:** Define the current (and planned) software packages. Which operating systems (MS-DOS, OS/2, Unix, etc.)? Graphic interface (GEM, Windows or XWindow)? Networking (Novell, IBM, 3Com, etc.) or stand-alone? Current CASE tools – if any? External programs i.e. Database, Wordprocessor?

❏ **Strategy:** Model the position of the organisation, say, in three years time. Guestimate (possibly with two sets of figures for best and worst estimates) the needed volume of on-going system design that could or should be using CASE products at that time. Volume figures could be based on the number of workstations, number of staff involved, etc. With a few simple assumptions, some approximate figure of total annual expenditure (based on current costs) could be arrived at. Then, for a rough rule-of-thumb, the initial foray into CASE systems currently being planned should be about one tenth of this figure. This assumption is based on about three years of doubling of the CASE expenditure as the usage and experience increases within the organisation. (If you cannot justify an annual doubling of expenditure over the three years from the original pilot scheme, then, perhaps, the introductory project is too ambitious or there has to be some other strategic reason for getting into CASE based design.)

❏ **Candidate:** Select one or more possible exercises that could be carried out using CASE technology. This could conveniently be part of the project (for example, a graphic design tool and dictionary to generate a product definition). Using a fairly approximate approach, establish the hardware, software and personnel requirements, along with time-to-complete estimates. These can be easily modelled into finance figures to give a first cut at the overall project cost. Then add in CASE related expenditure such as program outlay, training, and maintenance (see section on Costs below) to give a total budget projection. If this falls within the overall guideline limitation discussed in the previous paragraph, then start preparing the presentation material for appraisal by your higher management. If not, look for another candidate.

Compatibility

This is a follow-on from the previous section which defined the obvious physical and software interfaces that need to be matched. In this part we will discuss the hidden, and therefore potentially more serious, impact of adopting a CASE methodology. This is largely related to ensuring that the CASE tool usage will not interfere with the overall strategic procedures already in place.

❏ **Structured Design:** One of the unforeseen constraints of using CASE tools is that they all require the application of structured methods in some form or another. Now, if the current design philosophy is not based on some variant of DFDs or ERDs (see Chapter 2), then an added overhead will be the introduction and training in these methods – which is no small task in itself. Again, if the current approach is firmly based on ad hoc prototyping (section 3.4) without reference to any central model, there may well be some conflict between the needs of this style of approach and the CASE tools deliverables.

❏ **Existing Procedures:** If, for example, the current engineering office uses a well established method for handling and upgrading hard-copy drawings, then they will not always be co-operative in changing to a totally different way of processing graphic objects. Management by conflict does not have a good long-term track record, so a thorough review of the organisational changes involved in introducing CASE methods should be given a high priority. Either good work-rounds should be found along with co-operation and agreements on how to upgrade existing procedures, or the planned introduction should be dropped for the time being. It really is like that.

❏ **Configuration Management:** One of the major advantages of using the CASE approach is the speed with which changes can be implemented. The natural corollary is that many more changes are made to fine-tune the system or to make it that bit more attractive to the end-user. This concept of the continuous evolution of the system has the drawback that maintenance is made correspondingly more difficult. The problems start to arise, perhaps, on data entered a year ago which the system is no longer prepared to process. Does the error lie with a human error in the entry of data or with an incompatibility of the current version of the system with the earlier one? How to store all the variants of changing system implementations, and how to keep all the CASE related data will require serious review at the strategic level. In fact, it is something that can only be effectively controlled by implementing suitable Configuration Management procedures. The CASE product may or may not handle CM automatically, but, either way, it is a management requirement that should be kept firmly in mind (and there is more on this subject in Chapters 8 and 11).

Prior Experience

There are, perhaps, 40 to 140 CASE systems currently on the global market. It has to be said that selecting a CASE tool based on a vendor's sales brochure may not always be the best approach and this is backed up, to some extent, by one of the comments at the front of the chapter. The products themselves are very powerful and reliable tools, but there is no simple formula available at this stage that will allow you to short-list or identify the one product that would be best for your application. Even being offered a free trial for 30 days is not the real answer. In that time, you tend to find all the good things about the system without having established any of the underlying limitations. For all that, if a CASE tool is to be selected for a first time project, then some general guidelines can be applied (in descending order of priority):

❑ If any part of your organisation is already using a CASE tool, then select it. However good or bad it is, there will be someone in-house who has already solved the problems that you don't even know that you are about to have. Also, discussion with this other group will help you to avoid the more obvious mistakes that everyone makes the first time round.

❑ Failing in-house usage, if your consultant team recommends a package on the basis of having used it on other projects, then go for that one. They, at least, will have had some experience with it.

❑ Find a friend or colleague in your line of business who has already invested in a CASE tool. Talk about the problems that were met and why that particular system was chosen.

❑ Contact a professional organisation for advice on the subject. Remember that you are trying to home in from two different angles: the technical aspects of the CASE package, and the special factors related to your information system waiting to be designed. (It is not much use buying a system which is perfect for analysing the performance of fighter aircraft if you are in the business of selling cheese.)

❑ If you have a local agent who is sympathetic, talk it over with reference to the options open, the pros and cons of individual packages and a possible introduction to other people who have acquired them over the last six to twelve months.

❑ Finally, if there is no other way out, approach a vendor for assistance. As a beginner, choose one that advertises a lot, with well established service and training departments and which has been around for a few years. (The assumption being that they must have a reasonable product to have survived this long) Again, the more expensive the product, the more likely that it is full featured and will potentially satisfy your needs – but this has to be substantiated.

Costs

There is no doubt that CASE tools are expensive and difficult to justify for an introductory exercise. However, if it helps, look round the office at all the secretaries using their word processors and reflect on the wars and revolutions it took to replace all those perfectly serviceable type-writers – and how no-one would go back to them now. In three to five years time, virtually all information systems will be designed and implemented using some sort of CASE products. You have to consider if you (and your company) can afford to wait while your competitors invest now and gain the competitive edge.

❏ **Initial Outlay:** Tools can cost roughly between £500 and £500,000 depending on overall scope and services (at the time of writing -multiply roughly by 1.5 for US dollars and ECU, 2.5 for Swiss Francs, 3 for DM and 10 for French Francs). If you plan for an introduction on, say, a PC or similar machine then it would be reasonable to assume that a system from a known source, comprising graphic design tools and an interlinked dictionary, can be put together for about £1,500 to £9,000 for a single user pack. The unit price can drop dramatically with volume purchases.

❏ **Training:** Assume a figure of about 5 to 7 full days of training (possibly as 2 days on an introductory course, followed later by, say, 4 days on a design application). With a daily cost of about £150, then one can identify an outlay of about £1,000 per person – more or less independent of the cost of the tools.

❏ **Support:** This is the hot-line service, maintenance and upgrade contract with the vendor. Assume about 10 to 15% of the original outlay – per year.

❏ **Organisational Changes:** There will usually be added costs and delays involved in preparing or modifying the existing working procedures and practices to meet the requirements of the CASE approach (see the section on 'Compatibility' above). While the total cost will obviously depend on the nature of these changes, it is worth stressing that the full outlay in this area could well exceed the sum of all the other expenses combined.

Excelerator – A Typical CASE Product

As a representative of the more comprehensive tools, consider the product developed by Index Technology Corporation. (This is simply one example taken from a number of competitive products, and no endorsement is intended in the description that follows, which is based on the current version. The opinions expressed are, of course, my own.)

Market Penetration

Claimed to be in excess of 30% of the global market with more than 20,000 systems delivered. Judging by independent inputs from other sources – this is one of the group of leading CASE tools in the marketplace.

Costs

Could be on the high side for a PC based system. However, perhaps the features and facilities available still make it a good-value product.

❏ Single user purchase: about £5,500

❏ Training: roughly £150/day; say £900 per user.

❏ Maintenance, etc: 12% of initial outlay; say £650 per annum.

To set up one analyst with the hardware platform (say £2,000) and a set of CASE tools will cost a total of about £9,000, plus the cost of extra insurance. As said above, the unit cost drops for multi-licence deals.

External Interfaces

This is possibly more flexible than most equivalent products. It can be used on a reasonable range of hardware types, and interfaces with a variety of applications packages:

❏ **Basic platforms:** PC-AT (640 Kb RAM memory, mouse, monochrome or colour graphics), PS/2, Sun, Apollo workstations, VAX, VAXStation.

❏ **External text interfaces:** WordPerfect, MS-Word, Ventura, Pagemaker (etc.)

❏ **External databases:** DB2, Ingres, dBaseIII, Oracle Prime Information, CDD/Plus (etc.)

❏ **External code generators:** such as Micro Focus Workbench (COBOL format).

Methodology Support

Again there is a full set of options:

❏ **Graphic tools:** among a number of other standard layout generators, Data Flow Diagrams (DeMarco) and Entity Relation Diagrams (Chen) are supported.

❏ **The data dictionary:** There is good linking between the graphic packages and the data dictionary. Audits can be used to indicate discrepancies between them.

❑ **Structured design approach:** Excelerator supports a range of structured philosophies such as Information Engineering (James Martin) and SSADM (LSDM).

Major Features

The general style seems to be – provide a full set of facilities, but leave it to the designer whether to use them or not. Thus, there are no automatic mismatch, alarm or failure detectors, but the capability is there for the user to implement a sophisticated design plan.

❑ **Multi-user capability:** Available, but requires good partitioning of sections under design. There are locking mechanisms to prevent simultaneous working of the same material by different analysts, but no automatic 'deadlock' limitation (where A is waiting for code worked by B and B is waiting for code worked by A. Until released externally, both operators are paralysed in this situation.). Requires competent handling by the Project Librarian – i.e. the CASE tool supervisor.

❑ **Domain Control:** By using selected lists of sets at the dictionary level (DAY = {Mon, Tue, ... , Sun}) i.e. by manually defining the set of domain, the concept can be applied.

❑ **Configuration Management:** It does not provide CM directly and will require a separate application tool, or external system procedure of saving and storing the current dictionary, say, on a daily or weekly basis.

❑ **Security:** Access is controlled via password and username which are allocated by the Project Librarian. In addition, he or she will also control which parts of the overall project each user is allowed to work with.

❑ **Integrity:** Central to any method of system design is the need for an extensive set of checking tools to trap the inevitable individual or group human error. Excelerator seems well served in this area, although, again, there is no option for automatic alarm generation. Thus, if, for any reason, an entity is removed from an Entity Relation Diagram, there is no warning flag to indicate that the same entity is still present in a DFD or in the dictionary. However, reports can be readily generated which show any imbalance between the various diagrams and the dictionary. In addition, there are also, for example, tools which the analyst can use for level balancing (ensuring that the Data Flow Diagram is itself well structured), normalisation (eliminating redundancy in the construction of the system database tables) and record content analysis (checking completeness of the records and other project elements).

❑ **Presentation Material:** There are two important tools here. One which helps in the formative decision making process is the Presentation Graph. This is used to describe the overall system plan in a simple easy-to-read system plot. It is, if you like, a window into the design philosophy which enables the client and designer to enter into a dialogue to refine (or accept) the current definition of the overall objectives. Following on from this the system modelling is implemented, and another report generator can be used to directly assemble the resulting graphic and dictionary files into a *System Definition* report. This is largely an extraction of existing data items which fully defines all the sub-elements of the system. Since the definition is directly derived from the dictionary, this eliminates the introduction of any additional errors due to the manual generation of the document.

This abridged outline can only give some of the flavour of a product which, like a number of other CASE tools, is multi-featured, addresses more that one part of the system design life cycle, requires sound training for full exploitation, and which has the possibility of substantially reducing the cost of information system design and implementation. The scope and control available to the designer is outlined by the options shown on the main designer menu illustrated in Figure 3.7.

CASE Overview

We have touched briefly on some of the major aspects of using CASE tools. This is a new and growing field which has yet to provide well-defined operational standards and whose introduction could still give poor results in the wrong working environment. Thus, in spite of the very real advantages that CASE tools offer, they should only be considered for introduction where the probability of success is reasonably high, where there is a long term plan of gradual extension of the methodology and, above all, where the application of these tools is going to be well supported within the organisation.

Having said all that, it will be evident that CASE tools can offer advantages from two different directions. Technically, they can provide a quantum improvement in the processing of system design activities, although that improvement can only come from a thorough knowledge of both system design fundamentals and the workings of the selected application package. Secondly, they are a powerful source of management strategic information, since they are generally structured to provide a good reliable interface to the decision making body. However, once again, to be truly effective in this area, a sound understanding of the strengths and limitations of the tool is required. For anyone involved in a particular aspect of system design, time given to the study of CASE tools will well repay the investment.

3.5 Summary

This chapter has been concerned with the decision making that should occur at the beginning of any system development. These decisions are centred round each specific project and the conclusions will depend partly on the make-up of the decision making body, the objectives of the host organisation and on the prevailing political and financial climate. There are no *correct* answers – only honest endeavours and sensible projections that are thought to be best for the current situation.

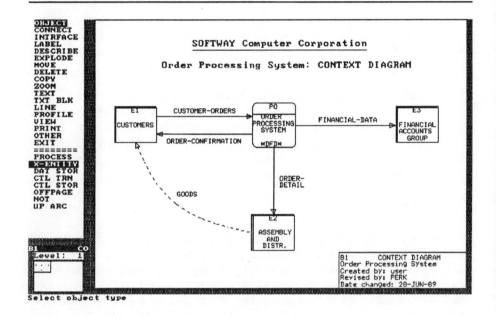

Figure 3.7: The Excelerator main designer menu

By now, it should be clear that the way the project is planned, costed, implemented, reported, and generally managed will be critically dependent on the strategic considerations discussed here.

In particular, we have addressed three major areas :

The System Development Life Cycle

The life cycle comprises all the activities undertaken to create a new operational system. It is important to recognise the scope of each of the constituent work phases in order to provide realistic cost and time project estimates, and these phases have been analysed and discussed. On a more long-term basis, we have covered the reason why systems continue to need upgrading even after successful completion and installation.

Structured Design

This section reviewed a number of alternative philosophies that can be applied for development of information systems. There are two main lines to follow and a third option consists of a mix of the other two :

Structured Methodology

This is the open-loop approach where a well-established sequence of set procedures will start from a feasibility study, generate a Requirement Specification and deliver the finished product reflecting that specification. The tasks are well defined; there are a number of effective error checking techniques; and the resulting projects are easily managed. On the other side, it can be an inflexible philosophy, where mid-design changes are not welcomed and the design process may take so long to implement that the original requirement is rendered obsolete.

Prototyping

A novel solution to some of the problems associated with using a structured methodology. The main advantages are that it is fast, providing first sample screens in a matter of days or weeks; the process maintains the full involvement and interest of the client in the design process; it can be responsive to changed requirements; and the continuous feedback ensures that the final result will match the expectation of the end-user. The disadvantages are that it is not easy to plan or forecast; performance testing may not be meaningful with just a prototype model; and it requires a disciplined management to ensure that project activities track all the changes so easily introduced.

Mixed Methodology

For the more adventurous souls, it is possible to use a mixture of the techniques outlined above. With careful planning, the objective will be to allow user testing of each system module – leading to system reworking where warranted. At the same time, the benefits of controlled project planning should be available. However, this style of operation will only be effective with projects where the system can be broken down into major modules that are sensibly independent of each other.

The Power Users

An important part of the chapter has been taken over with providing an outline of CASE tools, their properties and methods of application. In essence, they are a means to automate the development process with regard to system design. They are potentially very valuable in their functionality, but are still fairly novel, and, at this point, have no agreed standards or generic interworking capabilities. This should change over the next few years, but, until then, their selection, introduction and use should be carefully monitored at the management level. In particular, there should be a full evaluation of possible conflicts with the strategies and procedures already existing within the organisation. For all that, given the right working environment, a supportive management, and the appropriate project – CASE tools will prove enormously effective in time-to-complete factors and reduced error-injection rates.

In the final analysis, complex systems can be effectively processed using CASE tools. It is just a question of applying the standard three Cs : Caution, Competence, and (many cups of) Coffee.

3.6 CASE Usage by the Newtown and Universal Projects

The following examples illustrate one way in which the decision making process can be carried out, and how the specific working environments are evaluated. Remember that this is a subjective process and that more than one answer may be acceptable. Perhaps the best test to apply at the end of the day, could be to ask an independent management body : are the decisions, at minimum, *reasonable*?

Newtown General

❏ Life Cycle: The status of information systems in the medical world is undergoing enormous and rapid change. It would, therefore, be sensible to assume that the system under current review will be modified extensively in the near future to accommodate new strategies, new external sources and sinks (see Figure 2.1), and changed interfaces to other departments. It makes sense to model the system with the closed loop cycle of Figure 3.1b.

❏ Structured Methodology: Again, with short time spans, a fluid situation, and an uncertain, computer-illiterate workforce – it would seem fair to go for the prototype approach. This will involve the hospital staff early on in a positive way and ensure that they will be well motivated to operate the final installed system.

❏ CASE Tool: Application. A complex problem. If a single medical unit, in this case, the General Surgery Department, wants an information system to be operated at the local level, then it is almost certainly not worth the added outlay for an automated tool and extra training. If, however, the entire hospital (or, even better, the Local Area Health Authority) sees it as an introduction to a long-term grand strategy, then the sums involved become trivial, and the current project would be a good candidate. With the information available, however, this is taken to be a department driven requirement. Now, with just one analyst, the start up cost for the CASE tool discussed above would be about £9,000. With one system analyst, working for six months the overall resource costs with overheads will be in the region of £25,000. This gives a rough total outlay of about £35,000 for a small project. In following the application criterion of 10% of a possible future planned budget, the annual system-design budget for this one department should be of the order of £350,000. It sounds a shade unrealistic for this sort of funding to be supported by just one ward. Conclusion: in the absence of support from the central hospital authority, go for a manual implementation. As a corollary, special care should be taken to eliminate manually introduced errors.

Thus, Newtown would probably be advised to adopt a manually designed prototype approach, and to expect that a number of redesign cycles are likely to occur over the next few years.

Universal Solid State

❏ Life Cycle: This is a totally different type of business environment, where a heavy investment will usually be made in the latest techniques in order to improve overall productivity. There could well be an established data processing department that could implement the system design exercises. In this case, for historical reasons the analysts of this department would probably be happier with the open-loop version of Figure 3.1a.

❏ Structured Methodology: Again, in line with the disciplined approach that a DP department would be expected to use, the odds favour the application of a structured methodology such as SADT or SSADM. This will allow the formation of a well defined project with controllable cost and date estimates and good presentation tools for reporting back to senior management.

❏ CASE Tool Application: A different picture will emerge here – for two main reasons. In the first place, a single meeting between representatives from the research labs (Canada), manufacturing plant (Korea), and the sales outlets (Europe) would probably cost more in air fares than the cost of setting up one analyst with a CASE tool for a year. So the outlay is unlikely to be significant in terms of overall operating budgets. In the second place, the actual project i.e. providing information for management decisions on investment in new models, can only be a trivial part of the total possible applications of information systems within a hi-tech research/manufacturing/sales environment. In other words, it looks like a good pilot scheme and the initial outlay is well within acceptable limits. Here we see that the nature of the proposed development and its environment are again the prime factors in determining the strategic decisions. These will, in turn, establish how the project will be run.

In short, the Universal design team would probably select an open-loop life cycle with a structured methodology applied via an appropriate CASE tool.

This section has been concerned to give examples of how the strategic decisions might be reached. The approach has necessarily been superficial, but in real life the conclusions would only be reached after a great deal of care has been taken to fully evaluate all the necessary information. It is only by understanding the strategic implications of the options under discussion that the right decisions can be made for each particular design project. Arriving at these right decisions is probably the most crucial event in the entire project.

Questions

1. You have been asked to design and install a personal computer kit (i.e. the PC, printer, modem, media store, table and chair, etc.) in the home 'office' for a newly married young couple. Define the type and scope of activities to be undertaken, in terms of a classical life cycle.

2. Would you recommend prototyping in the case of question 1? Justify your decision. Then identify those areas of the design program where prototyping could be used. Describe how the end-user(s) would be involved in the process.

3. It is suggested that a CASE tool will materially help to automate the design procedure. Indicate the circumstances where it might be viable to use such a tool.

4. The actual client is a national organisation for helping the disabled, and the exercise of question 1 is something of a test case. Reappraise questions 2 and 3 in this light.

Personnel

DoE attacked for budget cover up

The Department of the Environment is under fire for allowing a key project to miss budgets and deadlines, and trying to speed it up by bringing in a (£)110,000 a year consultant.

. . . .

Trade union computer staff, angry that the post was not filled by a civil servant, took industrial action on January 16th, claiming that the consultant's fee was equivalent to the annual training budget for 120 of their members.

As a result, the DoE has dropped plans to draft in another consultant, and brought on four civil service computer staff instead.

Computer Weekly p.1 16.2.89

DSS battles to keep down staff turnover

The Department of Social Security is struggling to cope with staff turnover rates of 45% on the world's biggest civil computing project. Unions and suppliers say staff on this £2bn DSS computerisation project are leaving sooner than they can be trained.

. . . .

Rosie Eagleson, deputy group secretary of the NUPCS, says, 'There are definitely turnover problems both in the computer centres and among clerical staff learning to use desktop terminals.'

Computer Weekly p.1 8.3.90

Working mums left holding baby

Pregnant women and women with babies are being badly supported in the workplace at a time when employers need to attract more working mothers to offset skills shortages.

Philip Virgo, project manager for the group, said the only two computer firms which have effective programmes for women returning to work after having children are ICL and the FI Group.

"Most employers do not know how to organise returner programmes. They are only now beginning to explore the problem because of the worsening skills shortage." he said.

Datalink p.6 12.6.89

4.1 Introduction

The only thing that stands between you and the perfect information system is people. People who make, review and agree new proposals, people who manage and report on project progress, people who design and install, and, finally, people who actually use the new system for the greater corporate efficiency. They are all part of a long chain which, as always, is only as strong as the weakest link.

The Framework

This chapter is concerned with developing a set of tools. These tools are essentially techniques which can be applied to monitor the staff structure and interface networks for each project. They will also highlight where changes are needed to maximise the potential for a successful outcome to the project. In order to set up these techniques, we will need to review a number of important aspects related to the application of personnel in the system project environment:

❑ Identification of the people working on a project.

❑ Assessment of the factors causing demotivation and low morale at the individual and group level.

❑ Discussion of the friction caused by personality clashes at a common interface.

❑ Modelling of the typical behaviour patterns of an organisation.

❑ Providing a composite picture of the stresses that may be found in a project, and using this as a measure of the probable 'success' for that project.

The objective here is to identify and ultimately eliminate all the main causes of *inherent* friction and conflict within the workforce associated with information systems. That is to say, right at the start of the project, the framework should be designed to allow for smooth interworking of all the parties concerned.

Definitions

We are going to need a few definitions. So, for the purposes of the discussion that is to form the bulk of this chapter, consider the following terms:

activity: *a well defined set of tasks, with inputs from known sources and with outputs to known sinks. Examples could be 'write the design specification' or 'review the test procedure'.*

team: *a set of people with the main characteristics: they form a small interactive body ultimately responsible to some external authority; they were brought together to carry out specific activities; they operate* *within a defined environment; and it (the team) is always potentially subject to reformation or shut-down. Examples could the Berlin Philharmonic Orchestra, the School Sports Day Working Group, or the Finance Department.*

balance: *this is the measure that establishes the level of conflict (or agreement) between interested parties, such as individuals or teams, on the manner of carrying out given activities. Examples of these interested parties could be:*
Individuals and their assigned roles,
Members of a working team and other members of the same team,
Team A and team B both working in the same organisation,
Organisation I and organisation II working on some shared project.

This last topic, balance will have a major bearing on the project, since the real, if undeclared, productivity of the project teams is often related to how much time is spent sorting out misunderstandings, conflicts and frustrations due to poor interaction at the human level. If the whole area of human contact can be considered at the outset of the project, then a number of straightforward project strategies will help to cut out much of this wastage.

The Ground to be Covered

There are few hard certainties in the field of industrial sociology. For all that, a common sense approach to plugging all the possible loopholes in the area of interpersonal conflict will show an enormous benefit in any commercial development. So we will tackle the subject carefully, one step at a time. In the first place, we shall address the matter of who is going to be involved. This will provide an outline of all the parties who may expect to participate in the project, their potential roles, and the possible implications of ignoring their legitimate (or perceived legitimate) interests.

This will be followed up with a general review of the factors affecting workforce morale and the impact on the project. Consider, for example, the movement of the personnel allocated to the project. It is perfectly normal for staff to leave to get another position or move to another department. However, a mass migration not only says something about departmental morale, but is also a major disaster for the projects being designed there.

The next topic will be a short review of *role* as a source of friction. By identifying clear cases of poor interface, it will be possible to plan some low-level structural changes to the project which will reduce or eliminate these pockets of mismatch. As an example, Jennie who is careful if unimaginative may have a regular commercial contact with Shirley who has flair and is impulsive. Such an interface might be unavoidable but is unlikely to be productive.

Having covered these questions of personal and role conflicts, we can now look at the way large groups or organisations behave. Once we have a way of monitoring the characteristics of such groups, we can use this information to compare two potential partners for commonality of approach and potential for cooperation.

Finally, we can bring together all the topics that have been discussed to form a composite picture of balance. By using some simple plots, we can review a number of parameters, for each particular case, which will reflect the operational behaviour to be expected (both at the corporate and personal level). This will allow us to quantify the scope for potential problems in carrying out the project.

Once again, we will be discussing a number of important subjects in a restricted space. For this reason, the treatment has to be relatively limited, but more extensive treatments will be found in the bibliography.

4.2 Project Participants

Apart from any theoretical modelling, it is important to be aware of the numbers of people and groups who could be participants in a practical development exercise. This will ensure that the right representatives are included (or, at least, considered) for task allocation and/or review and acceptance activity. The major parties concerned with system design are:

❑ The client

❑ The designer

❑ The end-users

❑ The project managers

❑ The operations and management unit

❑ The interested outsider

The Client

In practice, there is no single entity which can be given this label. The term will usually include a number of completely different and possibly independent management roles. One of these could be, for example, the local finance director or comptroller who is responsible for funding the development activities. He is effectively the *client-paymaster*. Then there could be the local data processing department who will interface with the designers to ensure that the specifications are in line with the original objectives. They will also be concerned with product test, performance evaluation, documentation etc., and could be considered as the *client-consultants*. Finally, there could be the local departmental line managers under their relevant director who will need to keep in touch with the work in progress and participate in the installation plans. These are the *client-managers*. Each of these three roles – paymaster, consultant, manager – will need very different inputs from the projects (and possibly interface with totally different individuals) and these will need to be clearly identified from the outset.

The Designer

Once again, this term covers a number of different roles. At the top will be the *consultant*, who, hopefully, is well versed in all the tools and methodologies used to analyse and design the new system. Then, come the *analysts* who will carry out assignments defined by the consultant. These will usually comprise the design of specific sub-systems based on some master specification. The next stage would be to use *programmers* to implement in code the objectives defined by the analysts. Following on after all this, there might be a range of *support engineers* involved in aspects of test, performance, installation, training, and documentation. All these roles may be carried out by just one individual, or each function could be the responsibility of a whole department. The roles are always the same, it is only the implementation that varies according to the magnitude of the development activity.

The End-users

These are often the clerical staff who input and collect data from the system when installed. They have a certain importance, not always appreciated, in that only they really know how the old system worked and which changes would be effective.

"Japanese top managers never tire of reminding the employees that they, the workers, know the business best and that innovation and improvement must come from the genba *(where the action is)."* – Kenichi Ohmae, 'The Mind of the Strategist', p. 227, Penguin, 1986.

In turn, the cooperation and motivation of these end-users is important while sorting out the first few weeks of operating the new system. After all, it is a sobering thought that their lack of support can seriously retard or even stop the introduction of a new product (see, for example, one of the reports at the introduction of Chapter 10). In addition, there could be members of the data processing department regularly employed in the integration of the data inputs and providing summary or high-level reports. While the end-users obviously belong to the client's organisation, they have been separated from the block entitled 'Client', since their interface is usually at a totally different level.

The Project Managers

This may be one person working full time, part of one person's workload, or a team with members from both the design and client organisations. The concern will be with defining the overall strategies, overseeing all the necessary activities that have to be carried out, allocating equipment and resource to implement these activities such as to meet the master schedules, monitoring the progress up to the present and, where necessary, applying corrective actions where the planning has gone astray.

The Operations and Maintenance Unit

These are the persons concerned with the day-to-day administration and running of the computer equipment. The roles, however implemented, would include a *hardware* maintenance function – again, depending on the amount of work, carried out by one person (or part thereof), or a full team of engineers. There could be a *communications* role concerned with maintaining all the networks, modems, and other data links to the outside world. There will almost certainly be *site engineers*, responsible for the security and safety of the computer room area, along with responsibility for other electrical services such as air conditioning and power supply sources. Finally, there is the *administration* group concerned with the day-to-day operations and housekeeping for the site. All these people could be concerned with a single centralised location, or conversely with all the computer-based equipment distributed all over the site or sites. Again, they could be employed by the host company or brought in as an external service organisation (facilities management team). Whatever the situation, this group could be seriously affected by the proposed introduction of a new information system with its new hardware and software maintenance requirements.

The Outsider

This is another of those vague labels which catches everyone not included in some other list. For all that, the roles outlined here can take up a disproportionate amount of time and attention. In the first place, there could be the *union* official who may quite legitimately want to be satisfied that the work associated with the new system does not endanger or overload the staff. And perhaps to ensure that the remuneration levels are in line with any added responsibilities. Then there are the *external departments* who will also be using the new system and need to establish the proper interfaces. (In addition, they will usually be quite helpful in pointing out just why and where the new system is totally incompatible with existing corporate strategies and systems – which they fully support.) Representatives from *senior management* may descend from time to time to see where all the money is going and will want presentable material prepared for the appropriate meetings. Finally, and by no means least, there may be visits to the workplace from an outside *auditor* called in to assess the state of development and methods of operation. Whatever the reason for the visit, as much time as necessary will have to be spent in helping the auditor's investigations.

Although not directly involved in the project, these functions can have a major influence on the on-going strategy, and this is borne out by two reports given at the head of this chapter.

Summary

This section has enumerated some of the links in the chain mentioned in the opening paragraph of the chapter, and this information has been consolidated into the diagram given in Figure 4.1. It is worth repeating: if any of the roles indicated in this diagram have a negative attitude towards the design – or are simply ineffective, the impact on the progress of the development project could well be significant. While the management roles are particularly important, success means getting *all* these people to work together. This is where the real skill of project management comes in.

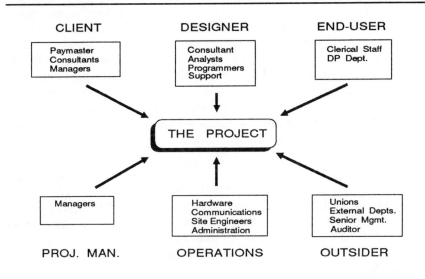

Figure 4.1: The project personnel

4.3 Morale in the Workforce

This section will outline some of the main reasons why staff morale can fall, and will look at the resulting knock-on effects that can appear in the office or workplace. In addition, we will discuss some of the possible solutions that can be applied as a remedy. Basically, all the sources of low morale being considered here are taken to be different aspects of *stress*. For our purposes, *stress* can be defined as 'any characteristic of the job environment which poses a threat to the individual.' Another view could be that 'stress refers to a misfit between the person and his environment' (reference 15, p. 63). Sometimes stress can be a stimulus to call for yet greater effort to overcome a problem, but, more often, it has a disabling and paralysing influence on the person concerned. Not only that: in communication with other colleagues, one person under stress – and therefore demotivated from a work point of view – can spread his or her disaffection with remarkable speed. The sooner the stress point is relieved, the better. After all, if the closing remarks of the last section have any relevance, then time spent reducing stress will offer handsome returns on investment. (It may even help the person concerned!) Among the frequently found stressors, or stress sources, that will affect the morale of an individual or group are:

❑ Fatigue and Burnout

❑ Political Stress

❑ Relocation

❑ Management

❑ Teleworking

❑ Minority Group

❑ Personal Problems

The question of salaries and other rewards or bonus payments can, of course, be a key issue – sometimes generating high frustration levels with the workforce. However, this is usually not within the control of the project manager. On the other hand, the job satisfaction and morale aspects covered in this section can have a substantial effect on the overall productivity of the design staff and are very much the concern of the manager.

Fatigue and Burnout

Unlike the other examples under review, this sort of problem does not appear over a short period of time. On the contrary, it is characterised by having the individual in an unchanging stressful situation over an extended period. It is a recognised risk among long-term teachers and social workers (reference 15, p. 102), but can occur wherever creative work is required in an continuing difficult environment. ("Why does Harry always ask me to join his detailed progress meeting – 10 minutes before it is due to start...") The person concerned will tend to show a number of symptoms of physical and emotional exhaustion, i.e. headaches, colds, sleeplessness and depression. While there are no quick-fixes, one possible solution would be to seek out the 'old-timers' and (tactfully and positively) change the nature of their work or the environment in which they operate.

Political Stress

You can have imposed on you a set of working conditions or objectives which are simply not acceptable. This could be more responsibility than is reasonable, a heavy travel commitment while a child or parent is sick, and so on. In particular, *role ambiguity* can be a major problem, where chains of command and scope of function have not been clearly defined (reference 15, p. 196). Since these stressors have originated within the organisation, presumably the load cannot be reduced. However, there is plenty of scope for management support. This could take the shape of temporary staff assistance, or a special travel allocation for weekend home trips, etc. Just knowing that someone is on your side can do wonders for the morale.

Relocation

Just as moving house is one of the major traumas for a family, so relocation within an organisation can be disruptive for the individual. It will be correspondingly worse if moving to another site, while that proposed three year stint in Alice Springs will take a bit of thinking about. Just being moved into a new department or being regrouped can cause severe disorientation. Again, in general terms, a corporate interested party or a personal-problem-consultant function can be useful in discussing the major impacts and changes that will occur. This could well include a video presentation, say, to cover all the issues, including support for the family on the move. As a final pointer, not many people have been too depressed with a relocation that involved substantial promotion and salary increases, while very few people have ever been much motivated without them.

Management

There is no getting away from it: working for an indifferent manager, or for someone who is only interested in playing politics, is no fun. While this will not apply to you, one could easily visualise managers in our company ABC who are so overloaded that they just can't find the time to chat informally with their equally overloaded staff on a regular basis. The resultant movement of staff will come as no surprise.

Teleworking

To those cramped up in an airless office which is only reached after an hour of uncomfortable commuting, the though of working at home must sound like something akin to paradise. It has been proposed by, among others, Alvin Toffler (see "The Third Wave", Pan Books, 1982, p. 210: The Telecommuters) and there are people who are currently working in this fashion with data and communication links into a central computer location. The advantages have been well publicised, but there are two problems which can result from working at home :

❏ *Distraction:* It can be difficult to maintain the flow of work if the children are replaying their holiday videos in the next room. Or, if you are asked to mend the washing machine. These sorts of natural distractions result in a dramatic loss of productivity.

❏ *Isolation:* The office can be seen as a social environment where the work can be freshened with coffee breaks and constructive meetings with colleagues (unlike with the children above). In this context, the home can appear disturbingly deadening and stimulation-free.

These problems can often be resolved by having some proportion of the time spent in the home and the rest spent in the office.

Minority Groups

There are four major groups that may consider themselves disadvantaged in comparison with the main working population in computer based industries: the post-young (to coin a phrase for the over 35s), women, the disabled, and people from the immigrant communities – in the UK this could be the Asians and Afro-Caribbeans, in Germany the Turkish community, and so on. Virtually every report claims that there will be a heavy demand for professional staff through the 90s, and there will have to be an increased take up of staff from these groups. Again, there are two factors to be considered:

❏ Organisations will have to plan special arrangements to bring these groups smoothly into the corporate fold. One problem area, concerning facilities for returning mothers and their young children, is aired at the front of the chapter.

❏ Bluntly speaking, the existing staff will have to exercise or be taught tact. An analyst is not expected to love the elderly, but, for example, " ... if you can still remember how to code, Grandad... " could be construed as a aggressive remark when offered to a returning ex-patriate on his first day.

Personal Problems

It is fairly obvious that someone in their late thirties facing an impending divorce will not be giving their wholehearted attention to the developments in the system design department. This applies equally to a number of other stressful situations outside the workplace where the person concerned is in serious overload. These problems are beyond the scope of this book and all that can be done is to be tolerant, until the pressure point has been removed. If it is really serious, approach the local medical department or some equivalent body for assistance.

Conclusion

All this discussion has been based on one assumption: it is advantageous to have a well motivated workforce with a high morale. The people will be strongly integrated as a team (or set of teams), will actually *enjoy* the challenge, and will work well together for the project. In turn, the last few pages have shown that such a workforce is likely to have a manager who takes the time to help and support staff in reducing their stress related problems. The underlying implication is that such a manager will probably have to have the support of *his* management in carrying out this policy.

Now, for some examples taken from the models. Let's look first at the level of stress in the hospital, where the staff will comprise, for our purposes, student nurses, staff nurses and junior doctors. They will probably not be strangers to fatigue. Burnout will be more familiar to the long term ward sisters, but is less likely to be a general problem. There may be considerable pressure on the junior doctors to perform responsibly under difficult circumstances. Finally, a fair number of the nursing staff may be employed from the immigrant communities, so the potential for minority pressures exist. (The actual degree of antagonism experienced will obviously vary considerably from location to location.) Again, these are judgmental values and in a real case it might take some time to reach a proper conclusion. However, for the moment, an initial estimate for the hospital junior staff would be that morale could be on the low side – perhaps reinforced by general considerations of salary.

The second example concerns the multinational hi-tech corporation. Fatigue is not going to be a problem (apart from workloads around budget presentation time, the rest of the year is reasonable). On the other hand, burnout can be a distinct possibility especially with the middle level managers who have stopped getting promoted. The political stress levels can vary considerably, but a multinational that keeps making good financial figures does not generate too much pressure on its staff. Relocation, however, can be a real issue. In the first place there may be disorientation in the new workplace, but, in addition, there can be the added pressure from the other members of the family who want to return to the former home or miss the old friends. The question of minority groups is not usually significant. This is due to the natural global outlook of the organisation as well as a sensitivity to pressure groups in the home country. Finally, with regard to his or her personal life, the ex-patriate may be susceptible to some loss of stability in coming to terms with the 'alien' culture of the foreign country. On weighing it all up, a first estimate of the average position on the 'morale scale' would be about half way up. We will be returning to this data in section 4.5.

Notice that, in addition to an overall evaluation of morale, the individual problem areas have to be identified on a case by case basis. Each particular mapping will then allow resource to be allocated specific to the defined area of stress.

4.4 Role Matching

This is a short section about recognising the obvious problems of 'round pegs in square holes' and taking sensible steps to alleviate the condition. Again, this is part of the piecemeal approach, where every section of the chain is examined for defects, and, where necessary, corrective action taken.

While the discussion on larger group interactions will be left to section 4.5, at this point we can go over two types of matches (or mismatches) that can be possible sources of friction:

❑ The nature of the role within the project being in conflict with the personality of the assignee. (Role to Person.)

❑ The interface between roles of individuals or groups, which have a natural lack of agreement. (Role to Role.)

Role to Person

It will be helpful to take a generalised look at the concept of *role* within the commercial environment. This can be defined as *'the typical behaviours that characterise a person in a social context'* (reference 13, p. 246). It is common wisdom, for example, that some roles will call for a fairly strong predetermined attitude by the person involved. Thus, a salesman is expected to be an outgoing character, an accountant should naturally give careful attention to detail, a negotiator will have smooth delivery and diplomacy, and so on. By the same token, people will have a natural *persona* which will tend to make them forceful, submissive, caring, indifferent to others, etc., and therefore better suited to some tasks than to others. Most of the time, people can successfully undertake a wide variety of roles, but just occasionally the gap may prove too much. Under those circumstances, the only crime is to leave the situation unchanged, so either move the person or modify the job.

Role to Role

It can be remarkably easy to set up an almost inevitable disaster. Consider the design analyst: a born problem solver, interested in elegant solutions, and quickly bored with the mundane. Now consider the clerical end-user: will go to endless effort to get the details right, will follow the book without once cutting corners and likes to take things step-by-step. Of course these are stereotypes, but it would be strange if you did not find similar people among your workstaff. Finally, let's take the reasonable situation where the analyst is expected to document a subsystem following design acceptance. It will be in the form of a handbook and outline how the system operates. From the analyst's point of view, this is the last desperately boring job before the intellectual challenge of the next project, and it is fairly obvious how the software works anyway. With this attitude in mind, the analyst spends a few terrible days putting together a number of hastily written and incomplete pages. As a result, the users gets a cramped, virtually incomprehensible, set of poorly written sheets which only frustrate their efforts to understand the operation of the new system. Both sides are demotivated and no information transfer really occurs. The mismatch is shown in outline in Figure 4.2a, which illustrates the absence of contact across the interface boundary.

One possible solution, among many, would be to interpose one or more technical writers between the two parties. They will be in a position to understand the 'shorthand' language of the analyst and transpose it into the required format for the end-user, and this new communication linkage is shown in Figure 4.2b. Notice that role/role mismatch is virtually independent of the people carrying out these roles, it is inherent in the nature of the roles themselves.

Addressing these matters will take a certain amount of time and effort at the beginning of the development exercise. The pay-off occurs further down the schedule in the way people will work together to get the system developed.

4.5 A Measure of Style

The first part of the chapter has discussed the nature of the people who could be involved in the project. The second discussed their attitude to it and the way individuals can affect the overall performance of the project. Now, we are going to take a brief look at group interactions and their importance.

Simply stated, a project with a management style that matches the aims and beliefs of the funding organisation is more likely to succeed than one which ignores these aims. To that end, it is evidently desirable to establish the nature of the organisation's operating philosophy. Two points arise:

❑ There are no right or wrong styles. There are only different styles.

❑ The way the work is carried out, internal to the system development project, is completely defined by the scope and needs of the project workers, and may have little in common with client practices. However, it is the *interfaces* with the client that should match the client's expectations.

We can start with a broad definition of *style*: the attitudes, values, opinions and beliefs that are generally held as valid or operational within the organisation (see Chapter 5 'Organisation Culture, Structure and Climate', p. 104 of reference 14). Decisions and management strategies will ultimately be based on these perceived truths of corporate style. What is needed is some simple assessment monitoring tool which will allow the behavioural patterns of the enterprise under review to be measured. There are all sorts of possible additional nuances, but in broad terms any

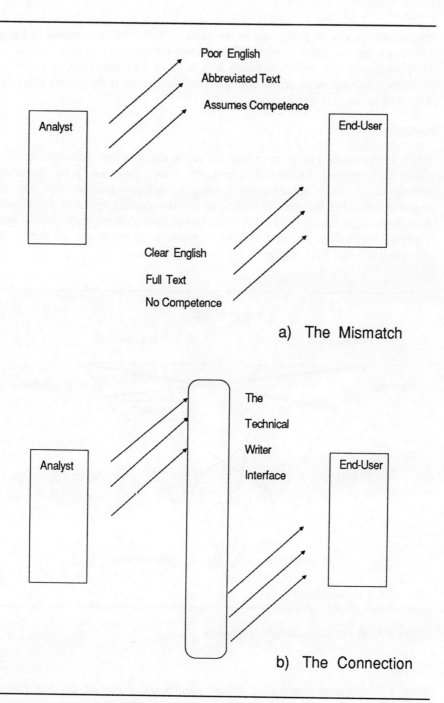

Poor English
Abbreviated Text
Assumes Competence

Analyst

End-User

Clear English
Full Text
No Competence

a) The Mismatch

Analyst

The
Technical
Writer
Interface

End-User

b) The Connection

Figure 4.2: The communication link

corporate entity can be positioned in the 'style triangle' which is shown in Figure 4.3. This is just one possible method for defining the nature of an organisation – in this case to plot the degree to which it is more or less autocratic; more or less entrepreneurial; and more or less homogeneous. Let's look at the general properties of each of the axes in the diagram:

Politics

This axis represents a measure of how the organisation is run. *Autocratic* tends to mean: well defined chains of command; good top-down poor bottom-up communications; firm adherence to existing procedures. This is often how the empire-builders and the early capitalists of the 19th century operated. Conversely, *democratic* might imply: fluid chain of command, decentralised management, good bilateral communications, and variable adherence to corporate standards. An example could be a 20th century multinational corporation.

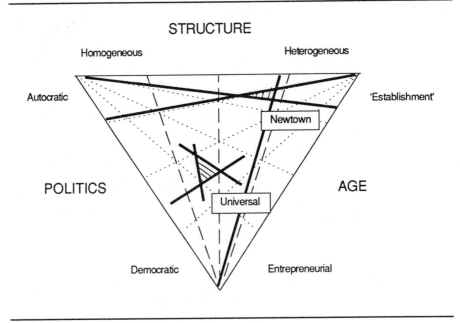

Figure 4.3: The organisation Style triangle

Age

When a commercial undertaking is just starting up, it has all the attributes of youth: it is an *entrepreneurial*, fast trading, seat-of-pants operation, corners are cut, and you stay with the job till completed. It tends to be stressful but exciting. This could be, for example, a start-up advertising agency. On the other hand, the large *establishment* company works in an orderly way, runs through established reporting procedures, has the resource for the really big jobs and the capability for long-term planning. Examples could be central government agencies or major banking authorities.

Structure

In an ideal world, everyone in the same organisation will share the same dreams and work together for the recognised common goal. In practice, a company can be torn apart by conflicting ideas on how to implement a given strategy. A *homogeneous* group will contain peer members or departments that more or less follow the same line on standard practices. Further, individuals with different levels of responsibility will accept working together cooperatively. An example might be the civilian workforce in a wartime factory. On the other side, the *heterogeneous* organisation will be a more difficult partner, since different attitudes and methods may be found among different peer groups while the ordinary workers may suffer from low morale and be less than satisfied with the competence of their management. The situation on the outward bound 'Bounty' would be an extreme case of such an organisation.

The values to be used in such a diagram are evaluated and established by the analyst as a result of observations, discussions and interviews with the project partner(s). While any assessment has to be subjective, there are some pointers which can be helpful in reaching an initial position -although again this would have to be backed up by confirmatory evidence:

❏ *Politics:* The company canteen or restaurant is usually a fair microcosm of the overall social conditions. The more autocratic organisation may have more than one restaurant for different strata of the workforce, and even if there is only one, then the different grades of personnel may assemble in different locations within the restaurant. From a different angle, the perceived administrative response to suggestions from the junior staff often indicates the nature and attitudes of the management approach.

❏ *Age:* The pointers for an entrepreneurial team are usually small size of operation in conjunction with high ambient noise level (a small quiet company could be so adult that it is practically dead). In addition, a marked absence of interest in areas such as Quality, Documentation, or Medical Facilities can suggest that spontaneous dynamism is the priority of the day. Conversely, when some time is spent in a meeting discussing the distribution list for the minutes, it is likely to be an 'establishment' organisation. Another strong indicator in this direction is any reference to anything like Company Standards on Information Technology, the Maintenance Cost Database, or a Qualification Test strategy.

❑ *Structure:* Not so easy to establish. Morale, respect for higher management, and cooperation within the peer group are all factors whose absence is only revealed over a relatively long period of observation. For all that, it is important to know if you, as the analyst, will have to play politics with the personnel involved with the project, and to determine the extent of the problem. Again, it is worth repeating, there is no criticism involved here. The objective is to successfully install a working system, and if you have to receive and send some decidedly peculiar phone-calls to different departments in order to meet that objective, then so be it. On the other hand, the situation will be more relaxed if the work force is sensibly unified in the organisation, since then a single style of interface can be used.

This section has identified some of the active parameters which can be used to monitor the operational style of an organisation. It is intended to be of value in forming an interface strategy with the project partner. The assumption is that friction in that interface will act to reduce the probability of success for the system under development. A good match, on the other hand, will only improve the chance for a satisfactory installation.

We can take a look at Newtown and Universal, now, to examine the positions that might be representative for them. The results and opinions will be subjective, confidential and liable to variation with time. In fact, the first appraisals may say more about the bias of the observer than anything else. However, with increasing contact, the results will be easily upgraded. They are certainly not for general discussion, since the opinions expressed can be fairly direct.

Newtown

The canteen rule probably breaks down here in that Doctors and Specialists may well choose to sit with certain student nurses over lunch, without any political intent whatsoever. However, as a first assumption, the hierarchy of committees, and the inter-departmental demarcations of authority may point to a highly autocratic organisation. This is represented on the diagram in Figure 4.3 by a straight line, starting from the POLITICS axis and continuing up to the opposite apex. In this case, the line will start reasonably near to the autocratic point. The current apparent frustration of some support staff, nurses and junior doctors with their working conditions suggests a heterogeneous personnel structure, and this is represented by another separate line on the drawing. Finally, the way in which hospitals (in the UK) have been tied together in District Health Authority groupings which in turn relate to Regional Health Authorities with common administrative procedures implies an 'establishment' or firmly regularised environment. This is again indicated by the position of the third straight line in the drawing.

In summary, an autocratic governing style; a well ordered operation; and a reasonably heterogeneous workforce. A first estimate of the overall style is therefore indicated by the shaded area formed by the intersection of the three lines representing these sub-elements of style.

Universal

Most North American multinationals are usually characterised by a fairly democratic outlook – at least as a early impression. First names are *de rigeur*, the janitor eats with the vice-president and "my door is always open ...". The underlying in-fighting may sometimes be brutal but, for all that, there is a reasonably democratic atmosphere. The overall corporate size can get rather large while still maintaining some of the trappings of the start-up origins of a decade or so ago. The commercial requirements for adherence to international standards along with the large size of operations mean that there is a strong overlay of formal procedures. However, there is still room for the bright maverick. Finally, unless actually over the hill, most high-tech organisations are usually work oriented with good group cooperation.

Thus, for an initial appraisal, this organisation is reasonably homogeneous; reasonably democratic; and still sensibly entrepreneurial. This is again shown via the three lines of intersection and corresponding shaded area for Universal in the diagram. For clarity, note that only those parts of the lines in the vicinity of the intersection have been indicated.

The technique has obvious application in assessing the nature of two potential partners. Assume that a university department wishes to improve its administrative systems and very naturally calls in a start-up consulting group situated in its own technology park. Very briefly, like most educational centres, the university will be very 'establishment' in that there is a well entrenched administrative structure; there will usually be fierce rivalries to get papers published and to obtain promotion to higher positions; and under differing situations the politics can vary from the completely autocratic to the freely democratic. On the other hand, the consultants will veer largely to the democratic, will provide all the characteristics of a start up company, and will not be able to afford the luxury of a divisive workforce. If the above suppositions are right, then these two styles of working are indicated in the diagram of Figure 4.4, and this clearly shows the wide gulf separating the two hypothetical models in terms of their styles of operation. This is not to suggest that these two organisations could not work together, but does imply that some care should be taken at the outset to define in detail the agreed lines of interworking.

Summing up, the style, or behaviour pattern, of any organisation can be expressed in a fairly simple way by means of a graphic tool. This will only give an approximate representation, but can still help to illustrate the state of the organisation, to point to the sort of inputs that would be acceptable to it, and to decode some of the possible responses that might result.

4.6 Planning for Success

We have now covered a number of topics related to the way in which people interact in a project, and this final section will bring all these topics together in a measure of how effective the project team is likely to be. This team will be a meld of personnel comprising, at minimum, staff from the consultant group and the client company and we can look at the different ways each of these groups would get things done. This can then be used as a measure of the likely friction or misunderstanding between the participants, which in turn will point to the probability of overall success in the project. Is there any justification for correlating a good match of outlook with successful interworking? Well, perhaps more importantly, it does seem clear that the converse is true, i.e. a bad match will cause poor interworking:

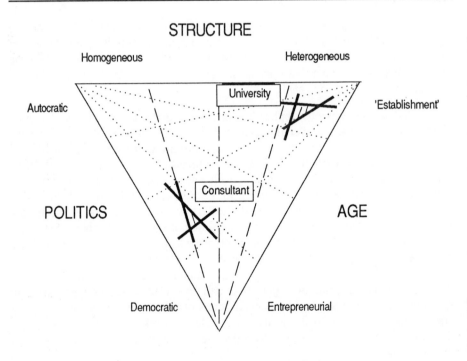

Figure 4.4: The Client/Consultant match

'Townsend watched the bureaucratisation of Avis with unconcealed gloat: 'It didn't take long,' he remarked, 'for the crap to start creeping in.' Avis moved to plush new headquarters, hired a staff of PR men, and began to look like other bits of ITT. Morrow, indignantly disputes Townsend's account of life with Avis: 'You couldn't save a company or run it with his methods', he said to me, 'Townie's not an administrator – he's not consistent enough. He's an artist.'

A. Sampson, The Sovereign State, p. 76, Hodder and Stoughton 1973.

The natural management style of ITT, in the above example, was completely at variance with the entrepreneurial whizz-bang approach of the company they took over (Avis). There could not be co-existence, so the style of Avis had to be radically modified.

The Nature of Balance

We are going to use another graphic method for assessing the overall balance of the project, and this, effectively, comprises a measure of just four parameters. In its favour, it is practical, easy to apply, and cost effective – all you need is a pencil and paper. The parameters to be used will be familiar as they have already been covered in previous discussion:

The Company/Consultant Match

If we return to Figure 4.4 for a moment, it will be evident that the more the separation between the two organisations on the chart, the greater the difference in style, and, correspondingly, the greater the potential for conflict and misunderstandings. The difficulties start to mount up if there is a team from the consultants working with the clients. Their methods of working will naturally match the style and expectation of their own organisation, which may be very different from that of the client. Just one representative, however, would tend to adopt the ways of working of the host company without too much effort.

Role Matching

In section 4.4 we went over some aspects of *role* in the organisation, department and project – at both the personal and group level. You will recall, for example, that a mismatch at the boundary between one group and another could have a serious overall impact. An appraisal of, let us say, the compatibility of the teams and their members with their assigned tasks should be carried out. This will provide a measure of the probable smooth working and co-operation to be expected from the workforce.

Common Strategy

This refers to the discussion back in section 1.4 of Chapter 1 relating to the level of agreement between the parties on the mechanics of carrying out the design process. This could be either a structured method or a prototyping method. Whatever is selected, it is desirable that both groups agree on the adopted method – or, at minimum, accept it in principle. If there is still no agreement on the way to go forward, then the future interworking may be confused.

Morale

Once again, if the morale of the host group is low then their work potential drops and more time and effort will be needed to get the same results.

These four parameters represent a convenient measure of the potential for success. A high value on all four will ensure an integrated team working in an effective environment, while a low value promises a very stormy trip. Now, we can draw four horizontal bars, where each one represents one of the parameters discussed above. Then for each bar, a mark can be made which indicates if the assessed value is low or high. Finally, we can take an overview of all four parameters and evaluate the potential for good interworking.

Application

We can illustrate the method by application to the Newtown/Universal models:

❏ **Company/Consultant:** You will recall from Chapter 1 that the same consultants were to be used for both projects. Assume that the consultant group is newly formed, and that it more or less conforms to the 'footprint' or location and shape of the consultant marker given in Figure 4.4. Then, comparing this with the equivalent results given in Figure 4.3 indicates that the distance on the graph from the consultants to Universal will be quite short. That is to say, the degree of match is high. Conversely, the separation from the Hospital marker will be considerable, which in turn implies a poor match. These representative values have been inserted in the first bar for each of the drawings of Figure 4.5.

❏ **Role Matching:** This is the rough and ready estimate of the way the workforce fits the various allocated functions within the project. This can only be subjective and will obviously vary from case to case -both at the personal and at the group level. An arbitrary value of about 50% has been given for both of the models.

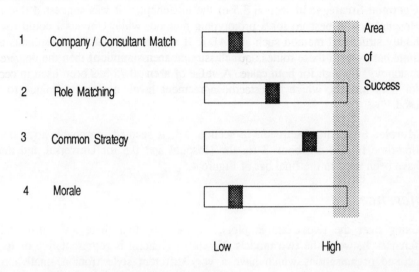

a) Newtown General Hospital

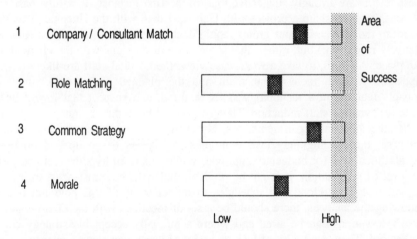

b) Universal Solid State

Figure 4.5: The nature of balance

❑ **Common Strategy:** In section 3.5 of the last chapter, it was suggested that the Hospital would best go for a prototyping method, while Universal could use a highly structured method such as SADT. If we assume that the consultants are quite happy with these routes, (which is quite an assumption) then the degree of match will be high for both cases. A value of about 0.75 has been used in bar 3 for both models, which reflects the agreement level, not the technique to be used.

❑ **Morale:** From the discussion in section 4.3, it seemed reasonable to allocate first-time figures of about .3 for the Hospital and 0.5 for Universal and these have been used in the final bar of Figure 4.5.

Inference

Looking over the two example plots, we can see that there are considerable differences between the two models. Newtown General is representative of large structured organisations which have a very different style from a small active consultant group, and which may suffer serious undercurrents of group rivalries and frustrations along with a relatively poor morale. Universal, on the other hand, will be more open to a flexible interface, and will have a reasonably common and supportive approach to getting the job done, and the morale will be higher (at least, compared to the Hospital).

These results are strongly suggestive that, in the first instance, it will be easier for the consultants to share a project with Universal than with the Hospital. This does not mean that the consultant group should decline to work with a client (that is a relatively rare event) but, rather, that some close discussions with the client should take place. After all, to take a worst-case view, the hospital staff are likely to be in opposition to both their management and the planned added work, they will probably fear the new technology skills required, and suspect that it will be the cause for eventual staff reduction. The group could be in direct strategic opposition to the other hospital departments, possibly even the computer operations group. In any case, the funding may take 6 months to 2 years to go up and down the organisational tree for budgetary approval. While this is all hypothetical and just at the level of supposition, it might be prudent, under the circumstances, to increase the anticipated workload and schedules to reflect some of this potential friction. Following the analysis, there should be a set of meetings with the client where all these reservations can be aired and where a mutually acceptable strategy can be worked out. Then, with a bit of luck and a lot of work, you stand a chance.

4.7 Summary

This chapter completes the section called Background. Its object has been to take a broad sweep across the material and techniques that can be usefully applied to the development of information systems.

In Chapter 2, we went over the various diagrams that can be used to describe the interaction of the sub-elements of a system. In particular, Data Flow Diagrams and Entity Relation Diagrams were evaluated along with the way they are all linked together via the Data Dictionary.

There are strategic options and decisions that have to be considered at the outset of every project, and these were reviewed in Chapter 3. The block elements of the Life Cycle, the choice between Structured Design and Prototyping, and the pros and cons of using a CASE tool were all given a sound airing.

Finally, the section has been completed with an overview of the way the project personnel can potentially affect the development program. After all, it is still quite normal for large discrepancies to occur between the first estimates of time, costs and performance as compared to the actual figures that emerge at a later date. Part of the reason for this has to be the ongoing misunderstandings and frictions that have not been routinely eliminated from the project. By analysing all the possible human interactions at the personal and team level, we can plan each project such that the conflicts that exist between individuals and groups will be significantly reduced.

Of course, it could be argued that there really is no problem, that all this concentration on the workforce (and their apparent sensitivity as human beings) is just a collection of sociological mumbo-jumbo with no proper application to system design activity. On the other hand, judging by the commonly found high staff turnover, recurring user dissatisfaction with the output systems, and the continuing high cost of corrective maintenance, there is a strong case for giving increased attention to the social needs of the staff. The approaches put forward here are sensibly practical in that they provide a low-cost monitor of some of today's personnel problems, and alert the developer to potential storms ahead. In particular, they enable the project management to focus attention on:

❑ Defining the participants

❑ Addressing issues of morale

❑ Exploring possible friction at the role interfaces

❑ Establishing the behavioural style of the client

❑ Estimating the scope of group interworking problems

Questions

1.   a) Define *your* role in your organisation (i.e. what is expected of a student, or analyst or treasurer, etc). Now write down the type of personality that will offer a good match with the above. Does it match your own personality?

b) Repeat the analysis for your boss or tutor (this could be considered as an exercise in tact and diplomacy).

c) Consider the position of Systems Manager in the Computer Centre at a university:

Give a job definition that is reasonably descriptive.

Give a job definition that is *role ambiguous*.

2. A successful ex-advertising woman decides on a change of job scene because of pressure from her growing children. She ends up as Test Laboratory Manager setting up standards, working mainly from home. Discuss any possible problem areas that may arise.

3. Make graphical-plot estimates of the probable *style* of:

a) A start-up airline company (two DC-3s and a re-engined Boeing 707).

b) International (triple-A rated) insurance company.

c) Management buy-out sophisticated fibre-optics plant.

4. The explosive success of a new young pop-group requires some sort of information systems control. They go for the best known and respected consultant group, which has been operating for a number of years across Europe and the US. Make an evaluation of the potential for successful collaboration between these two parties.

5

The System Environment

Marconi sues in fire fight

London's fire authority has received a High Court writ from its main supplier after years of wrangling over an £8 million system first commissioned in 1982.

. . . .

According to Marconi, numerous changes to a computerised command system ordered by the authority have contributed to delays of more than four years and have led to the original price of about £3.2m soaring to £8.09m.

Computer Weekly p.1 23.11.89

Benchmark fights begin again

The brief ceasefire in the IBM/DEC benchmark war ended this month with IBM issuing more figures for its mid-range systems.

But users seems unimpressed and are questioning the real value of proprietary benchmarks.

Chris Wallace, information systems manager at Minster Insurance, says the benchmarks are probably not worth the paper they are written on.

"Any users worth their salt will want to do their own evaluation anyway. Mips from proprietary benchmarks generally mean 'meaningless instructions per second'," he says.

Computer Weekly p.1 24.8.89

Business PCs are easy game for hackers

The UK's business personal computer world is a hacker's paradise, according to a survey on computer security among over 200 small system users.

Nearly 75% of anonymous respondents to a questionnaire by computer manufacturer Opus Technology admit that their systems are inadequately protected against hackers.

. . . .

Over 75% of respondents also report that they have lost data through power or hard disk failure, yet only one in four companies takes the precaution of making back-ups.

Computer Weekly p. 4 18.1.90

5.1 Introduction

The next two chapters will cover the groundwork that has to be carried out to ensure that the requirement specification reflects the real needs of the client. After all, system design, coding, testing, and installation is about creating a physical product that matches the parameters and constraints laid down in this basic specification. If the specification is wrong in the first place, then all that follows is wasted work. This sounds obvious, but under the start-up pressures of getting a system development off the ground, it may not be all that clear. This is underlined by the first report of this chapter which refers to a far from unique exercise that was originally specified on a fixed-price contract in 1982 and intended to go live in 1985.

This chapter sets out to identify the major elements that form a framework for getting an accurate requirement specification. As a consequence of this, they will also form the framework for all the resultant design activity. The material covered will typically comprise two types of activity: decisions and definitions.

The first is straightforward, in that it relates to the agreements made on the way in which the project will be carried out. These decisions will generally be a compromise between the desires of the client and the capability of the consultant group. Thus, there could be a conflict in the selection of the word processor to be used. For a PC system, for example, the client may have already standardised on WordStar while the consultant might favour Word. In this case, it is likely that the client's wishes would be accepted. Again, the client proposes that the database to be installed should be Paradox, because a friend of his is using it. On the other hand, the consultants regularly use dBase IV and have no prior experience with any other product. In this case, it is likely that the best approach would be to use the database favoured by the consultants. (Or change the consultants.) The other alternative is for the design group to carry out their learning activities on your project – a very daring if rather generous attitude. So, candidate proposals – and they are often on more serious matters than the above – have to be put forward, and they have to be discussed and reviewed. Ultimately the appropriate selection has to be accepted and *agreed.*

The second type of activity is more difficult to sort out. This is where the client may not be competent to join in the decision-making process. We are discussing areas which are difficult to quantify, but which could be crucial to the usage of the information system. For example, *Performance.* This is a much used and abused topic, it will critically affect the degree of user satisfaction, and yet it is hard for the client to define his needs before the system has been designed and installed. (As an indicator of how even experts differ, see the second report which is on benchmarks. These are intended to offer a performance comparison between different competitive packages.) This topic and others like it raise complex issues, but they still need to be addressed before the design activity is started.

In effect, we are going to establish the *scope* of the project by indicating how it is to be carried out and the interfaces to be used. In addition we will be seeking to define some of the design criteria which will be needed in order to start up the development process. The material will be covered in the following sections:

❏ The First-level Decisions   (decisions)

❏ System Parameters   (definitions)

❏ External Interfaces   (decisions)

5.2 The First-level Decisions

This section is concerned with the basic agreements that have to be made with respect to implementing the project and the tools that will be used in the process.

Design Philosophy

By now, having covered the subject in Chapter 3, it is just a matter of reaching agreement on the way forward. Both designer and end-user should have a good understanding of the merits of structured analysis versus prototyping, along with a clear recognition of the major pitfalls associated with each. It only remains to assess the merits of each approach for the specific project and to agree a common strategy. In Chapter 3 it was suggested, for example, that structured design would probably be best for the large multinational organisation. Conversely, prototyping will rapidly and positively involve the staff of the hospital ward, and lend itself to the more chaotic situation (from a computer point of view) that will be found there. However, note that in a practical situation, the reality could be the exact opposite. Each company and each project is unique and has to be analysed on its merits.

Components

This part is mainly concerned with bought-in software packages that will be used a) during the development as project tools and b) for applications which will be permanently linked to the system under development. Again, until clear agreements have been made in this area, there is little point in continuing serious work on the project.

Text Processor

It makes sense to have a common word processor. In this way, text files, i.e. proposals, specifications and reports can be transferred and possibly modified and returned to source, all using network communications, or floppy discs. It is useful, but not vital. In general terms, the product in current use with the client is the one to go for. There will usually be enough resentment and uncertainty about the new-fangled system, without adding to it with a new word processor to learn.

Database

This is a much more serious issue. The heart of the system to be installed will be a database product. The efficiency of this product, the speed of operation, the reliability and ease of extension will radically affect the way in which the final system is accepted. There are three main types that can be selected:

❏ **PC-based:** These are eminently suitable for the smaller project – from standalone machines to networked systems. The latest versions tend to have a relational structure, are well served with screens and menus and have good hot-line support. A popular example (although not fully relational) is dBase IV from Ashton Tate.

❏ **Portable:** Again, there are a number of powerful relational databases, that offer good (but not outstanding) performance. Their main advantage is that their table layout and SQL command structure can be ported across a wide range of machines – ranging from the mainframe down to the simplest IBM-PC format. They offer a useful flexibility and extendability for the larger project. A representative product would be the Oracle relational database system from the Oracle organisation.

❏ **Text-based:** These are the class of database important in the area of text recognition and retrieval. They find important application in areas such as libraries and cataloguing, where the conventional database is probably not the best solution. One such product is Cairs Library Management Systems from Leatherhead Food Research Association.

It is well worth taking some time to establish the optimum type for the intended application, and then selecting one of the competing products that appears best suited to the application. The sort of selection priority put forward for CASE tools in Chapter 3 is just as applicable here, but, to be fair, products in the same price range tend to have the same capabilities.

User Interfaces

This is not strictly a product that can be purchased. For all that, it will strongly influence the overall user-friendliness of the finished system, but will add to the work-load during the design phase. Thus, the user will generally find the use of visual aids such as graphic screens, icons, menus, and windows more attractive than a simple text-based command line interface. On the other hand, nothing is for free, and these features will take time and resource to design. So there is always a trade-off, and the compromises will have to be recognised and agreed at the outset of the design activity.

Project Tools

As we have discussed in Chapter 3, the use of some sort of CASE tool will materially help in generating the logical models of the existing and planned system. The major advantages and disadvantages were covered there, and it is just a matter of getting some agreement on the optimum approach for the project in question.

Additional assistance can now be found in application software related to project management. These are packages that will provide various graphic indicators of the state of the activities being undertaken in the project. Thus, they will generate Gantt charts, or PERT charts, or resource distribution histograms – or a suitable mix of all three. The same criteria apply as for CASE tools, in that these packages will take a certain amount of learning but offer advantages once you have grasped how to use them. In general, a small project within a large organisation can be run, without much penalty, with selected manual and automated project management tools running in parallel. That would be the ideal in terms of a limited risk introduction to this type of tool. For a review of some typical products see reference 26.

Linkages

If you are going to drive a network based system, then you need network software. If you don't know much about it, then choose one of the popular models. That way, you will not necessarily get the best product, but you are unlikely to get into much trouble. A good working approach is to estimate a realistic number of anticipated users – and then double it when evaluating network capabilities. The subject is outside the scope of this book, but for a discussion on network architecture and some of the more popular commercial product, see reference 17.

The same philosophy will be applicable to the communications requirements. However, this is also becoming a separate field of growing complexity, and expert guidance should be sought. The latest techniques are essentially concerned with the high speed transmission of digital data over national and international telephone networks. The application of products which conform to the latest protocols of OSI (Open Systems Interconnection) may require some care in the interfaces and the potential merits of following ISDN (Integrated Services Digital Network) standards will not always be obvious. Even the relatively well established Fax and Modem equipment may need to have modified interfaces in order to be linked to networks based on these new international standards. These are normally subjects that have a bearing for the larger organisations with a number of international plants and offices. Again, it is a specialist field, but for an introductory coverage of these and associated topics try reference 18.

Hardware

This is usually one of the prime factors to be discussed when the initial presentations are being made. For all that, it is one of the simpler, lower-cost decision areas to be evaluated.

Simple? Well, yes, especially compared to some of the real problems to be discussed in the next section.

Architecture

There are two ways of planning systems that influence the hardware configuration: centralised, i.e. one big processor unit and any number of dumb terminals; and networked, where PCs or work-stations can be linked together using a commercial network system. As a general rule, the [mips/operator]/dollar ratio, where mips stands for Million Instructions Per Second, tends to favour many small machines compared to one large one. Thus, 20 two mips single operator machines suitably networked will usually cost less than one machine equipped with 20 terminals giving an overall two mips performance. However, while this may be oversimplifying the pros and cons of distributed processing, it is noteworthy that there have been some very successful installations using either technique. This suggests that if someone has strong views on which way to structure the hardware, then go that way.

Size

The capacity of the machine (or machines) will clearly depend on the perceived usage. The items to be addressed are: the number of users; the amount of required storage memory (magtape and hard disc); the amount of operating memory (RAM); and the required 'mips' or performance capability. These are all fairly conjectural in terms of eventual use (and make no provision for performance constraints which will also affect the final decision), so the estimates should err on the generous side.

Cost Criticality

It was suggested above, that the cost of the hardware was low compared to the overall cost of the project.

Assume that there is disagreement over the purchase of one system of £100K (£100,000) and the rival competitor of £75K. Now, let us take an approximate cost (for the UK) of £20K for the salary of one senior analyst or operations engineer. Then with overheads (working space, pensions etc.) this will be approximately £40K per person employed. With a development team comprising five people working for one year, this will work out as an outlay of £200K. Now use one operations, communications and maintenance engineer for the three years before a serious redesign occurs. (In reality, it will probably be three or more engineers working from time to time on the system, but this is a fair approximation.) This will add a further three man-years or £120K to the personnel bill. Finally, assume that each of the 50 end-users, paid about £12.5K, will take about one month of retraining and use before they are gainfully redeployed on the new system. That is roughly four man-years loss of personnel and, with overheads, equivalent to, say, another £100K. This makes a total of about £420K for the personnel costs of the new system.

Now, ignoring any bought-in software costs, system software or site license costs, project management costs, or on-site rental, maintenance and insurance costs, we can return to the effectiveness of using a £75K hardware package or £100K package. If this model is only approximately correct, then the worries over the £25K difference in an overall cost model of roughly £500K (i.e. £420K labour costs + £75K hardware costs) are not all that pressing. Especially if it buys a substantial improvement in performance.

How valid is this model? The cost of a good hardware platform for a 50-user system continues to fall, and will probably be lower than than the one estimated above. More to the point, find out at your own site – check roughly on the people, overheads and hardware cost models for the last exercise, or obtain the cost estimates for the next project.

Conclusion

We have gone over a basic checklist of the bought-in items that will be have to be decided on before drawing up the system specification. The actual design will usually be able to accommodate a wide variety of the answers that result. What is important is to pose the questions in the first place, get the necessary decisions and, where warranted, place the orders immediately. A summary of all these topics is displayed in Figure 5.1.

5.3   System Parameters

It is unfortunately almost customary in the real world to establish two key facts some time after the system has been installed. In the first place, as a result of some design short cuts and general lack of documentation, the software is virtually unmaintainable. Secondly, the system is found to be incapable of performing all of its intended functions. This may be customary, but it is not cost effective.

As promised, we are going to discuss a number of topics which are not clear cut or easy to model with any confidence. Nevertheless, they are likely to have a major impact on the eventual cost of the system since they will figure largely in any rework considerations. In any case, they will have to be referenced in the coming Design Specification and they include the following subjects:

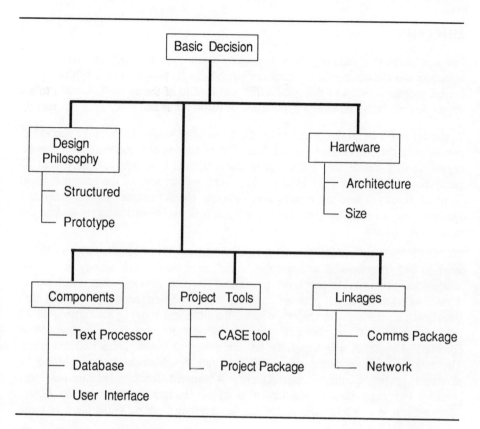

Figure 5.1: The initial decisions tree

❑ Integrity and Test Criteria

❑ Performance and Extendability

❑ Maintenance Objectives

❑ Make or Buy

Once again, it will be the objective to ensure that the right questions are asked rather than defining the nature of the particular answers. These answers will be the responsibility of the project partners who will have to evaluate them on a project by project basis. Nevertheless, by putting these issues on paper, you will be able to focus on the strategic issues before the design starts rather than after it has finished.

Integrity

For our purposes, integrity is a capability built into the system that will a) minimise the system conflict introduced by the design process itself, b) detect and inhibit user application of the system that will lead to a system malfunction, and c) detect and reject the input and application of incorrect data.

Examples could be a) the detection of the same label being accidentally applied to two entirely different entities or attributes; b) restricting the end-user such that he or she cannot delete any system files resident in a common directory; and c) preventing the input of JAN from the keyboard into an area of the screen marked 'Day_of_Week'. These are clearly very valuable characteristics of the system and the only way to establish that the integrity functions are operating is to test the system for failures.

Looking at the problem another way, how bug-free will the installed system be, or need to be? The answer will ultimately influence how much money has to be allocated to this task. At one level, Space and Defence developments will have an almost unlimited budget because there is an overriding need for reliable and surprise-free software. On the other hand, the little girl moving her turtle with an educational LOGO program will probably have a zero-rated test budget. Most commercial systems will hopefully lie somewhere between these two extremes. The real question is -what part of the overall development budget should be allocated to the Quality Control/Quality Assurance function within (or even outside) the organisation. Remember that this budget is provided to obtain adequate test and debug activity for the forthcoming system. Well, there is some advice on this topic:

"The increasing visibility of software as a system element and the attendant "costs" associated with a software failure are motivating forces for well planned, thorough testing. It is not unusual for a software development organisation to expend 40% of total project effort on testing."

Reference 3 page 289

"For some years I have been successfully using the following rule of thumb for scheduling a software task:
   1/3 planning
   1/6 coding
   1/4 component test and early system test
   1/4 system test, all components in hand.
   . . . .

In examining conventionally scheduled projects, I have found that few allowed one-half of the projected schedule for testing, but that most did indeed spend half of the actual schedule for that purpose."

Reference 4 page 20

Taking a reasonably sober view, about 30% of the overall budget should be gainfully allocated to the test and quality assurance role. (As stated above, it will be anyway, so why fight it?) Integrity is important, but it does not come cheap. However, reducing the test expenditure just adds a cost penalty to the post-installation phase and the resultant disadvantage of doing this will be discussed further in Chapter 11.

Performance

Once again, there is a problem of definition. In a subjective sense, it is a measure of the way in which the operation of the installed system matches the client's expectations. A more engineering approach would be to use benchmarks. However, meeting an industry-wide benchmark will generally say something about meeting that benchmark – and not much else. (The second report at the head of the chapter seems to support this view.) There is considerable activity by database suppliers, among others, to show that their system will run far more tps (transactions per second) than their nearest competitor. The results, although dramatic, often show a marked dependency on the way in which the test was set up, and the dedicated way the database was 'tweaked' to meet the specific tests of the benchmark. A possibly more useful benchmark might be one supplied by the client based on a set of operations which are typical of the intended application. The plus side is that the objective is tangible (carry out the suite of tests in so many seconds or minutes), but the minus side is that very few end-user organisations have the competence or interest to generate such a test vehicle.

So it is not easy to establish a physical test for good performance. Yet the user satisfaction will be critically dependent on having a fast response to the user inputs, even when fully loaded with all terminals in action. (See the reports in Chapter 10.) Fortunately, there are still some general factors that will help to build and maintain good performance into the system.

A Competent DBA

A good DBA (Database Administrator) will have the capacity to maintain the database in a well tuned condition, optimised to the overall way in which the database is being operated under system-live conditions.

A Competent Operations Manager

Will be able to optimise the operating system (i.e. VMS, Unix, MS-DOS etc) such as to maximise the capabilities of information input and retrieval. (See for example the report 'Tweaks yield massive boosts' Computer Weekly, p.11, 7.9.89)

A Good Database Designer

Will be able to design an optimum relational structure into the database which will eliminate or minimise redundancy in the tables. In addition, performance enhancing techniques, such as clustering or indexing, can be evaluated for potential use to improve the speed of data access and retrieval.

'Bell and Whistles' Control

The very features (the windows, icons, mouse, etc.) that make the system so approachable to the new user act to slow down a number of operations. While they should remain available for the novice, they should equally be designed to be removable for the more experienced user.

Summing up, performance can be more of a design philosophy or attitude than a specification, but its absence will often generate marked and open expressions of dissatisfaction by the end-user. By using qualified people in responsible positions, they will be able to optimise the performance of the system under widely varying conditions. On a more mechanistic level, a benchmark sequence of tests can be enormously helpful in evaluating a system under design, but if it is not directly related to the intended application then its value will diminish accordingly.

Maintenance

Over the last few years, it has become generally recognised that this subject is probably the cause of more grief than all the other problems in system development put together. The effective time to tackle a maintenance strategy is at the beginning of the project, not – as is more usual -following installation when the first user complaints or suggestions start to come in. It is too late by then. Although the chapter on this subject comes near the end of the book, it would be prudent to go over Chapter 11 now and then return here. In particular, the procedures and structure of standardised documentation handling, configuration management, test programs, and explicit comments inserted with the actual code should all be explored in the initial phase of the project. In this way, the suitable disciplines and ways of recording both the activities and the intent behind them, can be agreed and incorporated into the fabric of the project right from the beginning.

Maintenance is another of those areas which can only be handled with the clear support of the senior management. It is largely a question of investing more start-up activity in defining procedures and methods of operation, in order to gain the considerable benefit at the post-installation phase.

Make or Buy

This is the last of the grey areas which needs to be covered at this point. Again there are options which have to be evaluated for each system and each client organisation. In the main, they fall into two classes: buy-in or develop the product (whole or part of an overall system); and buy-in or develop the resource (personnel) to carry out the project-related activities.

Bought-in System Packages

There are dedicated packages available now to cover virtually every possible requirement. In spite of this, the majority of DP (Data Processing) and MIS (Management Information Services) departments have still survived and most of them are flourishing. The reason for this apparent conflict is mainly related to inertia in big organisations. The smaller companies will buy an Accounting or Order Processing package and *change their internal structure* to accommodate to the requirements and limitations of the package. The larger corporations do not have the resilience or flexibility for this approach, but can afford the time and effort to develop a system which exactly matches their more complex needs. Both approaches should be examined for potential benefits. In addition, there is the mixed philosophy whereby the major functions are carried out by some existing package while the more obscure requirements are satisfied with some bolt-on designed attachments. The major factors to be weighed up are largely self explanatory and are highlighted in Figure 5.2. Note that line 5 refers to the possibility of showing a number of typical user interface screens shortly after the start of the project. With a full custom built product, there will be a long delay before this situation is reached.

Custom Built	Mixed	Off-the-Peg
Full Control	No control in main areas	No control
Can be redefined	Partially modifiable	Cannot be changed
Non-standard Interface	Non-standard interface	Only standard Interfaces
Full Debug required	Full Debug required	Essentially bug free
Slow Prototyping	Fast prototyping	Fast prototyping

Figure 5.2: The make or buy table

Bought-in Personnel

Personnel will be needed to carry out the various roles identified in the project. These people can either be specifically taken on for the duration of the project or can be existing members of staff who will be trained to take on extra skills or increasing responsibilities. Again, there is no clear cut advantage either way, and the decision has to be considered on a case-by-case basis.

Permanent Staff	Contract Staff
In-house skills	No local skill gain
In-house redesign capability	Systems knowledge leaves the company
Good knowledge of local procedures	No local knowledge of local procedures
Cost of new training	Instant start up
Delays due to existing workload	Instant start up
Inflexible personnel selection	Completely flexible selection
Morale/Staff turnover	Loyalty/Staff turnover

Figure 5.3: The choice for personnel

The pros and cons are outlined in Figure 5.3, and the only ambiguous entries are the last two:

❑ Inflexible Selection: It is generally the case that the staff allocated to any given project will be the ones that have become available at that moment. Their suitability or competence are not usually significant factors in the selection mechanism.

❑ Morale/Turnover: A workforce with a poor morale will not work with anything like the efficiency and work output of a contract team. Conversely, the contract personnel cannot be expected to have any special loyalty to the company or the project. In both cases, the departure of key personnel will be an on-going fact of life.

Summary

We have been looking at the project as an undertaking to achieve certain objectives within the field of Information Technology. Some of these objectives might be difficult to quantify but require definition (or at least a fairly strong pointer). Following this, the designer can include them in the design framework and, at the same time, the client has some idea of what to expect. Only by defining these target objectives at the start can the project be configured to ensure that they are addressed during the development phase. It is rather like deciding, before the cooking begins, on how much of each main ingredient will be needed for a special recipe and this kitchen wisdom has been illustrated in Figure 5.4.

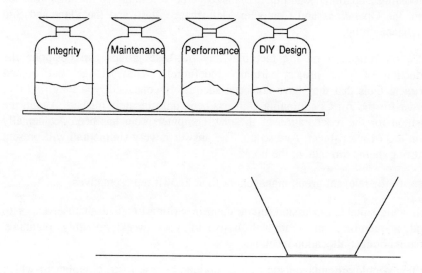

Figure 5.4: Get the project mix right

5.4 External Interfaces

This section is more concerned with tying up some of the remaining loose ends as opposed to discussing more fundamental issues. For all that, these 'loose ends' will have an important bearing on the way in which the project is handled and will be concerned with the interaction of the system with external equipment or people. The main topics to be covered are:

❏ Personnel

❏ Data Links

❏ Security

Personnel

The people directly concerned with the new development will be the System Consultant, Design Team, Project Manager, Client and End-users. These roles could be provided by the client organisation or by some mix between it and the selected design house. In any case, all these people will be well known within the project environment. In addition, as indicated in the last chapter, there will be third parties who are also likely to have an interest in the program. These may include other members of the client workforce, i.e the Senior Management, the neighbouring Departments and their Managers who will interface into the proposed system, the Operations and Computer Maintenance staff, and the Plant and Site Maintenance group.

It is worth reflecting on the fact that any of these groups can postpone the introduction of your project virtually indefinitely. Thus, if the last quoted department feels that they have not been adequately consulted, you may find that the order for the Air Conditioning Unit has been unfortunately mislaid. Again, the requisition for the redecoration of the new computer room has been accidentally filed in the wrong cabinet. And so on. The answer is very simple and will present a recurring theme throughout the book:

❑ Identify the relevant group managers or their known representatives.

❑ Following suitable discussion, invite them in writing to attend themselves, or to send a member, on a regular basis, to your weekly/monthly planning/ progress/budget-allocation meetings.

Very few people are antagonistic to a committee or task-force grouping to which they have been invited to attend. You may need a larger meeting room and distribution list as a result, but the exercise will be found to be well worth while.

As a final word of advice in this political slant on the project – maintain close contact with your good friend the manager of the Personnel Department. Sooner or later, extra staff will almost certainly be needed for a few days to solve some particular crisis. It is usually possible to 'borrow' a number of suitable staff from a distant department – but only with the active co-operation of this valued colleague, who just happens to know ...

Data Links

In section 5.2 you were encouraged to consider carefully the strategy to be adopted over communications. Well, having considered, now is the time to establish the exact nature of the products that will be used by the forthcoming system along with their transmission protocols, or hand-shaking conventions, to provide data communication between two or more sites. Very briefly, you may already be using or may decide to apply one or more of the following:

❑ **EDI:** Electronic Data Interchange. This is a means of transferring commercial messages between two parties, usually by means of a VAN (Value Added Network), which takes all the headache out of trying to establish a data link to two different hardware platforms which are also using different communication software. The main application is with formal preconfigured documents such as purchase order forms. The banks have been early users, and SWIFT is an example of such an EDI system.

❑ **E-MAIL:** As the name suggests, this is Electronic Mail which is much simpler to implement than EDI. It is frequently used on a local network where the organiser and administrator machine ('File Server') will save messages and inform the addressee when they next log on that there is a message waiting. It is simple, low cost, and very effective in communicating short messages over short distances – say within the building.

❑ **Fax:** A convenient means of transferring graphic images from site A to site B at relatively low cost in about one minute per page (excluding link-up time). These images can include, for example, a hand-written message or your signature as applied to a document or contract. A Fax card can be fitted to a personal computer with printer attached to provide a low-traffic low-cost facility. Without a scanner, of course, no paper information can be copied or transmitted.

❑ **Modem:** A piece of equipment (the MOdulator) which converts digital data so it can be sent reliably through an ordinary telephone network to equivalent remote equipment (the DEModulator) which turns the signal back into a format recognised by the distant computer. An absolutely basic piece of equipment for any communication via a telephone link.

All these products are based on a need to communicate with a distant or external partner in some undertaking. It may be another site of a your multinational enterprise, a commercial partner, a university looking at the same research, or your director working from home. Whatever is decided, planning to incorporate them into the design from the beginning will tend to provide the most effective use of these modern communication tools.

Security

So far, we have gone over all the external interfaces that are actually intended to be used. The natural corollary of this concerns all the external sources and links that are uncalled for and distinctly unwanted. In what way can we protect the system against the flow of data falling into a competitor's or criminal's hands? Perhaps we had better start off with a review of the general problem that is to be solved.

The Uninvited Guest

There are three major sources of computer crime: the hacker, the fraudulent user and the virus. In the past there has been a marked reluctance to alert the authorities when such a crime has been committed, although this practice is starting to change. In the case of hacking or fraud, there is the question of professional loss of face or openly revealing a lack of technical competence. (See the third report at the head of the chapter.) All the more reason for taking sensible precautions and building safeguards into the system while in the design phase.

❏ **Hacking:** This is the term for some person seeking to illegally enter your system for thrills or commercial profit. The image of the precocious teenager hacker 'just having fun' may be attractive but is probably far from the truth. The reality is that there are many people who will spend a considerable amount of effort in invading your privacy and reaching your data either to subvert it or to take it for gain. (See "Stalking the Wily Hacker", C. Stoll, Communications of the ACM, p. 484, May 1988.)

❏ **Fraud:** The rising use of computers by banks and other financial institutions has led to increasing risk of criminal application of the computer. There was, for example, the insurance company that just fabricated new policies which were being taken out by people who did not exist. The company shares moved ever higher – till the bubble burst. And it is not only software. It is estimated that one gang recently stole over £1,000,000 worth of equipment for export to a foreign country. This sort of crime is very often the result of an 'insider job'.

❏ **Virus:** This is where a small program is introduced into your non-volatile memory such that it can reappear, replicate itself, transfer itself to other systems via floppy or hard disks or tapes, and may subvert your data or take over all available memory. In a few words, it can destroy your site as an operational centre. It is well worth thinking about the damage that could be caused to your programs by this form of mindless sabotage.

Can these unwanted visitors be stopped? The answer has to be a qualified 'yes'. Much like home burglary, you will probably not be able to stop a really determined professional, but you certainly can discourage most other attempts – and for very little outlay. Whatever the approach, it is the responsibility of the system manager to achieve two main objectives:

❏ To ensure that the corporation's operations and commercially sensitive material are protected

❏ To provide adequate security to personal data stored in the system.

This latter obligation is imposed by the Data Protection Act in the UK and by the public law 100-235 for government agencies in the US. Most other countries have, or are about to have, similar legislation. It should come as no surprise by now to learn that the best way to tackle this problem is with a structured top-down approach:

❑ **Need:** You are unlikely to achieve very much without the clear recognition of need by the corporate senior management. So the first job is to convince them of the overall importance of developing a strategy related to data security.

❑ **Involvement:** Having obtained the support of your management, the next objective is to get the involvement of the staff who actually use the computer based equipment. Procedures and company practices are only as good as the readiness of the workforce to implement them. This may take a corporate campaign or a set of lectures explaining the reasoning behind the proposed changes.

❑ **Partition:** Introducing security will cost money, operational delays and some user inconvenience. For this reason, those parts of the system that require protection should be identified. Perhaps, there will be a need for a hierarchy of protection requirements where each level gets only the degree of security that is warranted. Thus, the security processes can be applied selectively, maintaining free entry to all other areas of the system.

❑ **Access:** If prevented from reaching a terminal, the criminal's scope for action is severely limited. Thus, allowing only designated authorised individuals into the computer room should become corporate policy. And the room should have locks or other physical means of limiting entry. Similarly, a visitor should never be left alone near a terminal or workstation which is still running. Entry to the computer area only after proof of identity. And so on.

❑ **Machine:** This is the final area to be addressed having worked progressively through all the others. Depending on need, it is possible to introduce hardware keys, software passwords, complete destruction of unwanted files (not just removing the header label), data encryption, audit facilities, and anti-virus detection. Again, an overall system set of requirements should be formulated. This can then be used to identify the nature of the products that are to be incorporated into the system. A number of these approaches along with the related products will be found in reference 19.

Overview

This section has reviewed some of the problems associated with preventing your data becoming public property without your permission. Making it hard for the potential criminal is not too difficult or even expensive. All it takes is some thought about the sensitivity of data being processed and the existing system weaknesses in terms of illegal entry. The object is the involvement of the whole organisation to make your system like a maze where the unwanted visitor has to fight through at each level. This approach has been highlighted in Figure 5.5

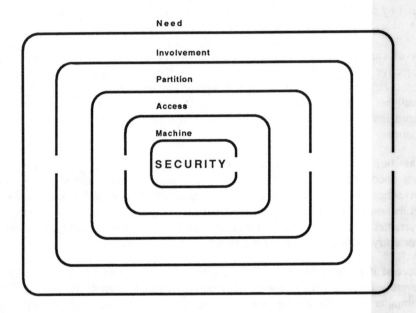

Figure 5.5: Unauthorised entry to the maze

5.5 Summary

The whole design and development activity is configured to meeting the objectives laid down in the Requirements Specification. To avoid spending large amounts of money on redesign, repeated test programs, upgrading systems after installation, it is clearly worth getting the Specification right in the first place. This chapter has concerned itself with defining the practical targets and physical elements that are to be incorporated into the system and, therefore, to be identified and designed in at the earliest possible stage.

At the simplest level, we have gone over a generalised check-list that has to be reviewed at the start of any development cycle:

❏ Design Philosophy; Application Programs; Project-based tools; Hardware selection.

❑ Test Objectives and Requirements; Performance criteria; Maintenance factors; Make or Buy decisions.

❑ External personnel; Communication links; Security.

All that remains, now, to complete the specification is the definition of the actual intended operation of the system within the organisation. This will be the subject of the next chapter.

Finally, let's look at the way the model organisations would approach the requirements defined here. They have been briefly listed in Figure 5.6 with typical commercial application programs that might possibly be applicable to the individual cases.

Hospital			Universal
Prototype	Design		**Structured (SSADM)**
-	Network		**Novell**
dBase IV	D'Base		**Oracle**
Word	W.P.		**Word perfect**
-	CASE		**Excelerator**
IBM 286 model	H./W		**IBM 386 model**
Demo on h/over Test report	Test		**Qualification Test Test programs Test report**
Hot-line support	M'nance		**Hot-line support On-site m'tenance (+ 12 % on cost)**
Make	Make/ Buy		**Make**
Local Area Health Authority Oncology Haematology Central Records ...	Ext'nals		**Factory 1,2 (Pusan) Factory 3 (Seoul) Research (Toronto) Europe H.Q. (Paris) ....**
Modem Email	Comms		**Email Fax**

Figure 5.6: The project environment

Once again, these have been merely inserted as representative examples and their use is not to be taken as recommendations in any way. In general, it should be clear that, as illustrated in this figure, the Universal project is assumed to have more money underpinning it than the Newtown Surgery Ward exercise and this is reflected in the facilities made available both as project tools and for the eventual system.

Questions

1. As a result of promotion, you have acquired a number of enthusiastic but non-expert staff to use for your design and operations team.

> What will be the result of using them for the Operations Manager, designer and DBA, etc.? What fallback options do you have in this position?

2. In what way will a lack of good design documentation potentially affect the maintenance of post-installed equipment?

3. Take the hypothetical case that your management does not perceive the advantages of building security into the project. What main topics would you cover in a general policy paper to a steering group on the subject?

4. Give possible examples of addressees if you are inviting external groups of users to your initial project progress meeting on a University Student Data System

5. In what way would you make it difficult for a stranger to gain physical access to your terminals and screens when:

> a) you have all the terminals and users in the computer room.
> b) you have networked PCs present in every office.

Base-line for Design

Passport planning slammed

The report, from management consultants Coopers and Lybrand, savages the Home Office for lack of imagination in drawing up the specification.

. . . .

The report also criticises the lack of time users had to make suggestions for alteration.

'This is undoubtedly one reason,' the report continues, 'why significant changes to the specifications were requested by the Pimis team after programming had commenced and in some cases after it had been completed.'

Datalink p.3 21.8.89

Ringside seat at the rocky horror project show

Another recent case involved me in discussions with a software house about a project that had to be finished in six months, in time for the launch of a new product. The company said I wasn't to be bothered about documentation too much.

. . . .

The phenomenon of hiding poor progress by skipping documentation can be detected easily because the programming will be very troublesome if the documentation is not right.

So why are these problems still occurring? To be frank I believe it is because most project and associated non-technical managers do not know how to manage large projects.

Computing p. 25-26 23.2.89

Unclear, irrelevant and too technical . . .

The documentation problem in IT has grown so bad that a fifth of end-users never refer to manuals supporting their systems: instead they hassle their DP department when they come unstuck.

. . . .

Programmers hate writing them as much as computer users hate reading them. As a result UK companies waste large amounts of money every year on useless system documentation

. . . .

Documentation remains, as ever, an afterthought.

Computer Weekly p. 26 14.9.89

6.1 Introduction

It is finally time to consider one of the key activities in the entire project: that of generating the Requirement Specification. In addition, there is one small task that we will also address at this stage. That is the ever popular subject of development documentation.

To start the ball rolling on the *need* for documentation, consider the following proposition:

Any project that runs without a coherent planned documentation set is doomed to severe cost overruns.

It appears a reasonable enough statement, the reports seem to back it up, common sense would support it, and most authorities would emphasise the need for documentation (look through the references). Even senior management agrees with it in principle. Their enthusiasm may not always stretch to extra funding, but most senior level managers will support the idea of planned documents to be written, reviewed and delivered as part of the total project activity. In today's development environment, it doesn't always work that way (and most projects correspondingly run well over target), but we will look at ways to set up an effective documentation strategy. Before that, it would be prudent to take a careful look at the contents of the requirement specification in terms of achievability. This, after all, is where the bulk of the eventual schedule slippage is introduced. The general cause of project overrun is attempting to design the fully comprehensive all-singing all-dancing product, or by incorporating the latest, most exciting, and least understood software tool.

However, in the first place we have to start with the project foundations. If they are not adequate for the job, then the whole project will collapse sooner or later under the strain and the exercise will have been largely wasted. We are talking about the Feasibility Study phase which will determine the make-up of all following objectives as defined within the specifications. This will naturally lead to the next phase involving all the activities needed to prepare a requirement specification. The specification is the pivotal point of the entire project and care and attention is needed in its formulation. Finally, the chapter will end with an overview of the need and possible realisation of a documentation plan.

The work to be described in this chapter will be largely carried out by members of the project team. Even if this team is only made up of design group members (a mixed team is to be preferred), the end users should still participate and ensure that the issues raised here are being properly addressed. At the very least, they should understand the mechanisms involved, and take a real part in any sign-off and acceptance procedures being used.

6.2 The Feasibility Study

This will comprise three major sections: information gathering; establishing the current system approach; and putting together the new requirements and improvements based on the old. The first is pure technique since it relates to interfacing (successfully or otherwise) with other human beings in what may be a very subjective or judgmental information transfer. The latter two are more skills-related in abstracting information from one location or format and placing it into another form that can be reviewed, critiqued or modified by other interested people. The totality of all these investigations will define the starting conditions of the project.

Information Collection

The main objective in this exercise will be to survey the workings of the existing system. In line with the material covered in Chapter 2, this will ultimately provide a report where the output will be in terms of the data entities, data flows and the sources and sinks of the input and output data. As an example, each user will ultimately describe the data modifications introduced as a result of his or her labour, e.g. take the incoming invoice number from Despatch, note today's date, and attach both to the Customer Invoice, along with the customer name and address taken from Customer Files. This can then be reduced to a basic Data Flow Diagram (as illustrated in Figure 6.1).

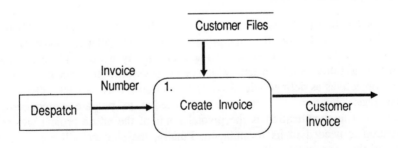

Figure 6.1: A current model data flow

We can break up the problem into two main factors: technical and interpersonal. The former relates to the mechanics of obtaining information, while the latter concerns the human factors which can radically influence the quality of the information that is to be delivered and assessed.

Technical

We are almost in the field of Market Research. Do you want in-depth interview facilities or will a large sample questionnaire approach provide what you want? And is enough known about the existing procedures to be able to formulate a questionnaire? Regardless of method, you will be applying a basic routine or algorithm, possibly along the following lines:

1. Model an outline of the current methods
2. Try the outline on different users
3. Update the model and return to step 2

Step 1 can be implemented by any convenient means – and does not have to be too accurate. Step 2 should give hours of innocent amusement to the users, but no matter – you have a thick skin and it will encourage them to try to educate you by telling 'how it really is'. Step 3 is the iteration which, along with step 2, is repeated until the level of possible update becomes negligible. At some time, say, after two to five cycles, that point has been reached and the task completed.

The mechanics of reaching out to the users, and possibly their managers, is open to choice. The option selected could be taken from one or more of the following approaches:

❑ **Interviews:** Conversations with end-user

❑ **Forms:** Fill in the blanks and return to..

❑ **Role-Playing:** End-users act out a process

❑ **Pilot Model:** Process simulation on screen

Interviews: These can be in the form of structured or more flowing conversations between an end-user and one interviewer, or as a group of end-users and interviewers round a table. The effectiveness of this approach will be modified, to some extent, by the impact of the questions in the interviewee. Thus, "Tell me what you do?" could be considered as a little open-ended, if not downright paralysing. On the other hand, "So what happens to form AT/23 when it arrives in your in-tray?" is more specific and allows the interviewee to give explicit explanations of his or her various functions.

Form-filling: This method is of value if there are a number of users involved in the same process, and the form generator knows exactly what information is required. To create a form for just one user will take more time than asking the user directly. Again, asking whether the end-user actually uses a pencil, a pen or a terminal to input data is only useful if this data, i.e method of input, is of interest in the overall process. Having said all that, and provided that enough recipients do not throw it away at the time of delivery, a questionnaire is a very cheap way of eliciting information from a group of people.

Role-playing: This is a very useful technique where a process involves the co-operative activity of a number of users. It is often easier to act out the process than to describe it and has the added advantage of more than one user commenting on the same process. Thus, a data-flow accidentally described in error can be modified or extended on the spot by the other users present.

Pilot Model: This is a form of prototyping where a simple model of the process can be put up on the screen for discussion and possible modification by the users involved. It is a good method, but requires the facility to rapidly generate and modify screens. In addition, users have to be on hand, or at the other end of a comms link, to view the screens and give a fast overview or opinion as to the way the model simulates the real process.

Remember, the objective is to reach an accurate picture of the system as it is currently applied. As stated in Chapter 1 (and backed-up in in the first quotation of this chapter), the most cost-effective approach is to spend sufficient time at the feasibility stage, getting the right information from the end-users. This will call for a certain amount of technical competence from the interviewer along with a capacity for going over the ground again and again until the method is absolutely clear. But that is not the end of the story. The end-users are unique because they have an important role to play in the system development and they cannot be replaced or interchanged even if considered unsatisfactory. What this means is that, if you cannot get a satisfactory response from the end-users, there is nowhere else to go. This is part of the reason why there is a social context to this problem.

Interpersonal

The essence of this phase is that someone asks the user some questions and it is assumed that the answers returned will be truthful and complete. This assumption should, at minimum, be open to review. Consider, for the moment, the staff belonging to the finance department of our sludge manufacturing company ABC. They do not have a lot of respect for their managers and relations generally are not all that good. One day, a perfect stranger comes along and wants to analyse their activities. He isn't offering them more money or more holidays, he is just looking for answers to some questions, please. All he wants to do is to increase their productivity and possibly reduce their overall numbers for the greater glory of their management staff. Wow!

A moment's thought will show that this is just a refined version of the classical time-and-motion study exercises carried out in the heavy industries. The workforce would sometimes go to considerable lengths to ensure that the data collected by the engineer favoured their side of the argument. In simple terms, the groundwork for a new system today will have to be *sold to*, not imposed on, the workforce of any organisation. In fact, we can identify some general guidelines for obtaining information from the workforce:

Motivation: There has to be some positive benefit to the workforce in the new project, if they are going to be involved and provide well intentioned and comprehensive answers to system queries. At the very least, they could be informed of the exciting retraining program they will have, to give them mastery of the latest technology in office data processing.

Comprehension: With the best will in the world, if the interviewee does not understand the question, the response is unlikely to be useful. Thus, the questions should be simple and couched in the language of the end-user. This minimises any chance of misunderstandings.

Numbers: Where possible, obtain duplicate information from two members of the staff with respect to the same questions. This checks that the responses are valid and that the question was understood.

Pressure: You cannot *force* anyone to tell you the truth – at least, at the levels under discussion. Similarly, crude political threats ("I'll tell your boss") or blackmail ("I'll tell your wife") will not guarantee any useful output from anyone.

Respect: This is another of those intangibles. However, the utility of the information that you obtain from the staff will always depend, to some extent, on the rapport that you have with the end-users. To put it frankly, if they think you are a clown, they will tend to tell you funny stories. Again, if you appear to be a boss's man, then prepare to get the silent treatment.

This is a very difficult subject, because it is the crucial first stage of a project and yet there is virtually no formal modelling of the process of information retrieval. In addition, the human interface can sometimes be counter-productive and can act to sabotage all the well-intentioned efforts to capture the current system. All this is another reason why, perhaps, some extra time and effort should be allotted to this phase to be confident that accurate capture has indeed taken place.

Model Existing System

This is the process where all the information obtained from the users is reduced to data flow diagrams and entity-relationship diagrams which act to completely model the system in current use. If the activity outlined in the preceding section has been effectively carried out, then this current process is largely a mechanical one. Apply more resource and the task is completed in a shorter time.

There are a number of supplementary questions which fall outside the scope of a data flow analysis, but which, nevertheless, will be of value in formulating the new upgrade. These may vary from site to site, but will usually include:

❑ The operating history of the current system

❑ The current hardware and related peripherals

❑ The application software used by the current system

❑ Reliability figures and performance criteria

❑ Physical interfaces to the outside world

❑ List of users and external sources and sinks

By the time you have established the model for the existing system and obtained answers to the above questions, you are finally in a position to generate the new model.

The New Requirement

After the mechanics of the last section, we are back in the open-ended unstructured free-flow sort of phase where skill and flair have to be used to resolve a number of conflicting requirements. As always, however, with the freedom comes responsibility. Remember that the bulk of cost overruns lie with the complexity and over-ambitious targets set in the design specification. The methodology in this section can be used to protect the budget and still generate a sensible requirement list with the following algorithm:

1. Justify the Change in the list
2. Establish the special constraints
3. Approve the Change
4. Discuss with the End-users
5. Revise the list
6. Return to stage 1.

Justification

Any change, of major or minor proportions, to the existing system cannot be introduced without a reason. There has to be a benefit, either to the workforce or to the management services. Or it is a legal requirement. If it cannot be argued, don't use it.

Constraints

Every sector of every industry has a set of special rules or laws that have to be followed. If you are not aware of any special limitations that apply to your project, keep looking – the odds are strongly against you. In addition, there are the legal constraints imposed at some political level – national or international. In this class is the Data Protection Act, or its local equivalent, discussed briefly in the last chapter. Further, from 1990, there will the requirement in Europe to conform to the new standard on the workstation environment in terms of minimising user stress (the ISO standard will be sensibly equivalent to the UK BSI standard 7179).

Approval

There has to be a role set up within the organisation that formally reviews and ultimately accepts (or rejects) the proposals as commercially worthwhile or legally acceptable. Note that both the proposal above and the resultant approval should be entered in a report and archived. This will be of enormous assistance to the up-graders who, perhaps a year or so later, always ask the agonised question "Why on earth did they do it *that* way?"

Discussion

Even though the modification is now acceptable to the management, it should still be filtered through the people who will actually have to use it. If they don't like the idea, then it is probably best to discard it. Conversely, if they have counterproposals then listen hard.

Revision

As a result of the above discussions, it will often be necessary to modify or enhance the original proposals. This is the point of iteration where each time a change is made it has to be justified and you go round the loop again. At some point there are no further changes. This is finally the time when the requirement list may be taken to be completed.

For the time being, this concludes the feasibility phase. The main deliverable has been a list of proposed improvements and this has taken a lot of time and effort to prepare. However, note that the list is not a specification. It is a definition of some carefully selected objectives and essentially defines the 'what' while saying little about the 'how'. This is a potential problem, in that the objectives may have been hammered out to be acceptable, but the implementation may still prove to be impossible, or at least take an uneconomic amount of time. This, then, is the problem that will be discussed in the next section. But for the present, we can end by picking some of the points of interest in this section and seeing how they might have been applied to the models in practice.

Newtown General: The end-users will generally consist of the staff nurses and junior doctors. Since they are usually heavily overstretched, the major problem will be stealing some of their time for interview purposes. The ward and operating-theatre sisters and more senior doctors should also be consulted. As already suggested, they may be somewhat overloaded on other tasks so a fairly positive attitude and soft-sell approach could well be needed for a good interface.

The external contacts (sources and sinks) will depend on the country and the current administrative structure for the medical services. Thus, for the Newtown surgery ward, there may be required data communication with other wards and clinics (X-ray, etc.), the hospital Central Records and Computer Department, the hospital Research Unit, the local FPC (Family Practitioners Committee) and possibly, among others, the DHA (District Health Authority).

Finally, take a look at the special constraint on this project. In the UK this largely comes down to the Körner report (see reference 22), which outlines the objectives of Information Systems within a medical environment. The local authorities were legally obliged to install Körner compatible systems by April 1987 and any systems under design today will have to conform to its main objectives.

Universal Solid State: A different situation. It is likely that most of the interested parties will be computer literate and will have a very clear idea of what improvements will help them in their daily work. In this type of situation, the parties are spread globally so regular review meetings are not practical. Fortunately, a phone call or a telex or fax message network will probably be sufficient to explore any new proposal and to accept or reject it.

The external contacts will usually be contained within the multi-national structure of Universal and could be, for example, the headquarters MIS department, finance and comptrollers offices, New Projects department, and so on.

The special constraints in this example might include the FCC requirement to minimise radio frequency noise from computer based equipment (see reference 23). This would apply to any equipment, made or bought, that is intended for data operation or communication within the US – along with general acceptance in many other locations.

6.3 The Requirement Specification

This is the key activity that has been promised throughout all the previous chapters. After all these preliminaries, we are finally there. Well, to be fair, not quite. What we are now ready to discuss is the final horse trading, the last political favours, and the ultimate shady compromises. Among other activities, we need to do *deals* to get a useful specification.

To understand this, we can take a rather jaundiced look at the traditional system development program (back, in our case, to the clients ABC and the consultants XYZ of Chapter 1). The lowest estimate frequently does get the job, and cutting corners is cost-effective in the short term even if quality-catastrophic in the long. Going down this route means that extra time, resource and costs provided at some later date may, perhaps, no longer rescue the project. In fact, if the project survives at all, the real outlay only begins with the maintenance phase after the system has been installed. In the middle of all this is the Requirement Specification which outlines the objectives of the development activity. It is these objectives which are often too ambitious for the skills or capacity of the development team working within the allotted time and budget. The results are usually partial deliverables, restrictions in the planned documentation and test activities, and non-productive schedule overruns.

This is why the modelling of the project, and the assembly of the specification that utilises results derived from the model are crucial to a successful system development plan. Both will be covered in this section. But, first, we will need to look carefully at the variables that will be used in the model.

Factors Affecting the Objective

This is where the wheeling and dealing comes in, where a specification can be modified and re-molded to establish a real chance of delivering client success. Let us look at some of the major factors that will be interactively involved in achieving the objectives of a new system:

❑ Administration

❑ Personnel

❑ Technology

❑ Requirement

❑ Schedule

❑ Budget

Administration

There are two factors which can affect the rate at which the project moves forward. In the first place, the degree of balance between the working partners will alter the effectiveness of interworking (see Chapter 4). If party A is forever snarling down the phone to party B, then the communication and co-operation between these two will tend to be minimal.

The second point relates to the relative ease of getting a decision. This is part of the normal requirements of any project and will dramatically affect the day-to-day operations. If, for example, the managers who are needed to formally sign-off a decision are travelling, or always in other meetings, or live in five separate time zones round the globe, then the ongoing and cumulative delays due to hung decisions are going to be serious. This is not to suggest that projects cannot be completed under these circumstances. They certainly can, but more time should be allocated where these conditions hold true.

Personnel

The number of people allocated to the development team will affect the time taken to complete all the designated tasks. However, the equation is not linear. First of all, the capabilities of the individual members of the team will vary widely. This can be both in terms of general system experience as well as particular expertise (or lack thereof) in the specific operating system, CASE tool, database language, etc. More to the point, you have a logistics problem comparable to running an army in a foreign country. For every five new system analysts, you will need added programmers (numbers dependent on the programming language used) and almost certainly an extra project leader or administrator. He will be yet another node in the project plan which will require additional updating. He will also be in the communication and decision making net which will only add additional delays. In addition, these new members of the team will need floor area, lighting, power, signal lines, tables and extra canteen space. And the added staff to maintain these extra corporate assets. (See pages 30 onwards in reference 4 for further discussion on this topic.)

All this goes some way to explaining why the management will tend to resist the application for every new person on the project. Equally, it explains why you cannot directly quantify the impact of one new system analyst on the schedule figures. As a crude starter, assume that one competent addition to a small team (three to eight people) will be about 0.6 to 0.7 of an effective person added to the workforce, in terms of schedule modifications. It may be true that he or she is an effective programmer, but every addition will contribute to the overall 'noise' present in the project and will require extra resource within the organisation – which is not necessarily good for the project. Thus, if four people together take 12 months to carry out some tasks, then one extra person could make that roughly 10.4 months (i.e. 48/4.6) rather than the expected 9.6 figure (i.e. 48/5). For someone who is less experienced – make that value about 0.4 to vector in the added training delay (that is to say, use 4.4 as the new divisor).

Technology

There is always a risk in assessing the relative difficulty of achieving a certain target. Consider, for example, the general requirement: a maximum delay of three seconds in providing an address from an installed customer list of 4,000, when up to 200 users are querying or updating the database. The only certain test is to build the entire system and monitor the actual delay over a period of several weeks with 200 operators using the system. It is difficult to simulate this type of test because it will depend on the hardware, software, application programs, design philosophy, and optimising skill of the operations manager and database administrator.

Experience suggests that a Cray supercomputer or a set of high-speed parallel computers will have no trouble with this task. Conversely, a 6 Mhz IBM PC XT clone is very unlikely to achieve it. Somewhere in between these extremes is your system running on the mini or mainframe machine utilised by your company.

If possible, this type of technical evaluation should be addressed during the feasibility phase, using small test routines to get a first approximation to the possible scale of the problem. If it does not look easy at the outset, then the odds are that it could be a source of considerable embarrassment later on.

Requirement

The list of system improvements or new requirements has been generated as outlined in section 6.2 above. However, each item on that list constitutes additional design activity in adding that item to the new system. It would be worthwhile to estimate the number of man-months, say, to implement each of the required changes in the list. Then to sum these amounts. This plus some figures for documentation, testing and installation is a crude indicator of the total time-to-complete in man-months Now, compare this figure with the allocated number of staff multiplied by the scheduled number of months to handover. (This is generous in that it assumes each member of staff is fully operational – see above comments on personnel.) By now, in the real world, there will usually be an enormous difference between the required time-to-complete figure and the allocated-by-schedule figure, the former being considerably larger than the latter. Under these circumstances, one of the possible solutions is to go over the requirement list again to reduce its scope.

Schedule

This is usually imposed fairly early on in the project. Part of the negotiating skill at this stage is to get the handover date treated as a system variable rather than a fixed constant. Or, at minimum, to explore what trade-offs are available if this figure can be modified.

Budget

Very often, the total expenditure on a development program is a fixed immutable figure. It was defined at the original presentation, and getting the job was dependent on that figure. However, sometimes it is rightly recognised as yet another complex variable that will vary as other parameters are changed. It all depends on the client's attitude.

Currently, costing for system design is a fairly straightforward exercise, and most proposals have pages full of cost models and financial analysis accurate to four decimal places. Looking back from the wisdom of, say, eighteen months into the program, it does seem a pity that so few of these estimates are ever within 50% of the final figure. By and large, the models were fine, it was just that some of the input data was dreamware.

So these are not constant parameters, but variables that have to be processed to make a coherent and realistic project. The model that you use may vary according to each client's or consultant's general philosophy, or with factors related to some special features of the system. All that matters is that a model should be used which takes the above elements into consideration.

Project Modelling

One simple estimating process is outlined in Figure 6.2. It provides a means of assessing the time required for the system implementation, the resource available to carry out the development, the schedule that follows from the above analysis and, finally, a rough cut at the budget based on these figures. A project model can be selected as a basic or a more complicated one. However, where a basic model is adopted, as shown below, then the drawbacks and limitations should be kept firmly in mind.

System Needs

Each of the tasks, finally defined and agreed in the previous section (the list of proposed improvements in section 6.2), is assessed by the designer who will have to provide that function. He or she provides a figure (Est_time_List_item) for the estimated-man-months-to-complete. In addition, the project manager or other review body may add a technical-difficulty factor for each task, in accordance with their own experience. Then, the total of all these products will be summed to generate the total man-months estimate needed to get all the elements of the project completed.

Note the built-in assumption that all elements of the project are treated as independent entities which will follow smoothly one on the other, with no hold ups or other restrictions. This is unlikely to happen in real life, but this assumption will allow a first estimate of the required development time.

Resource Definition

Each member of the team ('person' in Figure 6.2) is also assessed in relation to the experience that they will bring to the specific tasks that have been assigned to them. The special modifier is, again, an approximation. For the reasons outlined in the previous section under 'Personnel', an expert can be assumed to add about 0.7 or 0.75 of a work-force unit, whereas an untrained person may be as low as 0.3 of a work-force unit – although this could change after an initial period of acclimatisation. Where one person will have a number of different tasks during the project then the expertise-factor should be an average of the estimated figure for each task. This is obviously not easy to assess so it would be prudent to err on the

$$\text{Man\_Months} \quad = \quad \sum_{p = 1}^{p = n} \{ \text{Est\_time\_List\_Item}_p \ * \ \text{Tech\_difficulty} \}$$

$$\text{where} \quad 0.5 < \text{Tech\_difficulty} < 2.0$$

$$\text{Work\_Force} \quad = \quad \sum_{q = 1}^{q = m} \{ \text{Person}_q \ * \ \text{Expertise\_factor} \}$$

$$\text{where} \quad 0.3 < \text{Expertise\_factor} < 0.7$$

$$\text{Schedule} \quad = \quad \frac{\text{Man\_Months}}{\text{Work\_Force}}$$

$$\text{Budget} \quad = \quad 2 \ * \ \text{Schedule} \ * \ \sum_{q = 1}^{q = m} \{ \text{Person\_Salary}_q \} \quad +$$

$$\text{Hardware / Software Costs} \quad +$$

$$\text{Support Services}$$

Figure 6.2: The project model

side of caution and then to explain your reasons for this caution in the cover documentation.

Finally, adding all the individual figures in this area will give the total work force available to carry out the work.

Schedule

The third equation in 6.2 gives a simple figure for the schedule estimate, based on the available manpower and system design requirements.

Budget

Finally, the overall budget figure is generated with the fourth equation. Here, the cost per person (each individual salary treated on a monthly basis) is multiplied by the duration of the project established above. The result is further doubled to provide a rough estimate of the total cost per project-team employee including overheads such as building costs, pension plans, etc. This figure is then added to the outlay for the hardware and software required to run the system. Finally, the cost estimate of the site expenses, i.e. the maintenance and operations facilities required by the development group, is also added to the overall estimate to give the initial estimate of total outlay for the system.

The main thrust of this section has been to highlight how the requirements mesh into a complex relationship with other system parameters. Modify any one of them and that will put pressure on another variable or set of them. This calls for the negotiation and trading, indicated at the start of this section, such that the model can be consistent, i.e. that *those* improvements can probably be implemented with *these* design team members working for *that* time period and meeting *this* budget. You may have to trade with the budget controller, the MIS director, the client department and the personnel manager. This might result, for example, in reducing items in the the requirement list for a shorter schedule, which in turn will allow more people on the project for the same budget allocation.

There will be times when the development management will be forced to treat these variables as constants: this is the specification, here is the team, keep the costs below XXX and finish before YYYY. Under these inauspicious circumstances, take whatever steps that seem appropriate to you – but don't be surprised if the project runs into difficulties.

The Requirement Specification

By now, the planning for the entire project has been placed on some agreed and realistic basis (budget, personnel, implementation, objectives, etc.) and this will include the items in the requirement list. These items have been confirmed as the number of changes that will be made to the existing system. The data to be incorporated in the requirement specification is now available – having followed the activities outlined in Chapter 5 and Chapter 6 up to this point. It is finally time to generate the specification.

Specification Contents

In effect, all the work associated with preparing the requirement specification, i.e. the data defining the objectives and methods of implementation, has been completed. All that is needed now is the layout of the document. You will recall that the documentation format is also not a pre-determined structure: it is something assembled with the objective of satisfying the client, the client's operations group and the consultant design team. The only general proviso is that it should be clear and unambiguous in style of writing and layout. One possible format or starting point for the layout of the specification is given in Figure 6.3, where each left hand element is a section heading which is concerned with all the topics given on the right hand side.

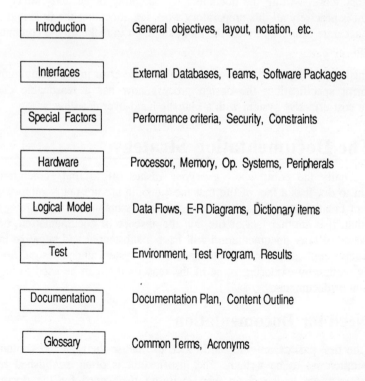

Figure 6.3: The format of the Requirement Specification

Authorisation

With the structure defined, the document comes to life with the data defined in the last two chapters being included in the body of the specification. That leaves one final activity required to make the specification a working document. The entire document has to be reviewed by the assigned review body or by the client users concerned, leading to the formal signing-off of the specification by all the different parties that will be linked in the project.

Note that any development work undertaken before obtaining formal approval of this document may well comprise wasted activity requiring a complete workround. By the same token, there is every incentive not to delay the meeting where this document is to be reviewed. The whole project is waiting.

We can see now that the emphasis, in previous chapters, on the importance of the requirements specification is not strictly well placed. In fact, after all the preparatory work, writing the document is something of an anti-climax. What *is* important is precisely all this preparatory work i.e. allocating the time and effort to provide accurate estimates for all the factors that go to make up the contents of this document.

In conclusion, having made every effort to minimise error in the formulation of the requirement specification, the design process now has a reasonable chance to deliver a cost-effective system with a realistic hand-over deadline.

6.4 The Documentation Strategy

This is usually the point where everyone rushes off to find something vitally important to do. It is a fact of life that most people are not really interested at the thought of creating or using a handbook, operator's manual or test strategy paper. For all that, it is another fact of life that the absence of documentation, or worse, the presence of poor documentation will have a substantial and negative influence on the future application and maintenance of the system under design. So we can start this section by exploring some of the reasons that can be used to justify the generation of documents.

The Need for Documentation

One of the first project activities is, in fact, to finalise the type and content of the documentation set to be written. The justification is often established by some designers or users in the chain who insist on *their* need for the document in question. Much like the proposed system changes of the last section, the document types and and their contents should be defended and attacked over a series of meetings. This will establish the commercial purpose in creating the document set; i.e that there is some project or system advantage to allocating funds, time and resource in generating these documents during the project phase. The justification

one proposed set is illustrated in Figure 6.4. Here, the document title and related distribution requirements are displayed. In general terms, the total work load could be contained in a single document called *System Documentation Listing* which carries all the relevant information about the documents to be written for this particular project. This could include the basic layout for each document as defined in existing procedures; a listing of related corporate standards; and an outline of the required review and update procedures. If such a list does not exist, then one of the first jobs of the project team will be to generate one, i.e. to define the need, nature and scope of each document to be written.

	Senior Management	Line Management	Users	External Users	Design Manager	Design Analysts	Operations	Maintenance	Archive
Doc. List		X	X		X	X			X
Feas. Study	X	X	X	X	X				X
Req. Spec.	X	X	X	X	X	X	X	X	X
Meet. Report		X			X				X
S / W Listing		X			X	X	X		X
Test Spec.		X	X		X	X	X	X	X
Test Report	X	X	X		X	X	X	X	X
Product Spec.	X	X	X	X	X		X	X	X
Installation		X	X		X		X		X
Training		X	X	X					X
User Manual		X	X	X			X	X	X

Figure 6.4: The documentation requirements

Document Standardisation

Over and above the need of any particular project and its team to have a set of coherent documents, is also a corporate need for standard document types and layout. This will allow other personnel, departments and plants to use documents from widely different sources. One solution to this whole problem of requiring standardised-format comments, reports, specifications and code is to establish a dedicated group that is purely associated with corporate documentation. This group can define and uphold the standards and procedures to be used, the documentation formats to be adopted, and hold review and sign-off meetings. Even where such an independent group cannot be justified, then its *role* can be defined and allocated to, say, some existing members of the team. This group could also be made responsible for setting up an archiving facility and configuration control ('what versions of the software packages were installed in Frankfurt in March 1988?').

Defining and accepting a standard document architecture has enormous advantages for the large national or international organisation, but is no small task. Consider, as an example, the negotiation that might be needed to define the first page of an arbitrary standard specification. It may, perhaps, be finally accepted to contain the following:

❏ Confidentiality status (optional)

❏ Permitted reader list (optional)

❏ Date, edition and review status level

❏ Author list (names, dept., and signed off)

❏ Review body list (names, dept., and signed off)

❏ Title of specification

❏ Document identification number

❏ Contents list: Scope
Related documents
Glossary of terms
Performance data
Mechanical requirements
Environmental requirements
Electrical interference

❏ Appendices: Supplementary

Each section in the contents list will then be further analysed and reviewed for optimum layout structure to meet the needs of the organisation.

For another approach, if good documentation is thought to be cost-effective, then it may be worthwhile to properly train the design staff to produce this valuable product on a regular basis. (If it is not thought to be of use, then don't waste their time in writing indifferent material – get them back to design.) Conversely, if the need is irregular, then perhaps specialised technical writers can be hired as and when required.

As a final comment, if you provide an effective environment for the generation of documents, you are more likely to get effective documentation. This could include: setting up and enforcing documentation standards, providing top-down support for documentation review as a necessary part of the product acceptance plan, educating the staff with seminars and other training tools, and encouraging a climate of opinion that makes it natural to associate work output with document output.

Documentation for Newtown and Universal

As in other areas, one might expect that the two model design projects would have a radically different position concerning documentation. But it doesn't have to be that way:

Newtown General

The current users are not all that interested in system documentation and, possibly, do not recognise its importance. However, if the hospital computer department is participating in the meetings, then it will almost certainly insist that a full complement of documents be made available before handover of the new system to the hospital. Again, the hospital Central Records may already be running some archiving scheme which will have to be superimposed on the project. The end result could be that a full set of controlled document deliverables is called for as a result of including these peripheral departments in the discussions.

Universal Solid State

With a more formal way of running projects through the Data Processing Department, Universal will be no stranger to structured documentation. As a result, they will insist on a hierarchical set of documents where all the subordinate products will have to be reviewed and signed-off before the top-level document can even be addressed. The cost will be higher and the quality of output will show a corresponding improvement.

6.5 Summary

We started the chapter with a review of the techniques to be applied in carrying out a feasibility study. Essentially, reliable information will be obtained from the existing users if the sample size is adequate and if the formal technique to be adopted, e.g. the use of interviews, matches the expectations and abilities of the end-users. In addition, the social impact of this study phase on the workforce should be taken into account. For a co-operative relationship, the existing users will need to be well motivated towards the new system and this may take some serious effort on the part of the management and the interviewer. For all its importance, this area of system design is not generally well defined, and some useful reports on this subject are given in references 20 and 21.

Following this analysis, a list of potential changes is drawn up that would significantly improve the existing system. With each change being justified, accepted and signed-off, there is a measure of practical control over the more exotic proposals.

At this point the major parameters of a project, such as size of design team or number and type of changes to be made, can be evaluated, modified and reassessed until a reasonable compromise solution to all the conflicting requirements has been found. Once that has been achieved, the remaining items on the improvement list can be entered into a formal Requirement Specification which can then be signed-off (or, if necessary, further modified) by all the parties who will participate in the project. This sort of analysis is ideally carried out at the beginning of the project. The more popular approach seems to be when the project is at the point of slipping six months and has become wildly over-budget. On the whole, the former is to be preferred.

The chapter ended with some coverage of a documentation strategy for the project. The possible application of documents throughout the system development was explored along with an outline of the type of documents that could be generated.

Questions

1. As part of the feasibility study, it will be necessary to interview the nurses and doctors in the Surgery ward of Newtown General. Discuss the pros and cons of sending in a) a junior analyst, b) a medical graduate, or using instead c) the ward sister.

2. You have carried out a first study proposal for the Universal work and the Headquarters New-projects Group have vetoed the project. As your boss would inevitably say: What can we do now ?

3. The day-to-day decision-making body for the Newtown General project has been agreed to comprise: the senior surgeon; the staff sister; the head of the hospital MIS department; and a representative of the Family Practitioners Committee. Criticise the choice, and offer an alternative membership which you suggest will be more effective in the given role.

4. The consultant has not included a 'Data Definition' document in the documentation set to be delivered. This is where each named entity and attribute is listed in terms of data type, no. of characters, where it occurs in the system, etc. Explain why you want it, and which groups will find it of value.

5. The client is hesitant about setting up an archive function, i.e. keeping every document and its upgrades and every software package version for the life of the system. Give some of the possible reasons for such a function.

7

Project Administration

Should training jump to a different beat?

In a world where competitive edge is everything, it is a depressing fact that US companies spend about five times as much per employee on training as we do in the UK. What this costs in terms of lost production is incalculable.

. . . .

A long term commitment to training is by no means a cheap option, but the contribution that it makes to increasing revenue more than compensates.

Computer Weekly p. 12 17.8.89

Radar kit faces axe

The Ministry of Defence may be forced to scrap up to 10 years software development work, worth £380 million, in an attempt to bring a vital project back on schedule.

The Integrated Command and Control System for the Improved UK Air Defence Ground Environment project has been in development for a decade. But it still does not meet MoD requirements and is already five years behind schedule.

Datalink p.2 19.6.89

When keyboards give you a pain in the neck

It is only recently that repetitive strain injuries have been discovered in IT workers. However, the data that seems to be emerging suggests that the problem is reaching epidemic proportions, and is not just affecting clerical staff such as batch-input operators, but white-collar staff too.

. . . .

Vdu operators are far more prone to repetitive strain injuries than operators of manual or electric keyboards because the vdus have light touch keys, extra function keys and screens. They also eliminate the valuable rests that result when paper has to be changed or a carriage return has to be waited for.

Computing p. 24 9.3.89

7.1 Introduction

This is the first chapter in the section entitled 'Managing the Design' which takes a look at the major issues of administration, communication and change control. All the emphasis to date has been on generating an accurate Requirement Specification. This has been because mistakes made during the feasibility phase or in drawing up the project plan will be more expensive to correct than mistakes made at any later date. For all that, the design phase still has to be managed, and a free wheeling and out-of-control development program will still prove a disastrous enterprise.

This chapter is concerned with the main aspects of technical administration during the design and test phase. This does not mean that there will be discussion of the system design activity itself, broken down into tasks, as carried out by the design team. This activity is fully explored by the numerous books on System Design and will be governed by the adopted methodology and technical skills of the development team. On the contrary, we are going to review the ongoing *management* of that team. The objective is that the daily running of the project should be, in a word, structured. Looked at another way, the planning of events should control the way the project runs, rather than responding to each crisis eruption with a stand-by fire-fighting force.

Since each design is sensibly unique, there can be no standard way to configure such an undertaking. However, there is a universal thread that does run through every phase of system development, and that is the decision making requirement. Every project should run smoothly on the decisions made each day which resolve the open questions thrown up at that particular point. Do we sign off the document at the front or the back? Do we add more resource to the test phase, modify the schedule or reduce the amount of testing? Shall we change the back-up equipment or increase the archive storage space? And so on. To sum up, good planning and effective, fast decision making are at the core of successful project administration – in whatever form it takes. In turn, both planning and decision making depend on the relevant procedures being in place and the ready availability of accurate information related to the project.

The nature of this information is the real subject of this chapter and will be defined and outlined in the pages that follow. It will constitute the envelope within which the decision making process can occur, i.e. where material can be accessed and subsequently prioritised in an effective and speedy process. The data under consideration been broken down into three main topics:

❏ Project deliverables

❏ Scope of the project

❏ Resource factors

The first will review the results and output objectives that are delivered to the client as a result of the development activity; the second will define the internal processes and procedures that will be applied to the running of the project itself; and the last item is concerned with the staff involvement and discusses some of the personnel factors that may be present in any particular project. As a further by-product of identifying all the objectives and tasks within the project, the workload of the project management role can itself be assessed and, if necessary, either prioritised or enhanced with added management personnel.

In summary, we need a basic listing of all the planned activities related to the project in order to have the data ready for fast efficient decision making, and to allocate the available management resource as effectively as possible.

7.2   Deliverables

Clearly, one of the more important aspects of the project is the definition of the agreed physical items and services that are to be developed and supplied to the client. The basic list is defined at the beginning of the project and constitutes the overall scope and justification of all the development activity that follows. It will always include the handover and installation of the designed software packages. Equally, there will be accompanying documentation which will describe the way in which these packages are meant to operate along with a full listing of the actual programming code. However, that is not the end of the story, and the full set of items to be handed over is outlined in Figure 7.1. Most of these items are covered in more detail elsewhere in the book, but it is convenient to discuss them together here and to spend a few lines as a reminder on each topic.

It is the totality of all these items performing interactively that will enable the system to be successfully installed and operated. So cutting back one to favour another may be something of a false economy. In any case, these items will constitute the major load on the project team, and it would be prudent to have a good idea of the initial work estimates to achieve each of the defined tasks. When schedules start slipping, the reason will almost certainly lie in one of the subjects discussed here, and tight reporting will enable a problem to be identified long before it becomes a crisis.

Software

The heart of the new system under development will comprise a number of software modules or packages designed using a particular programming language for application with a specific operating system (or systems). In addition, the software may need designated links to commercial application packages such as word processors, existing communication software and possible networking interfaces. All these will need to be defined in advance and working units transferred to the client on some agreed date.

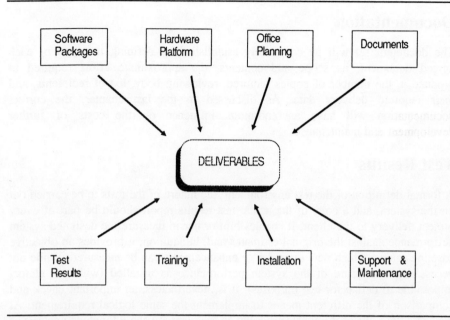

Figure 7.1: The development program outputs

Hardware

Again, the performance objectives of the hardware platform have to be defined at the start of the exercise, since they will have a critical cost and performance impact. The resulting equipment, including peripherals such as terminals, printers and memory storage units, communication and network hardware, and associated power supply systems will all need to be part of the tested and documented handover to the client.

Office Requirements

The client will have to be told what is needed, in terms of a working environment, such that the equipment can be operated to fulfill the required system application. Here, we are talking about required desks and chairs, the screens and keyboards, the air conditioning, the data signal wiring, emergency equipment and so on. It may be considered trailing-edge technology, but the system will still not work if someone from the development team has forgotten to install (or has not obtained) the required number of power points in the proposed work area. At the beginning, very few of these items can be defined. For all that, if the check-list is created at the start of the project, it can be updated regularly as more of the parameters become available.

Documentation

The document set will be completely established by defining the type of each agreed document, its scope and contents, the approximate effort required to produce it, the number of copies required, reviewing body, list of recipients, and their required delivery date. As discussed in the last chapter, the correct documentation will have an enormous influence on the costs of further development and maintenance.

Test Results

A formal definition of the test environment, the nature of the tests to be carried out on the system, and a copy of the actual test results report should be part of every project delivery to the client. It enables him or her to measure the designed system performance against the original estimates and, in addition, it provides an objective baseline against which new upgrades or enhancements can be measured. While not necessarily a measure of the system performance as installed (which is almost impossible to define for test purposes), it is, nevertheless, an important check and comparison of the different means to implement the same logical requirement. At the same time, the cost impacts are high, so the planning should include analysis of scope, schedule and resource estimates on this item in order to maximise the cost-effectiveness of the test function. In particular, conformance to existing corporate standards – if they exist – should be the major aim in this area.

Training and Ancillary Services

The value of user training has not always been fully appreciated in the past (see the first quotation at the beginning of the chapter). However, as part of the overall strategy on staff education, the specific training requirements of the project should be well defined. This could, for example, include regular meetings at each major milestone of the project. This would enable the staff to accustom themselves to the system over an extended period of time, rather than throw them in, at the conclusion of the project, with a three day intensive tutorial.

Installation

This subject will be covered in Chapter 10. For the present, it will be enough to mention that installation can be an effective and trouble-free operation. All it takes is comprehensive planning, sustained interworking, reliable communication and commitment right from the beginning of the project. That is all it takes.

Post Installation Activities

Again, this topic will be fully discussed in Chapter 11. The scope of this function will largely depend on the actual agreements made between the design group and the client. However, whatever these agreements, it would be sensible to record the expectations and responsibilities involved, such as the provision (or otherwise) of hot-line support or on-site consultant availability. This will be important in planning the forward allocation of resource as the project draws to a close.

This section has effectively identified the items that will have to be addressed some time during the life of the project. All of them will have to be delivered, in one form or another, to the end-user and all of them will need planning and resource to carry out the generation activity. It is recommended that a document, within the documentation set, is defined to list all the items discussed above. This will act as an indicator of the tasks accomplished as well as a reminder of the work that is still outstanding. The possible first pages of such a document, as applied to the Newtown project, have been symbolically outlined in Figure 7.2. Here the names of the Client and Design Managers for the project are indicated on page 1 along with a place for their signatures to indicate formal agreement with the contents of the document.

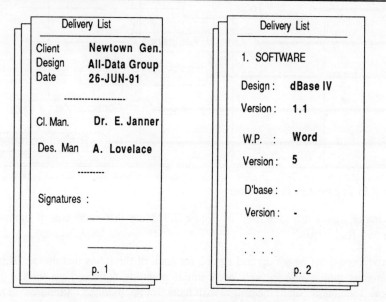

Figure 7.2: The deliverables checklist document

7.3   Scope of Project

When a builder constructs a house or office block, the tools he uses are of only minimal interest to the client. However, to the builder, the nature and quality of the tools, such as hammers and drills, will have a major impact on his overall performance. In a similar way, the system development process calls up a number of activities which are purely related to the smooth running of the project itself. The interaction with the client may be less frequent over these matters, but the problems arising may ultimately be of a more serious nature than the day-to-day queries of the last section. This section will identify various topics which concern the project, and which will be covered with agreed procedures and identified within suitable documents.

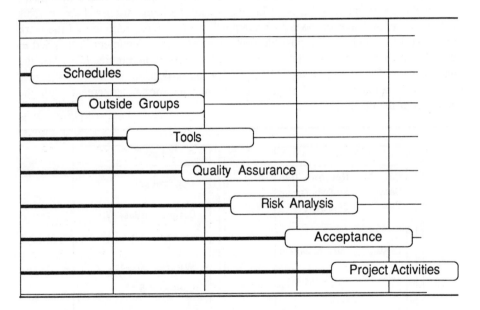

Figure 7.3: The project components

These major topics are identified in Figure 7.3. Note that each one of them will have a two-fold impact:

❏ A procedure must be set up and agreed for each of the items mentioned. Thus, it is obvious that *schedules* will need initial planning followed up with regular review meetings. Such meetings will have to be planned, attendees agreed, output defined, address list established, and so on. It will take a finite time to set up each of these procedures, and that time will have to be allocated by someone within the project or design staff. It does not come free.

❑ For each period, say, week or month, the regular agreed meetings, reviews etc. will have to take place. The additional time taken for these recurring activities will also have to be taken into account in the master planning.

Again, a few words concerning each topic will indicate the general approach to be adopted:

Schedules/Budgets

A significant number of all system design exercises, big or small, undertaken in the last few years appear to have gone wildly over the original estimates for cost and time to complete. The second example at the head of the chapter is only too characteristic of what appears to be a norm for the profession. While it takes little skill to have hindsight, getting the estimates right in the first place calls for a more disciplined style of analysis. A structured approach to system design, recognising the political content of the project, and including personnel aspects in the overall picture will all help to create estimates that have a reasonable probability of being met. This has been the subject matter of the last few chapters.

However, all that this work will provide is initial estimates – nothing more. There has to be continual feedback during the life of the project so that the figures can be modified or corrective action can be undertaken. The basic idea is to set up regular progress meetings where deviations from the original plans can be identified and suitable small workrounds put into operation. With more infrequent meetings, the deviations become gross, often requiring a more drastic, surgical solution.

It is true that there is no 'safe' or guaranteed method of management that will avoid costly overruns, but adopting a structured approach will certainly move the odds strongly your way. Regular meetings, fast decision making processes, and honest reporting to all the parties allows for good control of the schedule and budget figures – without too many unpleasant surprises. Again, it is assumed here that bad news does not have to be fudged for political reasons.

It is not really important that the schedules, for example, be rigidly maintained. What is crucial, however, is that full agreement continues to exist between the users and the design team regardless of any needed modifications to the priorities, schedules and budgets related to the project.

Outside Groups

One of the daily functions of a project is the distribution of information to interested parties who may not be part of the primary project team. This could be important either politically ('Why wasn't *I* informed?') or operationally (head office needs the revised cost figures). To ensure that all the right people are consulted, it is sensible to build up a list of topics related to the project, along with all the personnel who may have an interest in that topic. At a pragmatic level, this helps when inviting representatives to strategy/progress/crisis meetings, and also in drawing up distribution lists for printed material, or database access on the given subject.

Tools

This is another common sense listing. As pointed out at an earlier stage, there should be the same bought-in application programs standardised for use at every centre where the project is being used or worked on. If necessary, added packages should be purchased and installed at the different centres involved. In this context, distributing the list of the selected packages in use will tend to discourage someone trying to download data from a local PC card index file into, say, a distant relational database table. In particular, it should be made clear which programs, and which versions, are being used for the standard functions, as and where applicable. The list, for example, for Universal Solid State could be similar to the one given in Figure 7.4.

U.S.S. Application List

Function	Package	Version	Supplier
Wordprocessing	WordPerfect	5.1	WordPerfect
Database	Oracle	6	Oracle
Spreadsheet	Excel	2.1	Microsoft
Project Man.	Harvard P. Man.	3	Software Pub.
CASE tool	Excelerator	1.8	Excelerator
Network	Netware 386	3.1	Novell

Figure 7.4: The application programs list

In addition, the listing should contain details of the main hardware, peripherals (i.e. floppy disk drive, or magnetic tape, etc.), operating system and version level, and printers.

Quality Assurance

Contrary to popular opinion (and some corporate practices), it is possible to develop information systems and build in the quality at the same time. There are a number of tools or processes which can provide a methodology for precisely this purpose. Thus, for example, testability can be enhanced if the software under design is treated like the hardware, that is – compartmentalised into modules and submodules. Then each module can be tested and debugged in isolation on some suitable test harness. Large programs, consisting of lines of Pascal, Cobol or Ada language statements, can be analysed for underlying structure and programming violations. This can be done using tools such as LDRA Testbed available from Program Analysers Ltd. For full system testing, there are software test tools whose use will materially lower the eventual on-site maintenance costs. An example of such a product is the Verilog tool called ASA-PG which can support functional validation and system acceptance trials. Then there is the formal technical review technique, in which a small review team will assess a section of code or a specification document without any of the emotional bias of the person who generated the item under review. Finally, there should be an integration test plan which formally builds up the system in a controlled and testable manner. For further reading go to Chapter 12, p. 289 of reference 3 and Chapter 13, p. 141 of reference 4.

Quality assurance is more important than just a few lines describing some of the possible techniques that can be applied. It is central to reducing the overall costs of system application, but may take a long-term investment in time and expertise to make it effective. Much like structured design, quality aspects require the support of top management, the commitment and drive of the project leaders, and the technical inputs from the Q.A. manager or consultant. Quality may cost, but its absence costs more.

Risk Analysis

This is one of those subjects which will call for judgement based mainly on experience. In the first place, when the requirement specification was being written, all the proposals should have been considered for degree of risk within a realistic timeframe. Now, during the design phase, all the activities should be monitored for early signs of reduced or even negative progress in reaching defined targets. One criterion of potential problems is the 'condition of constant schedule'. This is reached when *independent of the date when the estimate is given, the number of man-months to achieve a given activity remains constant.* Such projects are not unknown, and there should be procedures in place for detecting the onset of this sort of problem, and there should be further procedures for handling that problem as soon as it arises. The output from such procedures may have to range from simply extending the schedule, to terminating the project.

This is another important topic and there are many examples given throughout this book where projects have either had to be shut down or caused heavy losses due to severe schedule overruns, or lack of delivery. We will return to this subject in Chapter 9.

Acceptance Procedures

At various places throughout the book, stress has been placed on maintaining cooperation between the client and the design staff. One implication of that is that decisions are agreed and not imposed. In order to underline that agreement, there have to be well defined procedures for legalising, as it were, the eventual results of a discussion, the decisions made at a meeting, or the finalising of a specification. Nothing is more time wasting than mutual recriminations about some misinterpreted decisions made six to twelve months ago. For the larger project, this can be largely avoided by formulating a number of high level review bodies. These will review for acceptance, for example, all the documents generated at a lower level. Another approach would be that all meetings are concluded with the formal acceptance and sign-off of the draft minutes. Again, there could be a standard comment inserted into all the minutes of any type of meetings: "Failure to comment within 20 days of receipt of this document will imply acceptance of the contents". Not only do these sort of techniques concentrate the mind wonderfully, they also prevent the corrosive exchanges that tend to occur at a much later date.

Project Activities

A PERT or Gantt chart is used to highlight some information related to the current status of the project. As such, it is of purely transient value, and will never figure as a system deliverable to the client. For all that, it takes time and effort to generate and will have a corresponding cost. Then add this to the cost of other activities such as the progress meeting, the progress meeting report, returned phone calls, replacing defective equipment, sub-contractor meetings, planning sessions, budget reduction analyses, and so on.

Section 6.3 (Personnel) in the last chapter showed that p people working for m months will not deliver $p.m$ man-months of work, but perhaps 60% of that estimate. Now, what we are saying is that not all of that will be applied to system design activity, since some part of the available time and resource will have to be used to administer the project. Perhaps it will cost another 25% of the available total resource and time, leaving only 45% of the original figure for actual system development. Clearly, some analysis on the anticipated project related activities and its cost impact in your organisation may help you to schedule events in a more accurate way.

This more or less completes the scope of the project activities. For more detail, try reference 24 – in particular Chapters 3, 4 and 5. Note that the manual tracking of some of these project functions can be a time consuming and error-prone activity. For this reason, it may be considered worthwhile to automate it with appropriate software tools and a number of the latest packages for project management and control have been reviewed in reference 26. However, like any other application tool, they will take time to learn and use effectively if the user is inexperienced.

Summing up the last few pages, an effectively managed project calls for thorough analysis of all the interlocking activities and is heavily labour intensive both in planning and carrying out all the assigned tasks. In addition, short cuts generally tend to be counter-productive. The needed attention to detail can be expensive, will take up valuable time and, from a technical point of view, is not particularly state-of-the-art or exciting. On the other hand, being one year over schedule is not particularly exciting, either.

7.4 Resource Factors

People, their skills and motivation are the prime asset of any organisation. They are probably even more important than the condition of the front foyer and visitor reception area. Yet the latter will tend to have considerable funds lavished on it, while the former is often ignored and taken for granted. This may not be the optimum strategic approach.

This section will touch on various topics related to personnel working on the project. The management style itself can radically affect the way people will respond to the corporate or departmental challenges and following the simple guidelines given below can dramatically enhance the overall productivity of the workforce. Note that all but the last topic cost absolutely nothing – it is just a matter of attitude.

The subjects to be covered here are:

❑ The Hawthorne Effect

❑ Support

❑ The HCI impact

❑ Role definition

❑ Training

The underlying premise of this section is that people who feel that their efforts are being appreciated, while working with a controlled amount of stress i.e. in a stimulating environment, and with a well defined position in the company will actually enjoy their work. This will lead to good motivation and a corresponding high productive output.

The Hawthorne Effect

This is a classic study in the field of industrial psychology carried out in the early part of this century. A production line team at the Western Electric Hawthorne plant in Chicago was monitored for the variation of output against improved working conditions. Taking a basic overview, the lighting was improved and production increased. Morning and afternoon teabreaks were introduced and production increased. A shorter working week was agreed and production increased. This program of improvements went on for a number of weeks, with the same trend being shown each week. Finally, all the benefits were withdrawn, and *production went up again*. The consultant in charge of the experiment, Elton Mayo, eventually established that the increased output was not related to the parametric changes in the workers environment, but *to the interest that was being taken in the workers themselves*. They enjoyed the attention being showered on them, and responded positively. While this is far from the complete story of the Hawthorne tests (see p. 17-20 in ref. 13), this simplified account says something illuminating about human nature in a working environment:

In the absence of other pressures, most people respond positively to external interest in their work progress, problem areas and current successes.

On this basis, our favourite companies ABC and XYZ could clearly improve productivity by insisting that the relevant manager(s) introduce regular two-way conversations with their members of the project team.

Support

This is about the problem of handling staff errors. The temptation, with all the other stresses of the moment, is for the manager to express his clear dissatisfaction in a very open manner. It is worth recalling that the staff undertaking system development work are expected to be highly motivated and creative and prepared to work through the night to finish the current software package. The remarkable thing is that most design staff will do just that – if they feel that their efforts are being appreciated. However, if the team are frustrated, angry, or think they are taken for granted, then the work output will plummet.

Consider the scenario where a junior analyst has just handed over a page of programming code without a single embedded REM statement (i.e. explanation of the function of each block of software). Now, you, the boss, can either:

❑ Bawl him out in front of the rest of the team, *or*

❑ Ask him to your office where you *praise* his design but point out why it is necessary to add remarks to help others to understand the code.

Maintaining morale looks obvious on paper, but somehow in real life making the effort to provide that extra support and understanding hardly seems worthwhile.

Just remember that the only thing that can generate a successful system development is your design team. Look after them.

The HCI Impact

HCI stands for Human Computer Interface. Up to a few years ago, that would have primarily meant the nature of the keys on the keyboard and the impact of the font and colour seen on the screen. Nowadays, there is more emphasis on the possible medical damage being done as a result of working at the terminal. At first glance, the operator keying in data at a terminal would appear to be working in a benign environment. Short working day, low noise levels, seated, clean air with no contact with toxic chemicals – it sounds like an ergonomic paradise. For all that, intensive use of computer terminals and similar equipment are bringing out some unforeseen medical problems. These problems are being addressed by means of an ergonomic standard which is currently being formulated by European standards organisations and which will be comparable to the BSI standard 7179. In particular, there are three specific areas areas of disquiet with the 'ergonomic paradise' and these are related to the keyboard, screen and the general work environment.

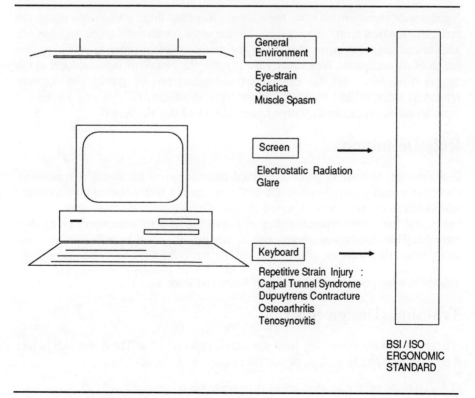

Figure 7.5: The medical aspects of HCI

The nature of the these problems are outlined in Figure 7.5. Taking each area in more detail:

KEYBOARD: Continued high-speed use of the keyboard can give rise to a number of diseases which are bundled under the loose heading of RSI -Repetitive Strain Injuries. The general effect is a growing loss of flexibility of the hand accompanied with either numbness or pain. (See the third quotation at the head of the chapter.)

SCREEN: There have been arguments put forward that the electrostatic radiation emitted by the VDU (Video Display Unit) is harmful to the long term health of the user sitting at the terminal. The usual result of extended exposure to this radiation is said to be some form of skin rash. However, for a considered view that the phenomenon, if it exists, is due to other causes, see reference 25.

GENERAL ENVIRONMENT: The bulk of the illnesses, possibly including the first group above, are potentially caused by some physical strain of the user. This might be caused by flickering fluorescent lighting; uncomfortable chairs; wrong height of the table or cramped workspace; overheating; overcooling; and so on.

Some senior management have been known to group these phenomena under the collective medical term 'imagination'. On the other hand, some union officials see a clear and urgent need to shut down the entire office in order to safeguard the health of its occupants. Whichever view is right, the morale of the workforce is the central issue here, and this can be seriously disturbed by gossip and rumours related to work related illnesses. At the very minimum, be prepared to discuss these topics sympathetically with a representative of the office staff.

Role Definition

If a member of staff is given a defined objective then he stands a reasonable chance of meeting that objective. Certainly he stands a better chance than someone who is left to guess what is expected of him. (One organisation had – and, for all I know, still has – the corporate policy of not telling its staff what salary grade they were on. That way, no-one knew exactly whether they had been promoted, what salary range they were in, or their level of responsibility.)

Tell them what you want and tell them when you want it.

Training (Design Staff)

It is worth looking at training from a strategic point of view. The down side is that it costs money and time. But, now reflect on some of the advantages:

❏ A corporate asset (the workforce) is improved and upvalued.

❏ The morale of the workforce is enhanced as it keeps up with all the latest technology inputs. (Ask anyone working in COBOL if they would like to go on a series of structured courses to learn SQL – the standard relational database language.)

❏ With planned programs of study stretching into the future, the rate of staff turnover diminishes as people stay in the department to finish the current, or even the next, course of study.

❏ The output systems always reflect the latest techniques. There is no built-in obsolescence.

In total, it sounds like a good deal for the company. While on the subject, there is a lot to be said for providing special technical training courses for the management, who were probably technical experts in their time – say, 15 years ago. One of the major advantages is that they will then be in a position to communicate technically with their own staff.

This completes the review of how the personnel can be positively motivated (or, at minimum, not demotivated) to carry out the assigned activities. It can all be summed up by the qualities of *respect* and *consideration*. They really are quite a cheap outlay in terms of the return on investment.

7.5 Summary

In this chapter we have briefly covered some of the principal aspects of project management. The emphasis has been on the technical side, because skill in that area is what will ultimately decide the success or failure of the entire development program. However, budgeting, forecasting, cost-management, the structure of the project administration and, frankly, wheeling and dealing to maintain political credibility within the organisation are all additional subjects that have be addressed at a very serious level.

The topics that have been discussed here are relatively unusual in that they basically only refer to the development team and its management. The client may or may not be interested in the day-to-day running of the project, he may want copies of all schedule meetings, but he does not really *participate* directly in the project.

Nevertheless, there is an important role that the client can play, and that is the role of Auditor. Tell it not in Gath, but the design team is composed of human beings and, as such, they are liable to make mistakes. In addition, these human beings are also usually being pushed to deliver twice the lines of code in half the time. As a result, it should come as no surprise to learn that serious errors can be introduced – both by the team and by the management of that team. On this basis, having an end-user representative monitoring the way the project is being run is something of an advantage all round, and can sometimes save a lot of time and wasted effort.

In short, monitoring the state of the technical development, maintaining control over the activities undertaken and taking rational decisions in the right timeframe – all this remains at the heart of good project management.

And one last point: look after the workforce. They are probably worth it.

Questions

1. Are these items 'Deliverables' or 'Project-related':

Design-team salary slips

Set up instructions for the test equipment

Air Conditioning purchase-order copy

Back-up tape of the complete installation schedule

The Resource Allocation Plan

The MTBF (Mean Time Between Failures) figures for the hardware items

2. A young programmer, who is clearly pregnant, comes to you saying that she is unhappy about working in front of the VDU screen because of the baby. What can you do?

3. Half way through the design phase, there is a re-organisation of the project (not an unknown phenomenon) and you are put in charge. How can you identify the major technical problem areas?

4. Half way through the two-year design phase, you are informed that the schedule will have to be modified to bring the formal handover to the users forward by six months. What practical proposals can be made back to the client management?

5. In the summary, it was suggested that an end-user should attend your meetings. What are the disadvantages of having such a client representative present at all your project meetings? How can you minimise the problems?

Communications

Changes that spell death for the middle manager

Becoming information-based means streamlining the company's organisation and speeding up internal functions. With a less bureaucratic structure, companies will be more responsive and competitive.

The information-based organisation does not actually require advanced information technology. All it needs is a willingness to ask "who requires what information, when, and where?" says Drucker.

Computer Weekly p. 15 12.4.90

Management study urges business rethink

Integration of systems and work groups is at the heart of many of the required changes, the report says.

"It is not just a matter of combining databases across all departments," it says. "It covers the wider issues of achieving close and effective working relationships between various parts of an organisation."

Computer Weekly p. 11 20.9.90

Runaway projects affect 60%

The causes of runaways were given as mainly managerial, not technical. Only 7% identified incorrect hardware or software as the culprit. Largest factor (32%) was inadequate project management and control, followed by failure to define system objectives (17%), lack of communication (20%) . . .

Computer Weekly p. 3 8.3.90

8.1 Introduction

In the nature of things, every system development project needs project management to organise and co-ordinate all the activities undertaken. However, this management just won't occur if you can't communicate. Again, a project is usually implemented with a team co-operating over key tasks. Inadequate communication will almost certainly destroy this co-operation. This may sound a little strange as, on a day-to-day basis, there is usually very little difficulty in communicating. In fact, there is almost too much of it with conversations, phone calls, messages, minutes of meetings, reports, faxes, E-mail, schedules, technical upgrades, mail shots *et al.* The real problem with all these possibilities, however, is to ensure that you are communicating effectively. To achieve that, you have to some understanding of the merits and disadvantages of each method. Before we get down to the nuts and bolts of the subject, this section will outline what is meant by communication, how its implementation can be enhanced, and what will cause it to become defective. But first, we will briefly return to the project in order to justify all this attention. Let's look at the basic format of a project, in terms of its workforce. This is given in Figure 8.1.

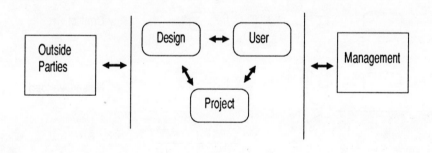

Figure 8.1: The make-up of a project

There are the three principal groups that go to make any project team and the two outer groups which have important interfaces with the main team. Notice how every two-way arrow represents a communication channel. (This is a clearly a simplification in that every group, for example 'Design', will itself comprise a number of sub-elements each of whom will seek to communicate within the group.) Now consider that any of the arrows shown in the drawing are not working properly – say, between 'Design' and 'Project'. At that point, in effect, you no longer have a viable project. Once the design workforce is isolated or acting independently from the project administration, then it becomes an exercise that is unlikely to be worth any further investment of time or effort. The only possible priority action remaining is to restore the link that was broken.

We are now in a position to offer another view of what is meant by a project:

A System Development Project is an assembly of active nodes directly linked by communication channels.

The 'active nodes' above are, of course, the relevant project teams implementing the activities defined in the schedule. However, for the moment, our interest is focussed on the channels between the nodes and the body of the chapter will be spent discussing some of the options available in forming, enhancing or maintaining them.

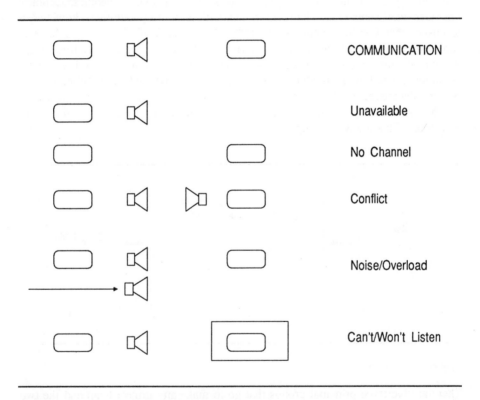

	COMMUNICATION
	Unavailable
	No Channel
	Conflict
	Noise/Overload
	Can't/Won't Listen

Figure 8.2: Communications models

In what way can these channels become defective? Consider the idealised model shown on the top line of Figure 8.2. Party A (the blob on the left hand side) wishes to communicate via the loudspeaker to party B on the right hand side, who is ready to receive the message. That is the ideal condition. Now consider some of the more familiar situations that can frequently prevent or inhibit this ideal state:

❑ B is unavailable, i.e. always at a meeting, travelling or in the restaurant.

❑ There is no loudspeaker. You may wish to contact a senior executive. But departmental procedures do not allow you to approach him directly, only through your boss – who is on holiday . . .

❑ B is not prepared to listen, since he has some communicating of his own to do, and he insists that his is more important.

❑ B would like to listen, but there are three other inputs coming in, and he can't make out what is being said.

❑ B has already made his mind up and will ignore any further inputs ("Don't confuse me with facts")

These examples illustrate when it is counter productive to try to get a message across. In any case, when you recognise that you are in one of these situations – stop transmitting and save your energy for the time when a proper communication link is available.

This is not the end of the problem. Assume that there is a clear link and B is set to receive. Then it is still possible to completely waste the transmission effort if the following have not been carefully considered:

❑ Relevance

❑ Density

❑ Boredom

Relevance

Do not go in for blanket distribution lists. Your 15 page report on software metrics may be the stuff dreams are made of, but, unless they are directly involved, most people will throw it straight in the waste bin. Worse still, the *next* time they get anything from you, they will be inclined to throw that away as well, without checking if it was for them or not.

Density

People can only absorb so much information in any given time. Take a simple slide prepared for a presentation. In rough terms, if it has more than about six lines of bullets or key information, then it is probably too dense to retain the interest of the audience. Again, the more 'white' or unused space there is on a written page, the higher the chance that anyone might bother to read it.

Boredom

The real killer. How do you stop the polite yawns and make the information interesting? Essentially, by recognising the danger and taking appropriate steps to liven up the material, or at least make it approachable. In this context, Figure 8.3 illustrates some of the techniques that can be applied in different media. Graphic enhancements, in particular, can be very dramatic and there is always the danger that the presentation technique becomes an end in itself. For all that, the attention span of the audience can be radically improved by spending some time on the display and layout of the message that they are to receive.

TEXT	Simple clear vocabulary Well constructed sentences Uncramped layout
GRAPHICS	Desktop publishing Presentation graphics Colour printing Animation
PROGRAM	Clear tutorial and handbook Good user interface (Menus, etc.) Bug-free Hotline facilities

Figure 8.3: Making the message interesting

In effect, the above discussion has been treating the subject as if it were a sub-set of Selling. This is largely fair, as 'getting the message across' is a familiar rallying cry at any Sales Convention. You are communicating with someone because you want to convince them that your idea is right and should be adopted. The better you target the audience and the better you express yourself on the subject, the more likely it is that message will indeed get across. With that concept in mind, we can now turn to the strategies, methods and message formats that can be utilised to achieve this objective.

8.2   Strategies

In any given situation, a strategy will provide a framework in which to provide a solution to a specific problem. Here, the framework is normally provided by the customs and habits of the host organisation (the 'style' – see Chapter 4, section

4.5), and these should be established and followed – at least overtly. The strategy usually follows one of three main categories:

❏ Vertical Communication

❏ Horizontal Communication

❏ Interlinking Nets

Vertical Communication

This is where you are expected to liaise with people above and below you in the organisational chart, and virtually no-one else. This is illustrated in Figure 8.4a where the senior analyst (among others) reports only to the project manager who in turn reports only to the chief engineer.

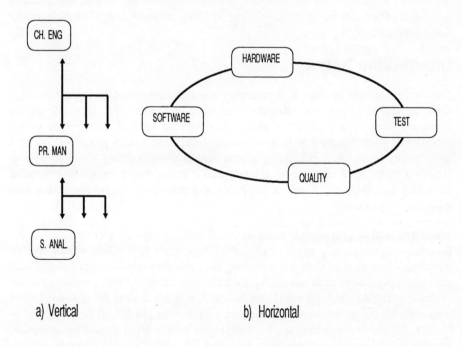

Figure 8.4: Communication channels

In an autocratic organisation, it has some advantages: you know what the staff who report to you are doing and it blocks any errors of the junior staff from being transmitted outside the department or company. Apart from that, it is very stifling and makes it hard for a Quality manager, for example, to send a report to his opposite numbers in the Hardware, Software, and Test departments. The official way is up through the chain of command until the level is reached where the message can come down another chain to the Hardware department, etc. The unofficial way is to walk round the building and let the intended addressees see the report 'off the record'.

Horizontal Communications

This covers the problems discussed in the last paragraph in that there is free access between all the departments – as shown in Figure 8.4b. The problem here is that papers are flying in all directions. Either each department is sent a message directly or it is sent a copy of some message tramsmitted to any other department. At the same time, the manager in every department is probably sending a copy to one of his own staff (for technical advice) while copying someone above him (for the record). It enables full and free distribution of information, but the theoretically paper-less office can be up to the ceiling in filing cabinets and processed conifer forest products.

Interlinking Nets

This is yet another attempt at a structure that can accommodate the information flow in an effective and efficient manner. This uses the idea of groups communicating only with other groups leaving the internal distribution to the group itself – see Figure 8.5. It is still hierarchical in that each group reports back to an upper level while requesting action from a corresponding lower level one. However, each level is multi-disciplinary and a group might comprise a member from Quality, Test, etc. It solves some of the problems discussed above but then adds some of its own.

Thus, it is hard to find an individual who will actually sign a paper or make a decision – they will only abide by an agreed input from their fellow committee members. This, in turn, calls for a meeting for virtually every decision, and, if staff are members of more than one group, then the time taken up with meetings can be overwhelming. Again, with travel and holidays, it is not always possible to obtain a quorum for the group, so the decision may have to be put off till next month. Finally, the group personnel may be changing as people move in and out of the organisation or project and this tends to prevent the group settling down as a coherent co-operative force. For all that, it has to be said that this philosophy can be made to work reasonably well for the larger projects where intercommunicating at a personal level can get unwieldy.

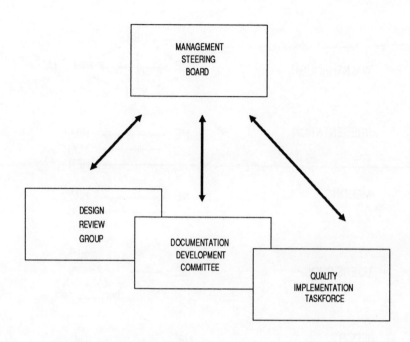

Figure 8.5: Group interlinking

We have gone through all these options to indicate what may be easily applied in any particular project. It is worth finding out the approach to be used, if only to consider the possible impact of its defects on the way your project is run. Note, in addition, that the communication linkages within a department or company will generally reflect the overall structure of the organisation. Thus a vertical style of communication only works well with a hierarchical reporting structure while the nets are a natural candidate for the larger more complex type of approach. Under these circumstances, there is a lot to be said for matching this corporate style in general to the structure of your system project in particular.

8.3   Transfer Methods

This section has been included as an *aide-memoire* in identifying the different ways in which information can be transferred within a system development environment. Once more, there is no right or wrong method, it is only a matter of selecting or planning an approach that offers a sensible response for the given requirement.

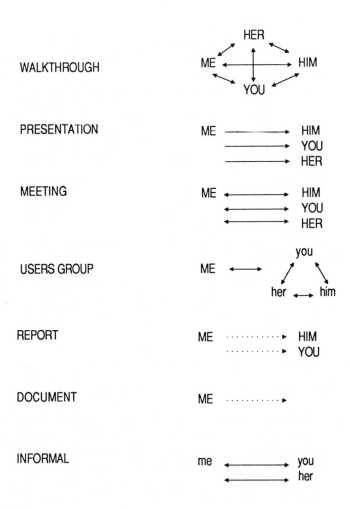

HER

WALKTHROUGH   ME ←————→ HIM
YOU

PRESENTATION   ME ————————→ HIM
————————→ YOU
————————→ HER

MEETING   ME ←————————→ HIM
←————————→ YOU
←————————→ HER

USERS GROUP   ME ←———→   you
her ←———→ him

REPORT   ME ·········▶ HIM
·········▶ YOU

DOCUMENT   ME ·········▶

INFORMAL   me ←————————→ you
←————————→ her

Figure 8.6: Different transfer methods

The key features have been outlined in Figure 8.6 and some of the pros and cons of each method will be given below. To make the material more approachable, (i.e. to sell the message), we can base the explanation on the 'real-life' documentation requirements of Universal Solid State and their consultant group All-Data:

Walkthrough

The details can vary, but the basic format for this sort of meeting is to have a free and unstructured 'barn-storming' session. Let us assume that the subject under discussion is the overall documentation plan for Universal. The project manager from the consultants All-Data has put together a proposal for review by his peers. Attendance is limited (otherwise it becomes a shouting match) and the participants could be, for example, the senior system analyst from All-Data; the maintenance and quality managers from Universal head-office in Toronto; operations manager from Brussels; and a planning manager from Seoul. These people are all sensibly on the same level of experience so criticism can be given and taken in a positive manner without generating conflict or aggrieved egos.

The nature of a walkthrough is essentially that of a free-for-all, so personal discipline is called for. The participants are expected to be competent, at the same level, and to contribute on virtually any aspect of the subject under review. It is like the last dress rehearsal where mistakes can be discussed while still among friends. The down side is the cost. Even without the travel expenses indicated here, under normal circumstances it may take four to six senior staff members, say, three hours for each of these type of meeting. This can be a severe penalty, especially if every department is calling for the same sort of meeting. Effective, but should be used with discretion.

Presentation

A popular method of disseminating information, this is basically a one-way flow of data – I speak and you listen. ("All questions at the end please" usually allows you a free flow without interruption – and will tend to ensure that most of the embarrassing questions get forgotten.) Another reason for its popularity it that it gives one an opportunity to create all those glorious presentation graphic slides. In spite of all this, there is a serious and useful side to presentations. It allows an efficient person-to-person transfer of information with minimum disruption. In the current case, the project manager has gone to Korea and will address senior representatives from each plant on the proposed individual documents and their contents. One person can directly communicate with up to 200 members of the audience who still have some chance to ask questions. In other words, the message is being spread, the cost is low, and there is even some limited feedback possible.

Meeting

This is possibly the most popular method of communicating in large organisations. The main difference between this and the walkthrough is that this is structured. There is usually someone controlling the meeting, perhaps the Chair or Chairperson, there is a formal agenda, and there is nearly always someone writing down the main points of discussion for the permanent record which will be sent to an agreed distribution list. For Universal, head-office has decided to provide the review body for the critical specifications as they are generated. Thus 6 to 15 managers will sit round a table and argue, clause by clause, the make up of the system requirement specification. The chairperson will control the discussion, moving the group on as required, and the rapporteur will take the main points down for eventual distribution to the attendees and other interested parties – not least the source of the specification. The down side is, once again, the cost. A meeting usually consists of sensibly senior, and therefore expensive, personnel sitting round all day discussing a few sheets of paper. This is legitimate for critical documents which may have a profound strategic impact, but each case will have to be justified in terms of the importance or critical nature of the subject under review.

User Group

A relatively recent innovation, a user group can be set up to provide a focussed pressure point for improving an existing situation or for acting as a collective interface back to a source. There are such organisations for virtually all the major computer manufacturers and they will readily complain about, for example, the performance, or lack thereof, of the latest upgrade. These groups can be enormously useful. On the one hand, they provide a tangible outlet for the pent-up frustration of the user who has spent the last four days trying to get through to the guaranteed open hot line. On the other hand, the person on the receiving end knows that there is a single source contact, usually the chairperson of the user group, who will provide a reasonably complete overview of all the users' responses. (This would cost a small fortune to obtain by any other means.) The internal structure of such groups is largely up to the members to establish. Thus, it could be formal or informal. The only basic limitation is that there has to be someone in the group who acts as the main contact.

In our case, Universal has set up a global New Product Documentation User Group, chaired by the test manager in Seoul. This was made feasible by setting up an E-mail link between all the main Universal offices who have put forward a representative for the group. Now all the users' responses can be channelled to one focal point. In turn, the chairperson can contact the project manager to feedback the problems that have arisen – and to get them addressed in a reasonable timescale.

Report

A report is probably the most cost-effective tool in the communication storehouse. There is no meeting to set up and attend, just an ordinary distribution list and some printed sheets. It is like an article in a corporate newspaper which has an open circulation for sending information round the company. It is certainly cheap, but there is a downside – much like a newspaper, there is no particular pressure for anyone to read it. On a good day, people will store a report, without looking at it, in their filing cabinet, while more often it will simply disappear into the waste bin. So, the value in distributing a report is, to some extent, dependent on the ability to get the addressees to treat it seriously. There is no perfect solution to this problem, only less imperfect ones. One way, is to pepper the document with Action Items – calling on the designated reader to carry out the specified activity within some defined time scale. This can be a political minefield – issuing actions to non-attendees of the meeting – but it will certainly force people to read the report. Another way is to request some blanket response from all the readers ('please telex your approval, or otherwise, for proposal 17, by the 5th of next month'). In nothing else, the number of returns will be a rough measure of your active readership.

As a multinational organisation, Universal would have a vested interest in making reports an effective communication channel. One possible indirect method of attack could be to modify the basic memo or request-for-information note-pads with boxes which are entitled 'source document' and 'section'. Then set out to pressure the writer of such memos to fill in these boxes with the appropriate material ('... without these source references being entered, there will be no obligation on the part of the addressee(s) to respond to the memo ...'). In other words, read up or shut up.

Document

If anything, the situation is even worse for a specification or a new procedure, in that there is no theoretical need for a distribution list. Equally, there is no obvious obligation for anyone to read it. The 'thing' is delivered to the library or standards centre, and there it sits – 48 pages of reviewed and thrice rewritten documentation – simply collecting dust. One possibility is to publicise it by means of a regular abstraction service. Thus, the library or quality department, say, could send out a monthly abstract of the new documents or standards received, their scope, and the current review status. Another approach is to ensure that all proposals are subject to audit by a senior review body which has a strong involvement with national and corporate standards. This body will not pass any proposal if there is no reference to the related standards. With even more effect, the senior management could seek to actively create a climate of opinion where such documents are automatically applied and accepted in the implementing of any new system or procedure.

Universal is sufficiently large to have an effective headquarters capability, so the setting up of a central audit board for all project related activity makes a lot of sense. It also slows down the decision making process which is a natural corollary of centralised control. On balance, it is probably the right way to go for globally applied systems.

In general, the information carried by specifications, documents and the like, ensures conformance to existing protocols and procedures, provides a groundplan for design and constitutes a point of reference for measuring the performance of the delivered product. Nevertheless, these documents may still need to be actively 'sold' to the designer and user.

Informal

With all the optimised structured methods and in-depth information strategies, one sometimes forgets that exchanging comments in a corridor can be a perfectly viable method of communicating. It is informal, cheap, fast and effective. There are limitations, but that should not blind one to some of the advantages. There are two main classes:

❑ Work related

❑ Leisure related

Work Related

Consider the following scenario: you have just received the agenda of the next meeting from Jerry and it has left out an agreed item of particular interest to you, say, safety requirements. Now you can wait until the meeting is held and then bring up the omission in AOB (any other business). This will put the matter into the minutes of the meeting with ongoing distribution round the company. Conversely, you can send a telex, or formal letter, to Jerry requesting that he correct his mistake, with copies to your boss and his. *Or you can pick up the phone and call him.*

The more informal approach is important as a way to minimise organisational conflict and will use face-to-face conversation, phoning, E-mail, or memo pad messages. These approaches are cheap, and usually connect to the intended recipient very effectively. Where the matter is confidential or does not call for publicity, this is the ideal approach. Where privacy is not an issue, however, then there is a disadvantage. There is often no permanent record, no thorough review of the subject, and the distribution of information is restricted to two or three persons at the time of the interchange. In this situation, one way round the problem is to follow up with a formal memo or letter distributed round the company recording the results of the informal discussion, etc.

This sort of minimised-conflict communication is very important in a distributed organisation where misunderstandings can get blown up into full-scale inter-departmental warfare. An international corporation like Universal will generally encourage the use of informal techniques to resolve problems or perceived difficulties. At the same time, there will have to be well recognised methods to formalise any agreements that may have occurred on the way. Otherwise, the information could be lost, or once again subject to further misinterpretation.

Leisure Related

This is an important area for communicating at the strategic level. There are two main types of application and they are typified by the working lunch ("Why don't we pop round to the club/pub/restaurant for a quick bite?") and the full leisure treatment ("We are having a barbecue/bridge evening/theatre party, next Saturday. Why don't you – and your wife – come round for little relaxation?"). These invitations could come from, say, a visiting vice president or executive from headquarters and in nearly all cases, the object is not 'a quick bite' or 'relaxation'. It is assessment. When a VP from Universal talks business in a leisure environment, the business can only be of secondary importance. There is no back up support, no validated data, no multi-disciplinary feedback, and probably no computer to model the 'what-if' scenarios. No, the importance here is the measure of 'comfortableness' that is communicated to him by your inputs. In the first place, if he doesn't know you, is he going to feel relaxed working alongside you. If he already has confidence in your manner, probity and competence, then he will be looking for your responses, *in principle*, to some strategic proposal. It has to be a first impression sort of discussion, as there is no possibility of detailed analysis in the restaurant. For all that, this sort of strategic exchange of views, which tends to occur before any formal proposals are put forward for general release, will often have a major impact in shaping the objectives of the organisation over the next few years. In this light, they should be handled carefully.

That really completes this overview of the different types of communication methods. In essence, they can involve verbal interchanges via meeting or presentations: these can be effective but very expensive. Then again, you can use written material distributed as reports (such as minutes, or meeting records) or specifications: these are low cost, but there is no guarantee that anyone out there is reading them. Finally there are the informal methods which can be effective at a

---

1. *Tell 'em what you are going to tell 'em*

2. *Tell 'em*

3. *Tell 'em what you told 'em*

Figure 8.7: The secret of successful communications

local level, but may be limited in application and may need a formal backup mechanism to validate the results.

Regardless of the method or methods adopted, there is still the question of the way in which the information is to be delivered. There are no existing rules for this topic, but you may possibly choose to follow the ancient wisdom on delivery. This is a three part process and has been more or less encapsulated in Figure 8.7. For the record, it is also the approach that has been generally followed in this book.

8.4   The Message Format

If the last section covered the *how* to communicate, then this section will go over the *what*. In other words, there are different ways to transmit information, and their relative advantages and disadvantages should be considered when selecting an optimum approach. We shall briefly review:

❑ Simple elements

❑ Integrated packets of information

Simple Elements

There are three simple elements that can be delivered as packets of data: verbal, text, or graphic messages. An outline of these elements have been illustrated in Figure 8.8 and the basic differences should be well understood:

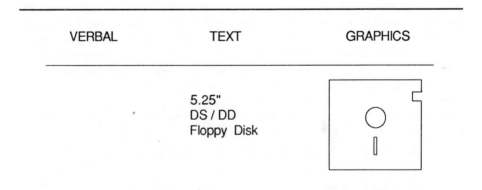

Figure 8.8: Simple message formats

Verbal

The main characteristic of verbal messages is clear from Figure 8.8: there is no permanent record. (If it were really necessary, you could use a tape recorder, but this is only done in exceptional circumstances.) This is an advantage for confidential discussions, but tends to leave misunderstandings at the end of the discussion very much in place – there is no corrective mechanism. It is quick and may be undertaken with virtually no preparation – or knowledge of typing. In short, it will be used where accuracy can be sacrificed for speed.

Text

Again, from Figure 8.8, you can see that text-based information is reproduceable and unambiguous. It is not visually interesting, but that is not a significant defect. It may contain fundamental errors, but that would not be the fault of the medium. What is wrong is that it can only be understood by someone who can read English. For the Arabic or Russian reader, it is literally meaningless. Notice that even text based messages can be incomplete. Here the application of logic will show that the capacity of the disk will be uniquely 360 Kb of memory. (If it were to have been 1.2 Mb of memory, it would have the designation DS/HD – Double Sided/High Density. Again, for 720 Kb of memory, the size would have to be 3.5".) On the other hand, there is no indication of which manufacturer is called for. Or whether the disk should be formatted, or even whether it should even contain stored files or programs. Thus, text files give you hard facts which can be readily upgraded, if so required, with additional text. On the other hand, they may be incomplete or inaccurate facts. In addition, they are definitely only available to the reading public who can understand the language of the original text.

Graphics

No problem with English here. An icon-based description can be universally understood (that is, people speaking different text languages can learn a standard icon descriptive language). On the other hand, notice how little information is given in roughly the same space on the page: the outline suggests a 5.25" type floppy disk, but there is no indication of capacity. With text, if so wished, you can write the comment 'formatted', but there is no universal modifier to indicate that the disk is formatted in the icon layout.

As compensation, it is more visually pleasing than the text equivalent.

Perhaps the optimum approach would be to transfer some information verbally for speed of access; then generate the equivalent text based material to unambiguously confirm the main points of discussion, and accompany this text with some graphic images to reinforce the comments and make them more acceptable to the reader.

Integrated Packets of Information

Simple messages, of any type, are not of sufficient complexity to satisfy today's needs for information transfer. For that reason, assemblies of information are are often created for transmission purposes. Such assemblies will be representative of the document type, the database model, and the system prototype which will be handed over to the end user for comments and approval.

Document

We have already discussed the document as a means of transfer, in section 8.3 above. Now, we can look at the document, in itself, as an actual deliverable. From the previous argument in this section, a document should ideally comprise a suitable mixture of text and graphics put together in some structured form. It is this structured form that provides the extra value to the organisation in that the standardised layout will make succeeding iterations and other documents familiar to the reader. Once you have stopped looking for the signature, date and revision level boxes for each specification, you can get on with with the real business of assessing the contents. If each document has a common layout, this 'business' will take a lot less time and key areas of interest can be identified and reviewed a great deal more effectively. As an example of one possible approach to the layout of the first page of a document see the remarks under *Document Standardisation* in Chapter 6.

Databases

Once again, this is not a matter of the *contents* or data resident in the database, but of the *format* or layout of the database tables and their interaction with the user. Databases are the central element in any system model, and their performance when being operated will have a critical impact on the way the system ultimately gets applied. For this reason, the user should be able to test the database as a 'black box' item and check that the inputs and outputs generate the data processed in a manner required, and, further, with a performance comparable to that proposed in the original requirement specification. The 'communication' in this case is the nature of the database structure and its suitability for the intended application.

Prototype

This is yet a further extension of the idea covered in the last paragraph. In this area of system appraisal it is the 'look and feel' that is passed to the end user for assessment. The user interface and the data report outputs need to be fully tested and reviewed by the workforce who will be operating the system. This feedback will lead to possible modification and recycling by the design team until the users are satisfied.

This brings to a close a sub-section where the communication is essentially between the design authority and the end-user appraisal team, while the nature of that communication is some part of the finished system under trial. This 'message' will then evoke a response providing feedback to the design team for further modification or enhancement. As a final comment, this particular link in the development chain plays an important part in providing user satisfaction with the eventual system, and it should not be treated lightly.

In fact, that last sentence constitutes a reasonable summary to the whole of this section on assembling elements of communications. The objective is always to formulate an attractive and digestible package to the user, and a little care in this area will dramatically reduce errors due to lack of comprehension or an imperfect transfer of information.

8.5 Storage

One of the key aspects of modern communication is that there shall be a readily available and permanent record of the data so generated. For this reason, we will briefly cover the concepts related to information storage and outline the main approaches to be adopted. The topic falls naturally into two areas:

❏ Configuration Management

❏ Archiving

Configuration Management

CM is an integral part of any maintenance strategy. This is true whether we are talking about the spares philosophy for all the versions of the Boeing 747 aeroplane, or the corporate finance system package installed in a city bank two months ago. One definition of CM could be:

The identification of a part or module, its version or iteration number, along with the identification of other parts or modules with which it interacts. All these parts will have been used together for some assembly or system (which then also has an identified version and date of assembly).

As an indication of how this might be carried out, consider the CM listing for some of the items to be used in the surgical ward system of Newtown General:

Operating System MS-DOS 3.3
Database   dBaseIV   1.1
Requirement Spec. 3.0
Test Spec   1st Draft
Design Minutes   22/4/91

This simple representative example shows that in the late spring of '91 these software packages and specifications were being used for design purposes. Now, when the system structure based on this implementation needs an upgrade in five years time, it will be vital to know both the version level of the database package and which other application packages and documents were also being used. And *their* version levels will also need to be recorded. Only when all this information is to hand, can you set about recreating the original design objectives and environment for test, evaluation and modification purposes.

In today's terms, it is virtually impossible to carry out CM without the aid of a computer based tool. When systems consist of hundreds and perhaps thousands of interlocking software modules, then it is not practical to manually monitor this version of this software which can be used with a particular version of that software. In addition, you will need to file all the related documents, (and their edition levels) and the hardware platforms and ancillary equipment. In something of an oversimplification, we can say that CM is concerned with storing the names and version (or edition) level of all the sub-system parts *and* the physical storage of all these related parts such that they can be reconstituted back into a working system. The first part, i.e. version control, can be processed by a dedicated CM package and a representative example of this could be SMS from Intasoft Limited. We shall be discussing this product in more detail in Chapter 11 on maintenance. The second part will be covered below.

Archiving

CM provides you with a unique vehicle for providing information to the future users and modifiers of the system. The actual *storage* of all this information will be carried out and maintained in a location called the archive. This is both a logical function and a physical address. It is logical, in that the system model can include the concept of an archival data store, and it is clearly physical in that some part of a building has to be assigned to holding the medium or media which carry the data. This could be paper, microfiche, or magnetic material, any of which could be used to store text or graphic information. In addition, actual application programs and dedicated code designed for the system will also be carried in some magnetic medium (or perhaps on an optical disk).

There is only one conceptual difficulty with archiving – and it is best addressed at the start-up of the project. The problem is one of getting the recognition-of-need and corresponding funding by the client organisation. This is because the optimum time for setting up an archive is when the agreement has been signed to begin system design activity.

In conclusion, CM is the principal tool to record all the reports and specification upgrades on the one hand, and every iteration level of the software modules on the other. The archive is the location where all this material is stored for future application. The resulting benefit of this activity, and it is considerable, will be obtained at some later time during the maintenance phase and this is fully evaluated in Chapter 11.

8.6   Summary

Communications is the glue that sticks all the working elements together in the development environment. To continue the analogy with adhesives, there are a number of specially manufactured types available, and there is usually an optimum selection for any given task.

In the first section, we saw that it can be relatively easy to block or degrade the communication path with a corresponding wastage of effort. It takes at least two willing parties to communicate. Even with this criterion satisfied, if the material being transferred is essentially boring or incomprehensible, then the information will still not get across. For this reason, it is worth giving some time to packaging the information, i.e. making it attractive, interesting and digestible. Trial runs with willing volunteers is a well practiced technique in political circles, and there is much to commend it in testing the user response to a chosen route.

In terms of the basic reporting approach, there are a number of options – although the usual recommendation would be to emulate the style of the host organisation. Using a horizontal reporting structure in a vertical environment (or vice versa) will provide a source of ongoing and probably unnecessary friction. Following on from this, we looked at some of the methods that can be used to disseminate information to a number of people. By recognising the pros and cons of each approach, the best method will usually become apparent for the majority of situations. (Where the selection is not obvious, then it is equally not important which one is adopted.) Again, the actual 'deliverable' or message format is open to selection, and, in this case, it is often useful to use more than one format mixed into the final package. This way, the message is reinforced by the different formats.

Finally, a brief description was given of the way in which all this information being transferred could be permanently stored. Configuration Management offers a structured methodology for storing various types of information which allows efficient recall for system modification at some later date.

Questions

1. How might you set out to make a presentation 'interesting'?

2. Imagine that you are involved in the Newtown Surgical Ward project. Draw a possible vertical reporting structure, indicating who is reporting to whom. And a possible horizontal one.

3. You are going to review the requirement specification with the hospital computer departmental representative, the ward sister, the consultant and the hospital comptroller.

> Discuss the relative merits of setting up a Walkthrough, a Presentation, or a Meeting.

4. A user group will generally be formed after a working system is installed.

> Propose possible advantages for forming the group during the design phase.

5. What security or safety factors would you explore if a mixed media (i.e. paper, magnetic tapes and disks) archive library is to be located:

> a) in the basement, b) on the top floor, c) by the kitchen and d) adjacent to the airport.

Change Control

Government code project dropped

A government department has had to abandon a project to produce accurate documentation for its existing systems because of lack of a propert software maintenance methadology.

. . . .

'After 18 months, they realised the project objectives could not be met,' said West. 'By that time, they had done work on six of the 30 logical sub-systems and only completed one.'

Computing p.5 22.9.88

Order and method lead to Case success

The introduction of Case tools needs careful thought and planning, McClure argued. Great industry interest a few years ago lead to a rash of cheque writing, but the PCs and tools bought have become "shelfware" and are simply not being used.

Other organisations may dither trying to select the right tool and end up doing nothing. McClure claimed that a branch of the US army spent two years and £100m looking at Case and never got anywhere.

Computer Weekly p.16 13.4.89

Foreign Office goes into red after system failure

The Foreign and Commonwealth Office was unable to balance its books for the last financial year because a new computer system ... failed to work properly.
The National Audit Office, the government watchdog, noted imbalances on different accounts totalling £77m and partly blames the £1m system for the discrepancy.

Memory Computer, which provided the software, went into liquidation last year while the system was sttil under trial. Shortly afterwards the old system broke down forcing the Foreign Office to rely on the new one.

Computer Weekly p.3 7.2.91

9.1 Introduction

There is only one universal constant that can be applied to any system development exercise. This is that change is inevitable. In addition, there is the corollary to this rule, and this nearly always holds true: change will be detrimental to the smooth progress of the project – and on a number of occasions will destroy it. Whether the objectives get modified, the timescale reduced, or the software upgraded, change is the daily, weekly, and monthly threat that never goes away.

On the other hand, change is the norm for any healthy system – biological or man-made, and it is the ability of the system to adapt to this change that promotes its survivability. This chapter will take a look at the major sources of change, how to detect them, and what action can be taken to nullify or minimise the adverse effects that may occur. In effect, overcoming the problems of change is all about having the right attitude of mind, and this chapter will, hopefully, give you that attitude to respond in a positive and constructive way.

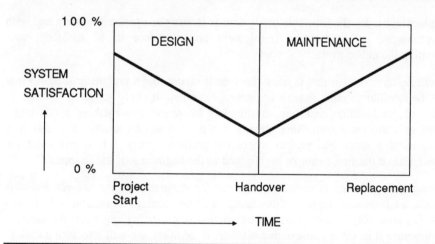

Figure 9.1: The Satisfaction function

However, first let us take a look at the model of a system development to see what makes change such a regular phenomenon. Consider Figure 9.1, which shows the standard pattern or shape for the function *System Satisfaction* plotted against time, as represented by the major project milestones. To understand why the shape can be described as 'standard', we will go over a typical real project and assess what happens as it progresses through its (simplified) life-cycle:

Start up: At the time of signing the contract, a requirement specification has been drawn up *and agreed* as a reflection of what the client wants, or thinks he wants. At this point, the perceived satisfaction level is probably maximum.

Design: As the design phase progresses – i.e. as the handover date gets closer – various drastic actions have to be undertaken to maintain the installation date or budgetary limitations. Perhaps your organisation is special, but for most practical purposes no project adheres to the original targets. (That is one of the main sources of change, in itself.) This is the time when extra functionality gets lopped off, documentation plans get slashed and test programs disappear to try to recover lost time or make some cost saving. And the closer to handover, the more severe are the actions that are taken, and the more the project will deviate from the original conception that had such a high satisfaction content.

Handover: Somehow the system gets installed and the end-users start to discover some of the deviations that were introduced. This phase lasts a few days or weeks, with increasing frustration as the prime defects are uncovered.

Maintenance: Now we are in the post installation phase, a program of 'product enhancement' can be undertaken. This will slowly remove the main sources of poor performance over an extended period of time. As a result, and with increasing user confidence to drive the system, the satisfaction level will gradually rise.

Replacement: By the time that the system is starting to operate smoothly and with effectiveness, it has become obsolescent and therefore to be replaced, thus repeating the entire cycle.

It will be obvious that this is not a theoretical model, but a pragmatic scenario that will be familiar to most system engineers. Note that at every stage, the change in value of the function represents a situation where either something needs to be done, or conversely something already has been done. Note also, that this is a scenario of a *successful* project where the problems were tackled and solutions found, unlike the first example highlighted at the beginning of the chapter.

Conceptually, change is inevitable, but can be dangerous to the project. For this reason, an important topic in this chapter will be 'damage limitation' which will describe some of the tools that can be applied in either 'rolling with' the change, or opposing it in some constructive manner. In addition, we will also take a look at the problems of handling a crisis. This is more than just change, this is where the project has reached the status of catastrophe. For all that, a structured and prepared position can still save the day. However, before we reach that position, (and the object, of course, is never to be in that position) it will be useful to become familiar with the various classes of change and to recognise, in good time, what form they may take. That way, corrective action has a good chance of being both low cost and effective. On that basis, we shall first take a look at some generic classes of change, and then follow this up with a more extended examination of the specific forms of change that can affect the project. Once we can diagnose the problem, we can get down to the business of correcting the fault or minimising its impact.

9.2   Generic Sources

There are a number of reasons why change is unavoidable in any practical situation, and these will be applicable to all system projects, however well funded, and for all participants, regardless of whether they are student or expert:

❑ Product Perception

❑ Objectives Enhancement

❑ Technology Obsolescence

❑ Error Correction

These characteristics will be present for every project, and the only sensible attitude to them is a marked lack of surprise, coupled with a readiness to handle the new inputs as and when they arise.

Product Perception

This will occur largely during the initial and design phases. It is a learning curve phenomenon, and relates to a closer understanding of the real targets and goals of the end product. Consider the process of learning to drive a car and the skills that are acquired. At first, the mechanics of the problem are overwhelming, such as how to change gear using the clutch and accelerator smoothly. Then comes the perception that the car is just one element among many in its working environment, i.e. other cars, vans, cyclists and pedestrians are all competing for the use of the same road. Finally, there comes the recognition that the most effective use of the entire system of road facilities, vehicles and human participants lies in following some complex codes of social interaction that relate to lane behaviour, car lighting and signalling, and deference to the perceived needs of others.

A similar sort of process will occur with the system project: at first, there will be concentration on the simple mechanical items, the tables and menus. Then, usually, a growing realisation that the system will be interacting with other systems in the organisation. Finally, there will come a recognition of the way the system will ultimately involve a full interplay of people, department procedures and organisational strategies. With each new layer of perception, modifications will be introduced to the previous model to bring it in line with the new thinking. Each of these modifications will, of course, have another potential impact on the system requirements, development timescales and overall costs.

Note that these new *realities* seen from the design side, are diametrically opposed by the equally evolving *realities* appearing on the side of the client group. Over the design period, the client will grow increasing worried about escalating costs and timescales, and will seek to correct these unwanted extensions with project cutbacks and budget freezes. All this tends to be in contrast to the relaxed atmosphere following the acceptance of the requirement specification proposals and the subsequent signing of a development contract. This new dynamic tension between the 'partners' is usually the first indication that the honeymoon is over. However, if this is seen as a natural and expected phase, then it can be readily handled with patient negotiation.

Objectives Enhancement

This is, in many ways, the equivalent to the above, only with the roles reversed and occurring during the post-installation phase. Here, for the first time, the client end-users discover the features that they consider necessary for effectively running the new or upgraded procedures and which are missing from the newly installed system. This is another learning-curve modification requirement that can only be established with a 'hands-on' approach to the system and is unlikely to be found from any theoretical overview. Again, the feedback will concern different layers of perception as the user gains increasing confidence in handling the package, and correspondingly becomes more aware of the larger issues involved in the system application. In turn, the developer will be reluctant to provide a team to implement these improvements as they are already occupied on some new project, and, in any case, there would be little or no additional funding to carry out the exercise.

So, once again, there will be tension between the two partners, and again it should be expected – with the resulting problems solved using reasonable negotiation.

Looking at both of these normal learning-curve sources of change, i.e. design modification and application enhancement, we can see how they go a large part of the way in determining the nature of the function illustrated in Figure 9.1.

Technology Obsolescence

Any project starts off based on an understanding of what is technically feasible at the time of generating the specifications. Conversely, the expectation of the client will be predicated by the technology available at the time of delivery or handover. The discrepancy between these two technology levels can give rise to some unfortunate conflict – especially when the project is expected to take a number of years, and when the project is IT based.

Perhaps this is where development projects involving Information Technology differ markedly from other engineering disciplines. The rate of change of products developed for computer application has been difficult to keep up with. It is certainly true that other technologies have shown remarkable advances, but nothing to match the scale of IT product evolution. Thus, aircraft construction or house building have shown significant technical improvements over the years but, at the most basic level, the cost of purchasing an aeroplane or a house have tended to rise by a certain amount each year. The added value (of technology improvement) has been matched by a rise in the purchase cost. Now, take a short look at the cost of some personal computer elements, based primarily on the IBM PC model or its clone, and a radically different picture emerges. The purchase costs for different PC related items, taken from advertisements in a popular English magazine, are shown in Figure 9.2.

	March 85	December 89
PC - AT	4706	899
Hard Disk (20 Mb)	1545	199
360 Kb Floppy (10)	24.00	8.00
Printer	980 *	950 **

* 15" / 150 d.p.i / 1 p/m   ** 10" / 300 d.p.i / 6 p/m

Figure 9.2: Technology changes

The quoted figures are in pounds sterling, but what is particularly interesting is the dramatic *fall* in price over a 4 to 5 year period for a more reliable, higher performance product. Even the printer example, where the price has hardly altered, shows a significant improvement in performance between the 1989 Laser printer and the 1985 24 pin Dot-matrix printer ('d.p.i.': dots per inch; 'p/m': pages per minute). There is no guarantee that these figures will continue to show a steady decline in the future, but, at minimum, it is a possibility.

These figures are good news for the buyer, but constitute fairly embarrassing reading for the system developer. If we return to the first paragraph of this section, we can see why. A PC based system honestly costed on 1985 prices, will look like serious and gross profiteering by 1989 standards. With any project where the design phase may take two or more years, the client will seek to negotiate an improved delivery based on his enhanced expectation. The technology has moved on, so why not reflect this in his system?

The reason why this causes problems is related to an important concept, well known in conventional projects, but not so easy to apply in software systems. This concept goes under the name of 'Design Freeze' or some equivalent label. At a specified and declared point in time, you will have to halt the fine-tuning of the design, and get on with the business of building the system. Now, if the client comes back every year with a new list of improvements based on the current technology, you, the developer, will have to return each time to the drawing-board and start again. Here, change can be a serious cause of disagreement between the development team and the client management, and the resulting problems have to be handled with some delicacy.

Error Correction

System design and development is an activity that, for the moment, is carried out uniquely by human beings. It is often a complex, poly-faceted, multi-disciplined, mega-funded activity and one that is also horrendously open to error. The wrong specification is used for reference; the wrong handbook gives the wrong printer set-up; the dimension is read as centimetres and not inches; and so on.

The basic difficulty arises when you discover an error five to eight months after it has been inserted into the system. At that point, it is not easy to evaluate the total work load required to eliminate the problem. You will have to locate the source of the error, carry out suitable corrective action, and establish the full impact or carryover of the error into other modules (and potentially correct those modules as and when required). There are some procedural techniques (see below) that can be used to minimise errors, but the more the effort, the higher the cost. Error minimisation is conceptually a question of investing a controlled amount of effort in the hope that it will reduce the introduction of errors to a *reasonable* level. Using structured methods, in general, will act to reduce the number of errors; working to thoroughly reviewed documents and checking all major inputs via walkthroughs will help to eliminate the more obvious mistakes; and a good set of test routines should capture and locate the bulk of the remaining problems.

All the above sources of change are guaranteed to occur in every project – there is no escape. For all that, they can all be anticipated, and corrective action exists in some form or another for every one of them.

9.3   Specific Factors

This section is concerned with identifying individual possible causes of change – or added workload – and outlining possible ways in which they can be contained and limited in their impact.

Application Upgrades

As a feature of the IT industry, both hardware and software suppliers offer regular upgrades to their products, frequently on a yearly basis. This is only one example of technology change that is often imposed on the design or user staff. The new selling points look very attractive, but the hidden penalties can sometimes nullify all the advantages.

Compatibility

Upgrades are intended to be compatible with the previous version of the product. This is usually true for *most* of the features of a particular package, but it is not generally tested for every possible application. The only thing that is truly 100% compatible with version 2.08 is version 2.08; all the rest are approximations, lying low just waiting for you to relax your guard. One way to minimise the risk of on-going upgrades is to use only the main features of any package. Another way, is to have a special strike force available which pulls to bits every new upgrade and reports on changes between the two versions along with full workrounds. Neither route is particularly cheap and in any case, the configuration management needs should also not be forgotten.

There is something to be said for deliberately not upgrading during the life of any given system.

Bugs

Every new upgrade seems to go through a period, lasting weeks or months, when it is rumoured to be falling apart from the bugs resident in the new software. In this case, the supplier is motivated to offer every possible assistance in helping you to clear the problem. Thus, if you do find something that seems non-standard or frankly perverse, there is a large and experienced workforce on your side for as long as it takes to solve the problem. The moral is, stay in close contact with the supplier – perhaps with the help of a user group channel.

Once again, only upgrade when you are confident that it is a worthwhile exercise.

Retraining

By definition, an upgrade implies that something is different. This difference will have to be perceived and learnt by the users if they are going to apply the new version with effectiveness. It is usually not enough to say 'read the handbook'; until one actually works through a tutorial example and marks the differences, the change will not sink in. When you know about both the change and the required solution, there is no difficulty; but meeting the problem head on when trouble is not anticipated can be very frustrating. As a trivial example, consider the keyboard modifier used within MS-DOS. Up to version 3.2 the English (as opposed to American) keyboard was called up with 'KEYBUK' and this command would be entered into the set-up batch file. However, for version 3.3, this became 'KEYB UK', i.e. with a space separator, and the batch file would need to be suitably modified. Now, this would be clearly indicated in the handbook, but if you were not specifically pointed towards it, the chances are that you would never see it.

The generalised solution here is regular retraining to keep the workforce in touch (noting the added cost and time penalties), and again keeping close contact with the supplier who should provide good tutorial material with each upgrade.

New Packages

Changing any working system element to one sourced by another supplier is a nerve wracking experience with possible effects lasting for up to two years after the change. Going from an IBM mainframe to a VAX machine, or from a VAX to a mini may well offer a substantial hardware cost saving for an acceptable drop in throughput, but the strain on the organisation will be enormous. Similarly, changing from, say, VMS to Unix as an operating system is an equally traumatic experience for the design and operations staff. This trauma should not stop transitions called up in response to different strategies, but the new technology justification should include consideration of the severe impact that the changeover will bring. Once again, the difficulties can be reduced by employing staff already well versed in the new technology, or by a solid program of training for the existing staff. In the latter case, it will be realistic to expect a long learning period to reach a good level of confidence.

Bringing in brand new applications can also be fraught with difficulty. Finding out what you can use from a new technology is far from easy and the investigation itself can get very expensive, as the second report at the head of the chapter illustrates. The last few pages have shown some of the problems that so-called progress or leading-edge enhancements can bring. However, perhaps we should keep in mind that IT products have literally revolutionised whole sectors of society, and effective systems have been successfully developed and used over the last 10 or 20 years. This may help to keep the scope of these problems in perspective.

User Interfaces

The previous section was all about the difficulties caused by external 'improvements'. This one concerns the self-induced problems, and is part of the "wouldn't it be nice if ..." syndrome. It is particularly prevalent with prototyping where the client can see exactly what is on offer, and rapidly gains an understanding of what he really wants. (Which is hardly ever what is on offer.) The subject under discussion may have an important bearing on how the user relates to both the system and the developer of that system (reference 12 p.117).

In a nutshell, there is yet another conflict developing between the client's growing appreciation of which menus, icons, screen layouts, etc., he would be pleased to work with, and the need of the designer to finalise the layouts and get on to the next task. This learning-curve feedback has been extolled in other parts of the book as a strong and constructive link between the user and the system developer. So it is, but it can also lead to a disaster from a scheduling point of view. Once again, the concept of 'design freeze' has to be held firmly in mind, and, at some point, the process of modification has to stop.

Administration

Here, we will discuss the impact of project related changes. These changes are interrelated and will generally affect the overall budget, personnel levels, schedule to handover and system functionality.

As an example of the sort of problems that occur, we can examine what happens when our friends ABC and XYZ agree to undertake a system development partnership. You will recall that they are not too professional, so perhaps it is an exaggerated case, but it will serve to illustrate the general principles. The typical fluctuations of the project parameters are shown in Figure 9.3. This figure can be taken as another view of the left hand side of Figure 9.1, and again we can look at time related values of each parameter. Note that every time there is a new value injected into the project model, this calls up extensive work in rescheduling, replanning, reallocating resource and so on.

Start of Project

At this point, all the variables have been assigned on some agreed basis (the budget will equal ..., etc.) and the parameters are represented in the figure with a set of normalised levels.

Half-way Point

What follows is just a useful pragmatic model of what might generally be expected to occur.

Some time into the design phase, a re-evaluation by the client ABC will tend to take place. Interest rates have moved up, or half year figures were disappointing or the new-projects director wants a re-evaluation – there is always a reason. (This does not happen every time, but it does seem to occur with a fair degree of regularity.) As a result of this new look at the project, some tighter project constraints are imposed by the ABC management. At the same time, the system requirements are being extended as the users develop a better perception of what capabilities are possible and 'wouldn't it be nice if ...'.

Although not shown in the figure, this is also generally the time when the design team XYZ has completed some first studies and recognise that they haven't got a realistic hope of meeting the original targets. Some additional work is carried out by their planning section and a new schedule, with required slippages, is put forward as a new proposal.

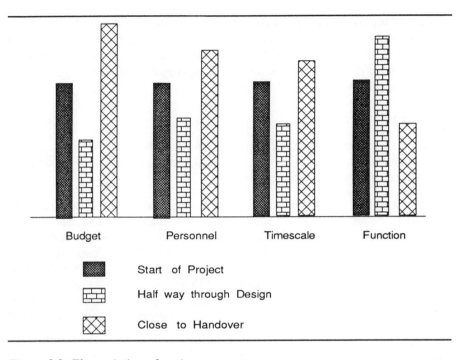

Figure 9.3: The variation of project parameters

The above conflict of positions is usually resolved to the satisfaction of the client, which leads to yet another re-evaluation of the project in terms of meeting the new targets. It is usually at this point that the official reported status and the project reality start to diverge rather badly.

Handover

The period leading up to installation of the system is an exciting time, with a lot of effort spent in rescheduling tasks as they remain uncompleted, and a lot of report writing to explain these upgrades to the schedule plan. By this time, the project has achieved the status of a 'red-flag item' when budgetary constraints take second place to schedule considerations and the measured values move to the positions shown in the third set of bars. Here the costs go up, the functionality goes down, and the quality goes out – but the installation is going to take place and the development team can look forward to the next job.

If we look over this rough ground-plan of what could happen during the design phase, we can see just how much wastage will occur with each change of objective. Every time there would be a new assessment of all the main project parameters and this will tend to occur on a number of separate occasions.

In the real world, project evolution is unavoidable. However, wastage can be minimised. It is possible to use a rigid system where nothing is allowed to be changed, or a flexible approach where the scheduling operates between wide limits. In either case good communication between the project partners will eliminate a lot of the unnecessary repetition and rework shown here.

Disasters

Any development program extending over a reasonable period of time is bound to be upset by some unplanned external event. Whether your software design house loses its chief designer, your hardware source has a fire in their factory, or your project manager's youngest child becomes gravely sick – all these represent a sudden step function change in the project environment.

There is no way to anticipate all the possible events that fate can and probably will throw at you. However, there are steps that can be taken to minimise the problems that they can cause and this will be discussed in the next section on 'damage limitation'.

Complexity

This is where we return to the 'anti-gravity platform' project. At some point, it will become apparent that whatever was thought to be fairly easy or feasible to design is proving to be the exact opposite. This book is littered with examples of this type of problem, where the usual life cycle is modified to: feasibility study, design, extended design, crisis evaluation, shutdown. It can often take up to five years to reach the final position, and by then it is a very costly and damaging exercise.

Again, the means to provide an early warning of this sort of trouble will be covered in the next section, but the real answer lies with the preparedness and competence of the senior management related to the project. Preparedness in the sense of close monitoring of the progress reports, and readiness to investigate closely any event that is looking suspicious. Competence in the ability to sum up a situation, to prepare potential workrounds well in advance of need, and, if necessary, to prematurely shut the program down. This last is well worth stressing as a low-cost option since it is always available, but seems never to be used until a threshold of about £5 million and 2 to 10 years wasted work has been reached.

Staff Mobility

There is normally another cycle of events operating within the project, especially during the pre-installation phases, and this relates to the changes of personnel who are directly concerned with the project. This cycle has been symbolised in Figure 9.4 where the start up condition shows eight staff, one manager, and one sheet representing administrative work.

Now let's go through the personnel cycle:

Added Responsibility

Due to new inputs and changes to the original program, the administrative workload is doubled, i.e. there are more progress reports, meetings, planning sessions, document reviews and so on. To assist you, one of the staff is promoted to help with the management function.

His or her first job is to replan the project to take account of the reduced numbers of active workers.

Staff Losses

Round about this time, one of your leading analysts leaves to have a baby and another one is stolen by another department – probably for a salary that you are not allowed to offer. Your assistant reworks the *Resource Allocation Plan* again, and you start demanding additional help.

New Intake

Your management has been listening, and takes on two new graduates to make up the numbers. You soon learn that the new staff see everything the wrong way round and have to be taught all the general principles, along with the specific details of the new project. This, in effect, reduces your staffing levels even lower as some of the old hands will have to spend time in tutoring the new recruits. Meanwhile, the management, having generously acceded to your requests, deems it only reasonable to add to the administrative workload. Your assistant starts preparing a new R.A.P. yet again.

Reorganisation

Half way through the design phase, the entire department is revamped to provide a leaner, more effective organisation. This will generally entail taking away one or two of your staff while adding slightly to the administrative responsibility. Your assistant saw all this coming and nimbly got himself 'reorganised' out of the project.

This scenario might be considered only applicable to the likes of companies such as ABC, but most or possibly all of these stages are likely to occur in every project which lasts for more than 18 months. It is always possible to carry out some short-term adjustments to smooth over a case of temporary hiccups. However, in the long run, a reduced staff means reduced work output. All you can do is make sure that the project management are fully aware of the implications of your changed staffing position. (On a more positive note, this may be the perfect

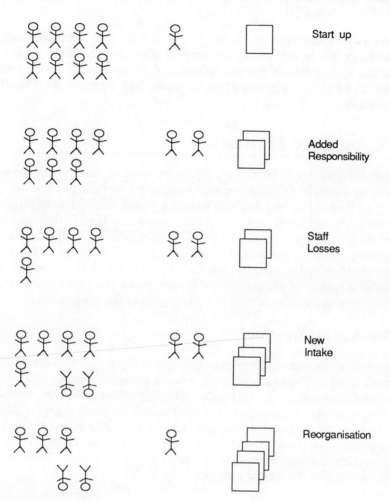

Figure 9.4: The personnel cycle

opportunity to extend the reported delivery dates due to your staff reductions, and use this to mask what was to be an inevitable slippage.)

Strategic Planning

This is another of those events where control is taken out of hands of the project management. If, for example, you happen to be working on a long-range social service package and a new government is voted in, you may expect radical changes to the original objectives of your project. However, frankly, with your loss of control goes loss of responsibility. Relax – it is no longer your problem.

The bulk of the chapter up to now has been spent in exploring a number of problems which can arise as a result of change. Whether applicable to all project operations as discussed in section 9.2, or due to some particular local factor covered in this section, change is bound to affect you and the way your project will run. Having thus established the nature of the challenge, it is now time to see what can be done in a *structured* way to control and overcome the difficulties that will follow.

9.4 Damage Limitation

There are a number of possibilities for buying peace of mind in a fast moving and changing situation. Of these, we shall concentrate on three processes or tools. If they are properly utilised they will introduce project monitors as an early warning system; they will set up insurance policies against day-to-day crises; and they will provide a vehicle for speedy action once the trouble has been identified. Note, however, that these processes will not offer any real advantage unless they have been installed *well in advance* and, like any other fire-fighting equipment, tested from time to time on a practice basis. For the serious project manager, a good time to set up these processes is right at the beginning of the design phase.

The Audit Function

This can be the first, and very powerful, line of defence in detecting the onset of project troubles. Too often, the audit, whether technical or managerial, is imposed by dissatisfied parties after the development program has gone wrong in some way. It may be wildly over budget, or just can't deliver the goods – see the third report at the head of the chapter. In this case, an external auditor is brought in to review and comment on the actual performance of a particular system, or to evaluate, say, the quality aspects of a certain development program. There are three characteristics of this type of exercise:

❏ The audit tends to be called after the event

❏ The event, whatever it was, was not good

❏ On the whole, blame is likely to be attributed.

The fact that important papers sometimes go 'missing' under these circumstances is hardly surprising.

By contrast, there is a role for the internal auditor, which has a different set of objectives. He has to be completely impartial in terms of the work under review, the persons concerned, and the readers of his report. In addition, he has to be capable of establishing the reality of the situation as opposed to the reported status – even if well hidden or disguised. These criteria are the same for any audit work. The difference from the usual function of the external auditor is that the investigations can be applied to work-in-progress; the results are intended as feedback to improve a situation that is improvable; and there is no blame assignment.

The role of Internal Audit Manager, or equivalent title, should be created as a senior position where the prime requirements are technical competence, communication skills, diplomacy, and experience. (This is stated for virtually every position, nowadays. However, it happens to be true for the auditor because he is, above all, the modern answer to the old question *quis custodiet ipsos custodes* – roughly: who will judge the judges?) The definition of his scope of activity is determined at some corporate level, and he should be capable of probing into virtually any area of interest, including management reporting structures, schedules, quality assurance, documentation, security, and sub-system design. He, or she, is not a problem solver; he is essentially a high-level technical/managerial analyst and reporter. His prime function will be to provide *accurate and dependable* status information which will then enable other parties to generate effective solutions. If so empowered, he can also be enormously useful in offering recommendations based on experience and 'feel' when some part of the organisation or system is felt to be potentially at risk.

He is the early warning system for the project.

Contingency Planning

This section could also have been called 'Insurance Strategy' in that it is concerned with preparing a source of reserves or recovery positions that can be called up in an emergency situation. It is not that items are required to be mothballed awaiting the call that may never come; rather that material, currently working under normal conditions, can be rapidly switched to some other role to solve the problem of the moment. In other cases, preventative maintenance can be applied, or even actual insurance against loss can be selectively applied. But first, as with any other insurance, you have to define the level of risk.

Risk Assessment

For any serious planning, it will be important to prioritise the possible problem areas for the whole project. This is a serious top-down study and, in effect, identifies the key areas where money or effort should be spent in ensuring the ongoing availability of the supplied function. Thus, there will be a significant difference in the replacement priority applied to the project manager as compared to a junior analyst.

Hardware

Again there will be critical items and less important ones. Thus, if six PC machines are all linked to one printer, then the printer failure will have a higher impact than one of the PCs. For hardware, selective redundancy is one useful solution, i.e. use two printers such that one can fail with no loss of system integrity. Another approach is to have a maintenance contract where a defective unit is guaranteed to be replaced within a fixed number of hours. (And test this claim out, say, once a year.)

Personnel

It is generally the most valuable people in the project who turn out to be the most mobile. Since people can sometimes leave in a hurry (plane crash, argument with boyfriend, etc) it is important to have the latest developments written up – at the time when they happen. As a fallback in this situation, a bilateral 'body-swap' agreement with another DP or MIS department may well help you out of a temporary shortage. In addition, some understanding with an agency who can supply instant contract staff will also be of value.

Funding

Most forms of trouble can be sorted out by finding the right approach, and then spending liberally in that direction (such as the contract staff above). However, for that to occur, there have to be some funds salted away somewhere for just such a rainy day. It could even be an agreement, in principle, with the company treasurer to release a certain sum for special purposes as and when required. Without that agreement, it might take two to five weeks to get the necessary permission for added expenditure – and that could mean project paralysis over that period.

Maintenance

Every piece of hardware will break down sooner or later, and each time the unexpected happens, someone has to work out what to do. By introducing a regular check up service, and replacement strategy after a certain period of time, a lot of the day-to-day problems and irritations will be alleviated. Treat your computer and office equipment with the same care as any vehicle in the company car pool.

Insurance

One of the simplest means to provide protection against accidents etc. is by selective insurance where applicable. This is a straightforward matter of discussing your possible areas of risk with an insurance company, getting quotes for defined policies, and deciding on a suitable compromise between expenditure and coverage. This may not help the project, but it could mean that the company is covered for any penalty clauses etc. that may arise.

Procedures

The last process to be discussed is the provision of a set of procedures that either act to prevent the project being damaged, or at least allow the effects of unwelcome events to be closely controlled. These procedures fall into the general category of 'good engineering practice'.

Security

If access to the equipment is made difficult with security entrances etc., then the possibility of strange hands 'borrowing' selected items is sharply reduced. Equally, the rigid application of properly applied passwords may not completely block access to confidential data, but it does make it a great deal more difficult for the interested hacker to worm his way in.

Safety

Again, due regard to the possible hazards of the physical world can act to prevent possible disaster. Here, the procedures should be generated for the proper application of fire safes, regular back-ups of all data, on-site and off-site storage and archiving of both data and documentation related to the project. And the back-up procedures should be tested every so often to show that data can be erased from the main memory and replaced using the back-up tape.

Error Checking

Anyone can make an error. However, if the procedure calls for every major decision to be checked automatically by some other review body (or even by the designer down the hall, while you check out his code for him), the chances of the error being undetected becomes correspondingly smaller. The penalty here is the extra resource or time used to carry out the same activity compared to the team that is not checking its own work. The pros and cons of this issue are something each project team or department has to analyse.

System Breakdown

From time to time the simplest sort of disaster, such as a fire or flood, will occur in the main development area. Under these circumstances, it may be weeks before the equipment is up and running effectively again. If this loss is unacceptable for commercial reasons or because of project schedules, it will be wise to enter into some agreement with a recovery service company. Within a few hours, they will guarantee to provide you with a replica of your hardware, allowing you to download your most recent data. This equipment may be at some external site or may, literally, be wheeled into your car park in a trailer.

Decision Making

Most troubles occur in August. This is due to yet another variant of Murphy's law which states that problems only arise when the means to solve them are not available. In this case, it is because senior executives are away for the Summer and therefore cannot be reached to sign off any expenditures or changes of strategy. For this reason, it would be wise to set up some decision-making body with a flexible membership ('...shall contain at least two vice-presidents or their representatives out of the six presently in office. ...') but with enough power vested in it to take decisions up to a certain expense level. This is not foolproof, but does address a large number of the problems.

Workrounds

Once again looking only at the high priority functions, the critical items could be analysed for failure on a 'what-if' basis, and possible alternatives could be examined and filed. In a high risk area, this is particularly useful, in that a list of options with pros and cons already exists, just waiting to be used. Where timing is of the essence, this will dramatically speed up the decision making process.

Let's see how all this might work in practice. Newtown General are insistent that their surgical patient system has to be reliable and they need the system designed and installed in a hurry. To allay the fears of the Newtown users, the following actions have been agreed on by Newtown and All-Data, the design consultants:

❑ The system manager of the Newtown General Computer Services department has accepted to take on the added responsibilities of Audit Manager for this project. It was further agreed that he will have full access to the All-Data personnel working on the hospital system.

❑ A Newtown System Co-ordinator is to be assigned at the Hospital to take care of daily issues related to keeping the project on track and meeting its objectives. After rejecting as candidates a staff nurse (interested, but already too overworked), or an outside contractor (very competent but too expensive), an M.Sc. student from the local Polytechnic agreed to take on the role as material for his thesis.

At this point, the change-related problems of Newtown are unlikely to be a cause for alarm. This is not to say that they will stop occurring, or even to suggest that they will no longer be serious. What has been achieved, however, is to allocate specific personnel to handle the problems as and when they arise. One person will solve the daily problems, while the other will keep a look out for the impending crisis, such that a early alert can be given.

That completes the review of techniques which can limit project exposure. A lot of it is common sense, plus an ability to invest now for tomorrow's benefit. For all that, there is a cost – whether it is extra resource requirement, or an extended schedule. It is all a matter of taking a calculated gamble. Either you spend your insurance money now, with possibly nothing to show for it at the end of the time; or you take a chance and possibly end-up with a real problem that has blown up out of all proportion because there were no safe-guards in place. The safe route is outlined in Figure 9.5, while the more dangerous trip, if you and your organisation can stand the excitement, is given in the next section.

9.5 Crisis Management

An emergency situation can be achieved by one of three routes: managerial ineptness or disinterest; competent leadership that took a calculated gamble to keep costs down – and lost; or sheer bad luck. The latter is probably the most usual. One such example might be that your hardware supplier goes bankrupt – leaving a large hole where your schedules used to be and some red faces in the finance department. Or the project manager has been taken on by a competitor – and promptly takes her entire team with her. Whatever the cause, there are two specific actions related to crisis management: the first is recognising that the condition has been reached, and the second is taking appropriate steps to meet it.

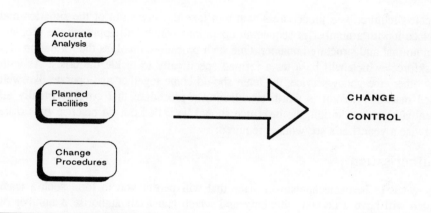

Figure 9.5: Establishing Change Control

Crisis Format

There can be no formal definition of what constitutes a crisis. It could be a case of creeping non-performance, where one day the level of frustration is suddenly seen to be unacceptable. This could be, for example, the weekly attempt to allocate the writing of urgently required test documentation. At some point you realise that it is never going to get written because nobody wants to write it, and the department is in total overload, anyway. On the other hand, the crisis could be a step function, such as when your software house has just been literally destroyed by a juggernaut lorry. Whatever the cause, there has to be a judgement or recognition that the current situation has overstepped the bounds of the normally acceptable, and that there is no procedure in place to handle it. This latter constraint is important in that some previously agreed procedure may have already considered the nature of the problem facing you, and provided the appropriate process to reach a solution. As an example, consider the redeveloper and his team of workers on the building site next to your building. In a fit of enthusiasm, he takes out your entire mains power supply. At this point you would be entitled to press the emergency button *unless* full back-up electrical generators had already been installed, with adequate capacity to cover the next few days.

In effect, a crisis exists at that point when *you* decide that the current situation is unacceptable.

The Taskforce

There are two opposed responses that can be considered as reasonably natural when facing a catastrophe – and they are to be avoided at all costs. The first is paralysis and the second is panic, and neither will prove sensibly cost-effective.

What is required is a procedure which will take the stress out of the situation and replace it with a number of sequential operations which will approach the problem in a normal and structured manner. One such procedure involves the formation of a 'taskforce' which will be a team formed specifically to tackle the crisis. As with any other emergency service, the team should come together and operate like well oiled machinery, so it is worth establishing a procedure that covers virtually all eventualities. In addition, the taskforce should be called out on practice runs once or twice a year. Let's see what is required:

Authorisation

There has to be a mechanism in place that will permit you to form such a team which will have a certain autonomy and which can itself authorise a number of activities and spend a defined amount of money. This permission has to be a high speed process (most crises contain pressures specifically related to time) and could be, say, authorisation from any local member of the executive steering board.

Current Work

The taskforce will comprise, say, five managers with an interest in the subject causing the problem. They will have been approached in the past and agreed to be members of such a team if so called upon. This means that one of the first sub-tasks will be the speedy re-allocation of work that they are carrying out at the time of the call. If they don't clear their own desks, they will hardly be able to commit all their time to clearing yours.

Stand-ins

Some of the intended members will not be available at the required time (its hard to be of assistance if you are travelling 5,000 Kilometres from the office). In this event, as another sub-task, all potential members should have designated stand-ins who have equally agreed to participate in the team if so requested.

Support Staff

The logistics of moving any military force usually involves moving more support staff than actual fighting men. In a similar manner, the team is going to need secretarial, clerical, and possibly senior programming services in order to create an efficient operational unit.

Facilities

One of the first jobs of the taskforce will be to define a workspace. This could be a room in the main plant, at another work location, or perhaps the local hotel. At the selected location should be found all the required equipment, e.g. desktop computers, printer, phones, faxes, modems, secretarial work stations, meeting desks, presentation slide material, and so on. Finally, a source of prepared food should be close by.

These are some of the main steps that will provide a fully working taskforce set up for emergency operations. Some or all of the above may be selected, depending on the exact nature of the problem. The first job of the taskforce will be to define its sphere of interest, required operations and interfaces:

Sphere of Interest

The limitation or boundaries related to the team should be spelt out at the first coming together of the members. Thus, the departments that can be called up or affected, the budgetry constraints, and projected time scales should all be clearly defined.

Operations

One of the first crucial jobs will be the exact definition of the problem that led to the creation of the team. Following on from this will be an approximate formulation of what is ideally required to solve the problem. This can be as formal or informal as thought necessary, and no solution should be excluded because it is unusual. Each proposal for a possible workround will have to identify the major advantages and disadvantages of using that particular approach. Each proposal will then be argued either by the team itself, or by a more senior review board. The ultimate result will be the selection of one option which will then be implemented to solve the problem which called up the taskforce in the first place.

The last job of the taskforce will be to organise the formal standing down of the team, once the work is considered to have been completed.

Interfaces

In the process of working towards a solution, requests for information and allocation of sub-tasks will go out to the rest of the organisation. In addition, a regular reporting procedure will be set up to senior management. All these activities will require the availability of suitable distribution lists, so that communication can be both speedy and effective.

This description of an emergency service has been roughly summarised in Figure 9.6 and can serve as an outline for a possibly customised procedure to suit the needs of your particular organisation. Whatever procedure is adopted, it is worth repeating that a full practice run should be carried out at least once a year to ensure that the procedure is effective and still operational.

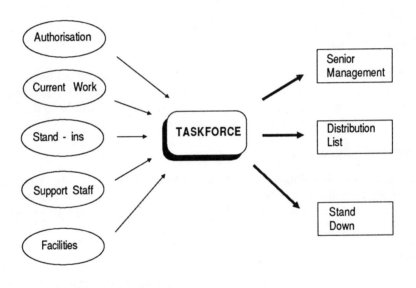

Figure 9.6: The factors relating to a taskforce

Now let's see how it might work for Universal. For whatever reason, there is an argument and the consultants All-Data have been summarily dismissed half way through the design phase. That sounds reasonably crisis-like and Universal's ESG4 (Emergency Strategy Group) was hastily assembled in Toronto. What can they do?

Well, among the first thing to be settled is the location of their workplace, and Brussels would seem to be the natural choice, since that was where the development work was going on. However, since the design organisation no longer needs to be considered, perhaps Toronto or Seoul could be a more convenient location. In the event, Toronto becomes the headquarters of the new group. They request and get two offices in the headquarters building along with all the peripheral services that they require.

What should they do next? Get over to Seoul and interview all the Universal staff involved with the project? Rush over to Europe to collect all the documentation that still exists? The first thing they decide to do is simply to put a framework or plan together of the required activities that they should undertake. In other words, the first action should be to formally discuss and prioritise the first actions in the coming days and weeks. Universal may have a crisis, but it is important for the group to treat it as just another management exercise. Having meetings is a lot less exciting than rushing round the world trying to be a miracle worker. However, it is *much* more likely to succeed

9.6 Summary

This chapter has sought to cover the potential impact of change on the smooth and continuing progress of the project. We started off with an overview of how a typical project can progressively trade-off performance against schedule as a better understanding of the true design requirements of the system becomes available. The installed poor performance can then get improved during the system application period. This may not be ideal, but is how it tends to happen in real life.

The underlying reasons for this style of operation were then discussed in section 9.2 where the main factors causing change were shown to be inevitable in the system development framework. Thus, you cannot anticipate the way commercially available technology will develop over the next few years, or, for that matter, which mistakes are going to be inadvertently introduced into the system as a part of the design process. All you can do is develop a flexible attitude, and prepare to act quickly to minimise any damage that may result.

The next section reviewed the more specific type of problems that are commonly to be found in most projects. These tend to occur in the areas of upgrades, user interfaces, administration, disaster events, complexity, staff mobility and strategic planning. All these have been covered to a greater or lesser extent along with a generalised guideline for the main possible areas of control or containment.

Following on from this, some specific tools were explored which can be set up to limit the impact of change on the project. The discussion centred on the internal audit facility, contingency planning and the laying down of preventative procedures. The last tool to be covered was a mechanism for the handling of real disasters, achieved by setting up taskforce to address the problem in a controlled and structured way.

Overall, the objective has been to illustrate how potential troubles can be identified as early as possible, and how to apply the tools which will effectively address these change-related problems.

This chapter also marks the end of the major topic 'Managing the Design' which has been divided into the chapters on Project Administration, Communications and Change Control. Here the intent has been to provide a review of the important tools used for command and control during the development cycle. It cannot make you an expert in, say, Unix or networking. For all that, these chapters will provide useful inputs for the *management* of business system projects and will be applicable from the generation of the Requirement Specification, through design and test, and up to Installation.

Questions

1. Halfway through the design cycle, your entire project team tells you that it will be leaving the organisation in one month's time.

> What proposals do you make? *(Input from your boss: any taskforce that you form will have a membership of one.)*

2. Your computer department has one processor and about 80 users on their terminals scattered throughout the building. The management is worried about the possibility of processor failure or shut down.

> Provide some ideas for reducing the risk, indicating the pros and cons of each approach.

3. All your group activities are run on IBM PCs, i.e. personal computers which use MS-DOS as the operating system. The new analyst requests that you purchase an Apple Macintosh for him, since it uses a graphical interface which would be useful to him.

> Give your reasons for refusing his request.

4. "I usually purchase an old application package, such as a spreadsheet, about one week after it has been replaced with a new version or upgrade".

> Discuss the pros and cons of this philosophy.

5. A particular user-interface software module is starting to look like an 'anti-gravity platform', i.e. it is looking impossible to design.

> What evidence would you look for to reinforce your suspicions, and what options are open to you?

10

Installation

Snail pace system dogs DHSS Lomp project

Social security offices face increasing backlogs of work from April because new benefits software runs up to eight times more slowly than current systems.

"It will slow work down, and that will pile up," says one DHSS office member who attended the Lomp training course in the past fortnight. "It could also make people against using the computer – they'll do it manually"

Computer Weekly p.3 3.3.88

Getting to grips with IT failure before the event

About 10% of IT projects are a success. "That is, they come in on time, on budget and sort of meet the specifications." So says Bob Charette, a US risk management consultant.

A high failure rate has dogged the computer industry since its beginnings and things haven't changed too much since. Too many projects combine unrealistic expectations with untested technology and so result in disappointment.

Computing p.28 29.11.90

Banking on a better design

The sad fact is that architects and building design professionals are often blind to the problem of introducing new information systems and computer networks into office space, overlooking the needs of IT and cabling, and forgetting that people have to work with equipment in the building they create.

Computer Weekly p. 26 11.10.90

10.1 Introduction

There is a time in every project life cycle when a sort of collective hysteria takes over, when frustrations and recriminations are the order of the day:

> *O Judgment, thou art fled to brutish beasts,*
> *And men have lost their reason!*

It is not clear whether Mark Antony was ever involved in system installation, but this does have a familiar ring to it.

The user response often indicates his frustration. This is the first time the user actually gets his hands on the new system in his own environment. He and his system have waited, perhaps a year or two, and between them have been interviewed, modified, postponed, reconfigured, retrained, tested and ultimately installed. At the end of it all, it is potentially a complete misfit and the disappointment starts to show through.

So let's begin again. Installation is an important and difficult operation which lends itself to a structured approach. Important, because it is a major step for the user, and also the opportunity for the developer to show off the full value of all his activity. Difficult, because the handover process is a minefield waiting to trap the careless operator. Every day lost is an added expense and frustration for the user and every mistake made by the developer is clearly observed (and related onward) by any number of the client's management and staff. It is an area where close co-operation, in-depth preparation, solid planning and the development of key contingencies will be handsomely rewarded. Above all, it is an area which should be driven by formal and agreed project planning, using a documented program which identifies all the main activities and their completion dates.

In effect, installation should be treated as a serious exercise in its own right, with a designated project team or manager and a well defined list of objectives. These should include a schedule plan, list of external dependencies, output reports: their types, frequencies and distribution lists, and a clear set of actions to be accomplished within the given timeframe. In addition, there will have to be a reviewing body for signing off or accepting the status of the given activities.

The structural elements required for this mini-project have been brought together in Figure 10.1 and we will take a brief look at the components below:

Team

The monitoring, controlling and reporting of events leading up to the system installation could be left to the existing project team – if this is acceptable and they have the capability in hand. Conversely, it could be agreed to form a special combined project team from members of the development group and the end-users.

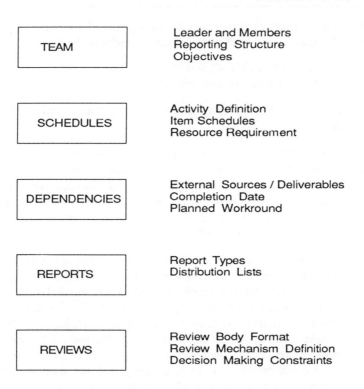

Figure 10.1: The installation elements

Whatever resource is to be applied, one person should be assigned as the installation manager.

Schedules

Building up a schedule chart is always a fairly risky business, but it is better to address the issue than to ignore it. The need to estimate the timescale for, say, wiring up the ward sister's office has two advantages: it forces you to think about the need and priority of this activity and, along with this, there has to be some evaluation of the required resource to implement the activity in the time allotted.

Dependencies

A listing of the dependencies will identify the principal external sources of risk to the overall schedule. This could be the delivery of the hardware from another department in the hospital, or possibly the documentation from some outside technical authors. Whatever the cause, it can be reasonably assumed that at least two out of ten such sources will fail to deliver on time, so fall-backs should be evaluated for most of them. Close monitoring of their individual progress may then help to provide an early warning of impending delays.

Reports

The progress in clearing the preliminary activities will be of interest to a large number of people. Problem areas can be highlighted and support rapidly obtained if the reporting structure circulates the current status of work to the right people. Again, honest reports with an effective distribution presupposes that this is a no-blame-attaches and an all-hands-to-the-pump sort of working environment.

Reviews

There has to be a mechanism for assessing the results of a set of activities within this mini-project. Either they are satisfactory and can be signed off, or further work will have to be called for in that area. In addition, a fast decision process will be needed when the installation team is faced with a number of different strategic options. Both these functions can be carried out by the project team itself, by the project manager or internal auditor, or by a higher review committee. In the hospital, this might be the senior registrar while for Universal they may go for a co-ordinating committee based in Toronto. The selected path will, to a certain extent, depend on the size of the project and the manpower available. Whichever route is adopted, the reviewing and decision making processes will have to be clearly defined. Perhaps this will need to be the first task of the review body.

As a general rule, successful installation consists of a great deal of preparation, relatively limited activity at the time of handover, and a lot of hand-holding in the weeks after the event. Let's assume that a team has been set up to monitor and manage the installation function. Then they will have to address a reasonable number of tasks to ensure that all the preparatory work has been carried out to a satisfactory level. In fact, this initial phase becomes the central focus for implementing the installation and every item, outlined in the sections that follow, should be considered as a possible source of risk. Not all of them may apply, but at least they should be thought about.

This is the point where the manager or team start their work. The first objective is to create an overall listing of all the activities that remain either to be monitored or to be implemented, along with a structured program or set of proposals for getting them completed. The possible problem areas will be reviewed here and have been grouped under three general headings – preliminaries, preparation, and change-over. The first is concerned with setting up monitors to check that the system fundamentals are moving in the right direction; the second discusses the work in preparing for the handover; while the last item relates to the installation itself.

10.2 Preliminaries

This is perhaps the most important section of the chapter. If the activities covered here have not been completed, the chances are that the installation will tend to follow the route illustrated in the reports at the head of the chapter. The items to be described fall into the broad classification of management monitors on the system and the intended site. They check that the system in is the right shape to be handed over and that there is somewhere suitable to receive it.

The fundamental approach is to assume that something will inevitably go wrong and the trouble spot has to be identified and eliminated before handover. This is based on the premise that rework is far cheaper when it is carried out on a system that has not left the development team. Once it has been handed over, the trouble-shooting costs on the user's site will go up steeply, in comparison.

Test Results

There are three types of test programmes which should be carried out before handing the system over to the client. Whatever the results, it is better to discuss them with the users before the formal installation rather than after.

System Performance

Some benchmark test specifications were agreed at the outset of the project, and the appropriate tests results should be available for review. The poor performance of installed systems is a recurring theme of user complaints, so it might as well be tackled at the earliest possible moment.

User Evaluation

Another familiar cry is 'but this isn't what we wanted'. Independent of the methodology, the users should be introduced to the basic screens and other system interfaces along with some sample methods of entering and extracting data. In the ultimate analysis, they have to approve of what has been done, otherwise they simply won't use it. The Universal users, for example, may want a simple but high speed command-line user interface with the system. If they cannot switch off the windows and menus which just slow them down, the irritation will be monitored round the globe. Conversely, it is likely that the hospital staff will want the exact opposite.

System Compatibility

The existing system will probably interface with a number of outside users and systems. Thus, the Ward data retrieval system will be linked to the Hospital central records system, and so on. It is important to make a final check that the system under design will, in fact, interface successfully with *all* the external data systems that are currently in use. If not, it is back to the drawing board.

Documentation

There is a human tendency to put off the documentation writing till the last possible moment. Well, that moment has arrived. Someone will have to check the *Document Deliverables Listing* to ensure that all the documents promised as part of the delivery package have been produced, and have been reviewed and accepted. If not, there will have to be yet another meeting to decide on either writing the missing item at once, or deferring it to some target date in the future. When all the documents are seen to be acceptable, then the required number of copies will have to be run off and stored until needed for distribution. As a reminder of the need for this activity, Figure 10.2 provides a skeleton outline of the documentation requirements for any information system handover.

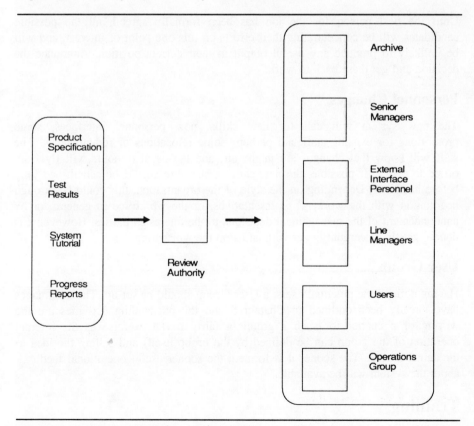

Figure 10.2: The basic documentation flow

Staff Changes

The introduction of any new system is going to cause changes in the structure of the workforce. This is clearly the responsibility of the host company, but they could be encouraged to get the various decisions out of the way. The changes will primarily affect three areas:

System Manager

In the first year of operation, there will be a lot of problems developed by or about the new system. Once it has been installed, there will be a need for one individual to be responsible for the fine-tuning and maintenance of the system, for providing feedback to the originating development team, to set up an advice centre for the end-users and to provide an interface to the external systems which use or prepare some of the data.

Until the best person for the job has been formally agreed, all the possible candidates will be concentrating their efforts on this one point of interest, and will be unlikely to produce any useful output in their current position. Announce the decision and get them back to work.

Personnel Changes

The new system will call for new skills, new personnel interfaces, some promotions for existing staff and perhaps some relocations or redundancies. The staff will know that changes are in the air, and the usual rumours will fly from office to office. If possible, the new staffing structure should be established long before handover. Depending on the style of the organisation, this could be through negotiation with the workers' representatives, or the workforce in general, or by announcement of the management decisions to the interested parties. However it is done – get the uncertainty over with and stop the whispering.

User Group

Having defined the potential users, a User Group should be set up. The advantages have already been outlined in Chapter 8 and the outstanding activities are the writing of a charter for such a group (a fairly trivial exercise as the internal operation of the group can be defined by the group itself) and selling the idea to the actual users. The sooner it is formed, the sooner useful operational feedback about the system will be available.

Training

There are two main courses which should be under development, and these relate to the users and managers of the system. The users will need to gain confidence in the day-to-day entry and retrieval of data, along with the appearance of screens and interfaces. On the other hand, the managers will want to familiarise themselves with the possible report generation and consolidation capabilities that are being offered. Thus, there will be a need to write and to run two entirely separate courses for two entirely separate groups of staff. In the hospital case, the nurses and junior doctors should be no trouble, but organising the ward sister, consultants and surgeons to attend a management presentation or course at some defined time – this may require a certain time and effort to set in motion.

Reception Site

It is remarkably easy to make an oversight about the intended location of the hardware for the new system. To combat this, a series of simple checks will at least ensure that all the major questions have been addressed.

Size

In some situations, the client will be strangely reluctant to allocate enough space. Thus, if the Universal Electronics site is to be located in a down-town Brussels high-rise office, someone will be estimating the added office costs per square metre. Conversely, if a PC is being added in the ward sister's room, she will not be pleased at the intrusion into her working space.

First estimate the number of people that will be expected to work in the given area. Now add about 20% to allow for natural expansion. In an ideal world, this is the number of desks and chairs that should be fittable into the new site. If there isn't enough room then flag your apprehensions about the new site to your senior staff, but go on to check the possibility of fitting the current number of people in. If that still doesn't work, sound the red alert.

Security

The site should be capable of meeting the security objectives laid out in the requirement specification. Thus the location may be need the entrances to be rebuilt to ensure that access to the site conforms to that requirement, and a number of intruder alarms should be installed if so required.

Safety

The site should be examined for proximity to sources of fire, flood or electronic interference. The first, for example, could be a canteen, the second the company toilets and the third could be an adjacent radar or communications laboratory. If a source of potential danger does exist, then added precautions should be introduced. Again, to cater for the possibility of a fire, the exit signs and directions should be well illuminated (at head height and floor level) and the exit passages planned to be well defined and unobstructed. You will usually need to get Fire Authority approval and it is important to bring them in at a very early stage.

Back-up and Archive

There will have to be an additional area allocated for back-up material. In addition, the archive will need some defined physical space for its location. For the hospital, for example, this could be a few square metres in the Central Records basement office. In general, this will have to take inactive documentation as well as digital tapes, which may cause the floor loading figures to be exceeded. Again, the storage material in their appropriate cabinets may need a controlled or air-conditioned environment.

Site Preparation

If the place is being modified and redecorated before the installation occurs, then it would be as well to check that it really will be completed in time. If the place requires false flooring, new electrical installations, central heating or air-conditioning, then, again, the progress should be closely monitored. The Gods do not seem to view this sort of labour with any great enthusiasm, and the chances are that it will be several weeks late. And check male/female toilets availability!

Law and Insurance

These are simple matters but they can be easily overlooked. On the one hand, the system will probably need to be registered in conformance with the laws on privacy and data protection; while in the other, the extra equipment being introduced should be covered with additional insurance taken out by the user organisation. This is not the same as the insurance taken out by the system design team against liability for late delivery, for any reason – see Chapter 9.

Communication

This is not strictly necessary, but any new site or new system introduction will be a source of some interest and uncertainty for the workforce. For a limited outlay, a regular communication or news-sheet could be printed to inform them, say bi-weekly or monthly, on the progress with the installation, the problems and the successes. There is nothing like the media to generate *involvement*.

This completes the check-out required to ensure that there are no basic problems in going ahead with the handover. In fact, reaching a satisfactory position with all the above items would be something of a major achievement for the project. More usually, you will go ahead with about 80% of the above sensibly completed and with a clear indication of what has been carried over for on-going attention.

10.3 Preparation

The last section was a check on items that should have been started some time in the past and could, in principle, already be completed. By contrast, this section will discuss the specific actions that will have to be undertaken to enable the installation itself to be carried out. Most of these actions will probably be planned to take place over the last three months before handover. Because of this late start-up, they will be particularly at risk, since any unplanned delays will have an immediate impact on the overall schedule. Again, close monitoring will be required to ensure that these schedule aspects can be addressed before they turn into problems, or even crises.

Power

For this topic, it will be necessary to answer three apparently trivial questions: how much; what protection; and has it been installed? In fact, the potential for serious oversight and resulting embarrassment exists with all the activities in this section. Thus, as a general rule, nothing should be taken for granted and each point ought to be covered with some care and thoroughness.

Quantity

The overall power requirements for the site should be roughly estimated. The consumption calculations should be based on the power requirements per terminal, power for the processor unit, and all planned peripherals along with possible expansion, and power for the lighting and possibly for the air-conditioning or central heating if electricity is used as the power source. Whatever the total figure, it would be sensible to allow a safety margin by doubling this number. This, then, is the minimum capability that should be available from the mains source. In an existing computer centre this, of course, will be the *added* requirement to the existing supplies. Any problem in meeting this target should be reported to the senior management for comment and action.

Protection

There are a range of possible philosophies related to protecting the equipment from variation in the mains input. These variations can include sudden voltage surges or transient spikes as other equipment is switched on and off; radio frequency interference transmitted down the mains cabling; and sudden loss of power. The options open to reduce the impact of these phenomena are:

a) Surge and spike supressor

b) Uninterruptible Power Supply (UPS)

c) A battery room for extended independence

Item a) is a low cost option that will act to limit or minimise the surge passed through to the computer equipment. The UPS option, b), will provide a limited continuation of power when the mains have been accidentally removed – say 10 or 20 minutes. The idea is that it will give you enough time to power down the entire system with no loss of data or introduction of error. The last option, c), is for high security installations where the equipment *must* continue to operate. In this case, a bank of rechargeable batteries and associated electronics can keep the equipment operating for a number of hours or days without external power. The strategy for the system in question should be well established and the appropriate equipment selected.

Status

Bringing adequate power to the system installation site is largely the responsibility of the plant or site manager. For that reason, he or she should be alerted, fairly early on, with respect to any new requirements and to the scheduled time when this power should be available. The same applies to installing central heating or air-conditioning. On the other hand, locating the actual points where power sockets will be available is strictly an internal matter of planning the physical layout of the staff, and this equally should not be left to the last minute. Large open-plan sites will require a more flexible approach to distribution, but these will still need some sort of floor plan worked out on a suitable grid pattern.

Data Distribution

Whatever types of data communication services are to be used, usually there will have to be a connection capability to each user wherever he or she is located. This will apply whether the user is linking his terminal to a mainframe, attaching the PC to the local network, or sending data via a modem to a distant site. Once again, there can be some unexpected strategic and tactical problems to be addressed.

Cabling Strategy

In any large installation, there are advantages to having a comprehensive cabling approach that will accommodate to the variations in number of users and differing applications. To cater for this need, there are a number of products which act as a structured wiring system. Current examples are IBM's Cabling System and British Telecom's Open Systems Cabling Architecture. Whatever philosophy is to be adopted, the basic decisions should have been made fairly early on in the project.

Another problem is related to the anticipated data traffic of the system. As more and more data is transmitted, so additional strain is thrown on the existing facilities. This leads to a strategic conflict because tomorrow's anticipated high density usage suggests fibre optics cabling as the optimum transmission medium. However, this option will have to be paid for at today's high prices, as compared to co-axial cabling costs (or even cheaper, the twisted pair linkage). However, there are all sorts of technical performance impacts depending on which type of cabling is selected, so someone will have made this sort of decision long before before the installation stage has been reached

Practical Cabling Problems

Where older buildings are being modified to handle modern applications, some unexpected problems may surface. Thus, in city centres, some banking and insurance companies are finding that their central offices are considered of historical interest. As such, the possible changes to the fabric of the building may be severely limited. This can pose special problems for cable ducting being fitted throughout the building , and may force the selection of optical fibre cabling as the least-space option.

On a different aspect of the subject, the nature of the required cable ducting will depend on whether false floors are being used or not. For modern office buildings, these floors are virtually standardised. However, for the older building, installing false floors can be an expensive and time consuming exercise – even if it is allowed. This is yet another decision to be established before the final wiring is undertaken.

Finally, when the cabling has been installed – in whatever form – a separate test program should be planned to confirm that the facility works and to show that signals of a suitable quality can be transmitted and received across the cable runs.

Computer Equipment

There will almost certainly be unexpected problems with the system installation program. In an effort to minimise the generation of faulty diagnoses due to multiple errors, the hardware platform and operating system should be debugged and made fully operational before the system is loaded. One possible approach to the testing and acceptance of hardware, is to plan a two phase exercise. In phase 1, a few weeks or months before handover, the hardware is fully tested on site. The first task will be to establish a suitable test area, say, by clearing one corner office of the Brussels location. Then the processors and peripherals can be delivered to this office and set up for the incoming inspection and test. The operating system can also be installed and tested at this stage. The hardware and operating system can now be tested and fully debugged with the possible assistance of experienced staff from the supplier. This can often take anything up to three to six weeks but will occur without any of the pressure that every day lost is another disaster. When the debugging is finally considered complete, or the remaining fault areas clearly defined, then the hardware can be disassembled and put into store. The office can now be returned to normal use.

Phase 2 would be the reassembly and checkout of the equipment at the final office site at the time just prior to system installation.

Office Equipment

While not exactly leading-edge technology, someone has to select, order, receive, inspect, sign-off and store all the required tables and chairs, lighting units, carpeting (non-static-generating), shelves and cupboards, phones, fax machines, copiers, fire safes, notice boards, coffee dispensing machines and hatstands. Furthermore, in order to have a well defined chain of responsibility, that 'someone' should be clearly designated by the installation team.

User Formats

Much like the power requirements, the user system environment will have to be adapted to meet the needs of the new system. One area of modification will concern the data inputs and output. Because the system will address the business of the organisation from a new viewpoint, the actual data sources and sinks as well as the data content could all change from that used in the past. These changes will need to be well defined such that the requirements of the organisation and the capabilities of the system to be installed match at all levels.

Again, the system inputs and outputs will frequently use dedicated paper forms to carry the information beyond the system. Thus a weekly time sheet will be prepared to carry just the required information to be loaded into a salary database. Change the database structure and it is most likely that the time sheet form will also need to be modified. Thus, all the existing forms and stationary related to the old system will need to be examined and if necessary modified to bring them in line with the new requirements. If these forms, say patient records, are going to external users, say Central Records, then changes to the way the data is handled will need to be discussed and agreed.

Data Compatibility

This is a requirement which, to a certain extent, is completely artificial in that it has no long term bearing on the success or failure of the system. However, in the short term there will almost certainly be a pilot test of the new system to prove that it processes data in a way that matches the output of the old system. This test will require the old and new system data to be compatible – i.e. that apples are compared with apples.

One approach to this pilot test requirement will be to run the same data in parallel on both the old and the new systems. By comparing the data processing outputs from both routes it will be possible to show that they produce identical results, thereby proving the validity of the new system in processing data. This logical argument has its limitations (all that can be reasonably inferred from this test is that the new improved system can be reduced in capability to match the performance of the old) but will illustrate to the user that the old and new systems can be made to be compatible. However, this particular approach will only work if both systems will accept and output essentially the same data. For this to be so, the new system data inputs and outputs will have to be specially analysed and possibly modified to meet this criterion. Without this analysis, such a test may be difficult to implement and expensive to run.

An alternative method which will enable comparison tests to be carried out involves the planning of special reconciliation reports. These will be designed to automate the comparison of data processing results obtained by different methods which used non-identical inputs and outputs. Such a testing philosophy will also enable a first simplified comparison of performance to be obtained.

The 'Power Down' Plan

At some point the new equipment and software will be installed, tested and debugged. While this is happening, a complicated ballet of groups and individuals will take place, as different aspects of the transfer process require different areas of expertise. To choreograph this activity calls for special planning to ensure that the business of the organisation carries on while the transfer is taking place. Largely independent of the resource allocation (see next item) and change-over strategy (see next section), the business will continue to need personnel and facilities – perhaps using different staff on a temporary basis who may be working at a different location. Whatever temporary conditions will be set up, they will need to be carefully planned as yet another sub-project to the main installation program.

Resource Allocation

One of the most important activities related to handover is planning the availability of a suitable workforce and ensuring that an adequate number of people will be on the site at the time required. Part of this planning will also include the provision of staff reserves on a contingency basis. (If the handover is in Summer, everyone is on holiday, if in Winter, they are all at home with the flu. There is always something.) The main parties involved with all the activities discussed in this section are shown in Figure 10.3, which is one possible plan based on the various milestones related to installation. Planning and getting agreement for each party to be available at the required time in the required numbers is one part of the exercise. Laying down fall-back plans on the assumption that they do not turn up as promised – albeit for the best possible reasons – is another.

Preparation Overview

Once again, the main requirement illustrated in this section can be summed up: attention to detail. By identifying all the activities that are going to be called up, by including them in some structured plan, and by ensuring that adequate resource is available to implement them in the proper sequence, there is a reasonable probability that the program will go forward smoothly and effectively.

10.4 Change-over

By the time that the actual installation date has arrived, the bulk of the work has already been done. What has still to be agreed is the manner of the transition – for which, unfortunately, no perfect solution exists, only less imperfect ones. Whatever method is selected, the new software programs are loaded onto the hardware platform, and the whole system has then to be debugged. This is where the system is queried with a typical question, in the expectation that it will generate what seems to be a reasonable answer. If not, further exploration will be needed to understand, and possibly correct, the unexpected response. This input/output regime is applied to successive areas until the entire system has been covered. Once the whole system is operating in accordance with your expectations, it can sensibly be said to be debugged.

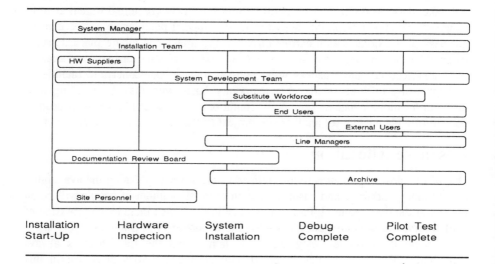

| Installation Start-Up | Hardware Inspection | System Installation | Debug Complete | Pilot Test Complete |

Figure 10.3: The personnel involved with installation

Finally, a pilot test scheme is implemented to provide confidence that the new system will in fact process the data to provide a valid commercial output with a performance that is, at minimum, no worse that the previous method.

The Structured Transition

The different options that can be considered are outlined in Figure 10.4. They look straightforward on paper, but they all have their drawbacks, so some care should be given to selecting the mode of transfer:

Switch

This is the simplest and cheapest approach. At some arbitrary point, the old method is stopped and, within hours or possibly days, the new system installed. There are two main problems: a) the staff have to be fully trained to operate the new system from the switchover point, and b) if the new system fails to operate properly, *there is no going back*. This is clearly a strategy for the courageous.

Parallel

This method gets round the problems of the straight switch, but only at some increase in resource usage and overall cost. While the new programs are being debugged, enhanced, or tested, for however long it takes, the old system is there to take the commercial load. This is the positive aspect. What is less clear is – who is running, managing and paying for these duplicated systems. The temporary extra staff needed will be newly trained to run either the old system (a cost that is hard to justify) or the new system (ditto). Perhaps a task force of external system users could be press-ganged to take up the new system role, perhaps a little earlier than

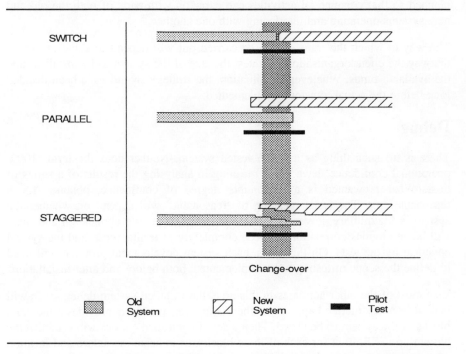

Figure 10.4: The change-over options

expected. However, even this may be difficult as the 'volunteers' would still need the agreement of their line managers, who might not be convinced of the advantages of this method.

Staggered

The larger installation may well be carried out one digestible bite at a time. Thus, the sales department could go over to the new system, which gets installed, debugged, and tested. Only after this, will the purchasing department make the transition, and so on. This will keep the risk associated with the new software contained to only one part of the organisation at any one time. In addition, the total number of duplicated staff will be kept within reasonable bounds. The down side is related to the system integration. If the entire system contains interlocked elements then attempting to apply it to individual departments is not going to be easy. As an example, consider a typical trading environment where the purchase requests are sent to a supplier and the sales orders are received from the customers. These are both dependent on the current stock control listings from the warehouse. In this case, installing a purchase request system – without linking it to a stock reporting system and possibly the financial control system – will only lead to chaos.

A staggered transfer has a lot of advantages. However, it will need to be carefully planned so that commercial activities can carry on with parts of both the old and new systems operating and interfacing with one another.

The way in which the transfer will be carried out will depend to some extent on the way the client organisation operates, the size of the system to be installed, and the available funds. Whatever the situation, the strategy should have been decided long before the actual transfer is implemented.

Debug

There is no such thing as a 100% tested system. Neither does the term '100% operational confidence' have much meaning in analysing the results of a series of tests. What is wanted is a *reasonable* degree of confidence, obtained for a reasonable cost. The exact meaning of 'reasonable' will depend on whether the system is for military, governmental, commercial or private application and there will be an obvious correlation between complexity of testing, cost, and the system coverage by the tests. On this basis, each system development program will need to define the scope of testing to be implemented, both before and after installation.

Like most of the other activities in this area, the installed system debug cycle will benefit from a structured approach, where a top-down analysis provides a the main blocks of the system to be tested. Then a set of controlled queries will establish the bottom-up verification for each of these blocks, or indicate the nature and location of the trouble. It is often not as simple at this, in that system software may interact with other application software, and both in turn may malfunction as a result of some limitation of the operating system. This complexity can lead to severe delays in providing a full debug service, although a thorough test cycle before delivery should have eliminated most of the trouble-spots.

Testing

The post-installation test phase is effectively part of the system transfer activity and cannot be easily separated from it. There are three central parts:

System

There will have to be some evaluation of the system's on-line capabilities, its interaction with other existing systems in the organisation, and the impact, positive or negative, on the majority of the end-users. Usually, the key parameters for the latter will be the 'performance' and the degree of 'user-friendliness' perceived when in use.

Comparison

As discussed earlier, the pilot evaluation will have to include testing with live data, taken from the daily work situation, to validate the new system. This will generally take the form of comparing the outputs from the previous method to the new system and showing that the same results are obtained, independent of method.

Workrounds

Somewhere in the testing cycle, a particular input/output sequence is going to provide poor results and will require corrective treatment (and a retest to show the improved condition). This is not serious, provided that the situation was anticipated. It will need to be handled, perhaps with a task force, much like the approach for controlling a crisis discussed in Chapter 9. Thus, a team is set up to to define the scope of the malfunction, to establish a program to clear it, and to provide the resource to carry out the proposed program.

10.5 Summary

In this chapter, we have reviewed some of the important activities that will enable a smooth introduction of the new system at the client's site. A structured approach, with emphasis on planning, preparation and co-operation will radically reduce the number of problems that are usually met.

In the introduction to this chapter, the need for a installation team or equivalent planning body was outlined, along with the definition of objectives for such a body.

In the next section, the preliminaries to handover were reviewed. These are items that lay down the essential framework for an installation program, and they should be closely monitored to ensure that no problems arise that could delay the overall installation process.

Following on from this, we covered all the physical items that have to be selected, bought, assembled and checked so that the intended site is fully prepared for the actual setting up of the equipment and end-users. In addition, some coverage was given to organising the various specialists who will be required at different points in the plan.

The final section was given over to the installation itself, to reviewing the possible strategy options, and outlining the objectives of the pilot tests. As a brief overview, if the planning and preparations have all been carefully carried out, this phase should prove readily manageable and problem-free.

Questions

1. You propose setting up an Installation Co-ordinating Committee with mixed membership from the client and the design groups.

> Elaborate on the advantages of combining members from different sources for this activity.

2. You have just been made 'Fire Security Officer' for the new site.

> The system manager requires your first feedback on a) site fire-prevention features, b) regular fire procedures and c) recommended site rules for all personnel.

3. As system manager, you learn that the proposed ceiling tiles for the new site have just been declared a 'fire hazard' by the fire security officer. Site preparation is already over schedule and over budget.

> Discuss the options open to you.

4. Twelve PC clones (equivalent to IBM PC – 286 machines) are on order for a networked system, but the supplier has problems. At the last minute and at no extra cost, he offers you a more expensive machine which uses the Unix operating system as a substitute for the MS-DOS based clones.

> a) Discuss the impact of a late change of operating system on your project.

> b) Prepare a fall-back paper with an action check-list and new program to get round this potential problem.

5. Two weeks after installation, the client requests a 50% expansion in the number of users who can access the system.

> a) Indicate the possible areas of added work this would require.

> b) Put forward some suggestions why this might not be a good idea in any case.

11

Maintenance

Maintenance is not a soft option

The UK spends over £1 bn a year on software maintenance. Survey data puts the figure at 49% of the total DP budget in 1979, rising to 65% in 1986, and there is every indication that this is getting worse. It is clear that in many DP departments software maintenance exceeds development costs.

One of the major problems associated with the maintenance of existing software systems is a lack of documentation which should have been produced with the source code.

Computer Weekly p.28 2.11.89

Birthrate fall poses maintenance threat

Software maintenance work is going to be severely hit by Europe's falling birthrate in the 1990s, with only a third of the necessary work getting done, according to new UK research. The shrinking number of school leavers over the next 10 years will produce a shortfall in staffing levels in software maintenance organisations which could result in "dramatic deterioration" in service levels, according to Ian Reid, chief consultant at systems consultancy Data Logic.

Computer Weekly p. 3 21.9.89

Merger aggravates Alliance headache

The Alliance & Leicester building society faces the problem of juggling Girobank's IBM-based systems with its own Unisys strategy after it takes over the bank.

The building society's £130 million offer last week for Girobank has come just one month after the completion of five years' work by Girobank on a £30 million banking system. For the Alliance & Leicester the move means hurling itself into another dp merger, having not yet finished merging its own two computer centres.

Computing p.1 27.4.89

11.1 Introduction

Running through this book has been the sense that all roads lead to maintenance and that it is the most critical activity in the whole development cycle. If it is, then there is remarkably little printed about it, at least compared to the design and test activities, where whole shelves of texts exist. For all that, as the first report suggests, it has become the most expensive part of the life cycle, and, perhaps, the least recognised.

It is a discipline which, one way or another, affects every part of the data processing function within an organisation. Until it has reached the point of being totally replaced, a system can never be considered as 'finished' or 'completed'. At any one time, it is either being prepared for the next upgrade or recovering from the last one. Or both. Looked at from the organisation's point of view, the procedures related to maintenance activities will say more about the company's attitudes to information technology than virtually any other single factor. However, before we get into the corporate strategy side of maintenance, it might be useful go over some basic definitions. Then we can follow that up with a short reminder of just why the subject is and will remain so important.

The emphasis in this chapter will be on software maintenance as a prime constituent of the overall system development life cycle (SDLC). Every required change, after installation. may need to loop back to some point in the original life cycle, as shown in Figure 11.1.

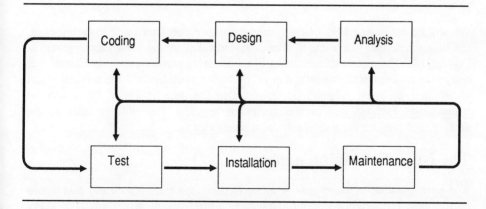

Figure 11.1: The Life Cycle – maintenance style

This is a maintenance oriented modification of the basic diagram of Chapter 3, where:

Maintenance is the debugging, modification and upgrading of any information system already installed for application by the end-user.

Here, *debugging* relates to the detection and removal of coding errors or performance malfunctions introduced accidentally into the system. *Modification* is the changing of the system to respond to some external stimulus – for example, new outputs required to meet a change in health reporting legislation. Finally, *upgrading* will be the improvement in the system called up by the client due to better perception of either his needs or the possibilities of the system. Notice that this definition of maintenance gives the potential of reaching a performance level far in excess of the original product.

The work breaks down into two further subdivisions, of which the second appears more frequently – at least up to the present:

Structured Maintenance is the activity carried out when the existing system was developed according to structured methods. The development documentation has been written and stored, the code has been fully commented (i.e. explanatory remarks inserted for every few lines of code) and understanding the main thrust of the design is correspondingly easy. As a result, applying modifications and benchmark testing the output will be cheap and effective.

Unstructured Maintenance occurs where a change is needed for some uncommented and undocumented code, typically COBOL, of some two to five years standing. The most important and frustrating phase is trying to analyse the raw code to decipher what the original intent of the designer was. The results are, at best, approximate. The resulting modified code is then tested in a manner which may, or may not, reflect the original test, if indeed there ever was an original test phase.

We will be discussing both of these modes of operation later on. For the moment, the major activities for each of them are indicated in the flow charts given in Figure 11.2. The main difference lies in the analysis phase on the right hand side, where the redesign will critically depend on trying to understand the original intent of the first designer. Again, note how part of the deliverables of the structured maintenance exercise will be the document upgrade. This will go back to the archive, and prepare the way for the next modification.

The Need for Maintenance

If it were possible to avoid reworking an existing system, then clearly this would be the most cost-effective option. However, a brief review will show how every system will inevitably need to evolve to match the changes that are going on around it. At some time or another these changes will include:

❑ Unavoidable upgrades in hardware, operating system and bought-in application programs. These tend to happen about once every year or so and will call for careful re-examination of the system interfaces to these items.

❏ Unavoidable modifications to the system objectives as the external world changes. This could be due to a new tax structure or examination syllabus.

❏ Unavoidable enhancement as the client's expectation is raised (or dashed!). The system will be modified to become more (or less) sophisticated in line with the client's hands-on experience, or that of his friends and colleagues.

❏ Unavoidable changes as the client's operating environment changes. Thus, the Newtown system could be extended to more wards or even linked across to another hospital.

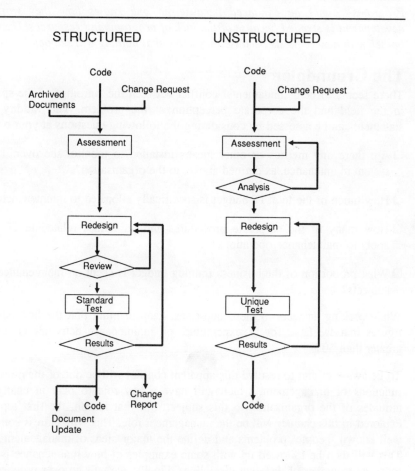

Figure 11.2: The maintenance flow plan

Even the most perfect system, when handed over, will experience these pressures and sooner or later will require that the system be modified. In addition, the majority of systems are far from perfect and will almost certainly contain embedded errors. These, too, will require urgent attention as and when the effects become apparent.

It seems virtually guaranteed that any system currently in design or already in use will need a great deal of further attention over its active life. If every system ever designed still needs on-going support, then this could spell out a lot of problems for the data processing industry. Take the opening words from reference 29:

'Maintenance is an epidemic which is threatening almost all DP organisations. Programs cannot be enhanced because no one knows how they work. New development is stymied because of the lack of programming resources. Users don't bother with new requests because they know that nothing will happen for years.'

The Groundplan

There seems to be a fundamental conflict between the warnings of the specialists in the field and the corporate perception of the problem. The validity of this statement can be assessed by considering the following questions at your own site:

❏ Are there any metrics or other means installed to monitor the overall cost of system maintenance, as defined above, to the organisation?

❏ How much of the total IT budget is specifically allocated to maintenance?

❏ How many of the corporate procedures and guidelines related to IT actually apply to maintenance operations?

❏ What proportion of the business training budget is spent on maintenance related subjects?

While seeking answers to these questions, keep in mind that the best percentage figures that we have for IT expenditure on maintenance activities is something greater than 50%.

To be aware of and to resolve this apparent conflict will be one of the more critical functions of management, which will have a key role to play in changing the attitudes of the organisation to this subject. For that reason, the first topic to be explored in this chapter will be the management role. This will address some of the well known 'people' problems and define the major areas of management interest. This will then be followed up with some examples of how maintenance is applied today to a number of different disciplines. Finally, we will go over proposals for a more effective maintenance plan which will establish the tools, rules and deliverables to be applied or generated during design. These will then permit low-cost but effective control of systems during the remainder of their future life span.

11.2 The Management Role

There are a number of problems concerning maintenance which are related to the way it is perceived in the organisation. Thus, it is often poorly paid, compared to development; it is not considered advanced technology and therefore not exciting, unlike development; there is a high staff turnover, and low job satisfaction; and, in the most general terms, it is not supported or appreciated by senior management or the executive. (Don't accept my word for it, check this out with *your* source of job advertising. Count the number of attractive-looking design jobs. Then count up the exciting, blue sky, meet-the-challenge, leading-edge maintenance related positions on offer.)

This, then, is the environment within which the maintenance manager has to operate, and the principal management task will be – to change that environment. In that context, the subject will be treated with reference to four main subject headings:

❑ Guidelines and Procedures

❑ Maintenance Team

❑ Senior Management

❑ External Interfaces

Guidelines and Procedures

In an ideal world, the obvious approach would be to design systems on the basis that they will need to be maintained. It may be obvious, but for most of the industry this remains an unachieved objective. We will be discussing an appropriate methodology to meet this goal in the second half of the chapter. However, for the moment, the applications of the type discussed in section 11.3 will need some working framework for resolving the problems that are currently being met. Each corporate and departmental environment will call up a specific set of procedures that will match their overall style of operation, but the maintenance set should include most of the following:

❑ In the first place, there has to be a defined procedure for the review, assessment, classification and acceptance of incoming maintenance jobs. The classification should define the scope of the job, e.g. 'quick and dirty', full scale module replacement, documentation update.

❑ The budget, schedule and resource requirements should be estimated and then reviewed and accepted by a higher review body, in line with some standard review format.

❑ The entire body of available information about that part of the system under redesign should be assembled and distributed to the design team. One copy should go to the archive. (If an archive does not exist, set one up.) This package may only be the coding printout, or it may include full existing documentation.

❑ The maintenance job specifications, test reports and project updates should comprise a standard and well defined set of documents which are to be reviewed, accepted and archived.

❑ Regular progress reviews with defined objectives should be set up. At all times, the ability to shut down the job should remain a viable option.

❑ Interface meetings should be established where all groups potentially affected by the planned modification or upgrade can be kept informed of the possible exposures and changes that they face.

The Maintenance Team

For the present, a relatively low-cost philosophy is the temporary reassignment of one or two design analysts (those who cannot plead a 'priority-red' status for their project) to sort out the latest maintenance problem. They will resent being moved, will probably know little about the programming language version under review, and will care even less. Under these circumstances, the potential for a competent solution is not too high. For an alternative, more professional approach, there should be set up a dedicated team which is respected, motivated and competent:

Justification

Cost-effective maintenance requires experts and specialists: specialists in debugging and repairing software systems. Even managers will be needed who have the qualities to manage maintenance projects and personnel. Setting up such a team will have a number of major advantages:

❑ It releases the design staff to do what they do best.

❑ The team will repeatedly use and be familiar with the standard procedures and document layouts.

❑ Each solution will be optimised and fast as experienced maintainers carry out the work.

❑ It will establish norms that external consultants will be able to follow. These consultants are usually called in to provide added expertise under peak overload conditions.

Motivation

Without any formal organisation or departmental status, those working in maintenance on a temporary basis are unlikely to have any high morale or motivation for the job. This, in turn, will lead to indifferent output which generates high error rates and poor documentation. It is true that the work itself is arduous and can be frustrating. But then so is front line ambulance work in times of war, and yet morale or lack of dedication has rarely been a problem in that particular field of endeavour.

What is needed is overt corporate recognition, both financial and social; the *camaraderie* of fellow colleagues working in the same discipline; and the self satisfaction that comes from seeing the job well done. For efficient processing of maintenance related problems, i.e. out of enlightened self-interest, the company should address the first of these points and set up an appropriate group or department, suitably funded. Then, over time, the second point above will automatically resolve itself. The last point is related to the competence and confidence of the workforce in carrying out its objectives, and that can only be generated and enhanced by suitable training.

Training

Maintenance is *not* a natural extension of the design process, it is a discipline in its own right. As such, there is an important need for formal teaching of the decision making skills and work techniques that go to make up maintenance. That leads to the next problem – there are not a lot of suitable tutorial courses available on the open market.

'Then how do most data processing professionals receive their training in maintenance? They give themselves on-the-job training (OJT), which in essence is no training at all. Many programmers never learn effective or even correct techniques of program maintenance.' (Reference 28 p. 243)

The choice may be limited. If the local higher education centre cannot help with a series of lectures, then set up your own internal seminar or equivalent, using the skilled personnel already present. In summary, a properly instituted and funded maintenance team is probably the second most important step taken by any organisation for getting the maintenance costs under control.

Senior Management

The *first* most important step has to be convincing the senior management that this is a serious problem worthy of their time, interest and commitment. Without this understanding, any improvements in the existing maintenance strategy are unlikely to occur.

The basic difficulty is that the benefits from setting up a maintenance group, formal procedures and training programs are only going to be realised in the long term. On the other hand, setting up these items could involve a significant capital outlay *here and now*. So the case had better be well prepared.

In broad terms, there are two main strategic objectives:

❑ Establish, both in principle and in practice, that a complete set of maintenance procedures should be instituted and funded. These should include the setting up of a formal trained group to address maintenance related problems.

❑ Obtain agreement that all future systems will be designed using some fully structured methodology. This will enable the system to be effectively maintained during its active life.

The first one will help to make the current work more efficient. This work will probably be concerned with undocumented and unstructured systems. Conversely, the second objective will ensure that maintenance carried out on systems under current and future design will be faster, much cheaper and more effective.

External Interfaces

Making changes to existing programs and systems may have some unfortunate side-effects on other system packages, operating system file management (and related subroutines), and application programs as well as to the hardware performance. It will be impossible to completely eliminate these interactive mismatches, but careful review of the impact of potential changes will help to keep these added problems to a minimum. For that reason, good contact should be kept with:

End Users

These are the people who have the definitive knowledge on the current problem. Whether it is fault removal or function enhancement, only the users can completely describe why a change is considered necessary. In addition, they will probably have a good idea of the impact that any particular proposed solution will have on the system in use.

External Users

No system works as an independent island. It will interact with, say, corporate headquarters costings, the central student examinations database, the area oncology records unit and so on. Any change made to a working system will have to be analysed and tested for possible effects on all of the peripheral systems. The best persons to do that will be the external users.

Suppliers

The only people who really understand application programs are the suppliers. If your system utilises or interacts with these programs in some way, then check with the customer-support group for final clearance before going ahead with any proposed amendments to the interface.

Archive

Procedures should be in place which allow for ease of access to the archive for a 'browse' facility. This is equivalent to scanning through the index or microfiche at the public library for references to a required topic of interest. Ideally there should be a text-based archive index which can be queried to list articles or documents containing a given character string, say, *maintenance* or *failure mechanisms* and so on. In any case, the archive will play a central role in any maintenance feasibility studies and should be located at a convenient site close to the maintenance work area.

In this section, we have outlined some of the tasks, objectives and contacts that will be part of the job for any maintenance manager. More particularly, we have discussed the potential procedures and guidelines that will be needed in a maintenance environment; the formulation of a team that could carry out the work in a professional and cost-effective manner; the strategic objectives that will require support from senior management; and the personal contacts, who will help to ensure that the system modifications will generate no obvious mismatches with other systems and programs.

Independent of any advertised job description, the role of maintenance manager *is* potentially a challenging, multi-disciplinary and very hi-tech position. In the current maintenance climate, it will also need a high calibre candidate to make a success of it.

11.3 Applications

It is not always possible to wait for ideal conditions before starting some new maintenance exercise or task. The personnel may not be available, or the work site has still to be agreed – there is always one signature outstanding. For all that, there has to be some practical way to process and resolve existing maintenance problems under the current conditions.

This section will review some examples of the way maintenance can be implemented in a number of different disciplines. We will look briefly at equipment maintenance, third-party agreements, and maintenance applied to long-term policies. The final item will provide a basis for carrying out changes in an unstructured maintenance environment.

Equipment Maintenance

For all but the largest organisations, there is little point in carrying an in-house Maintenance Department to handle the running repairs to the hardware. The problem is that it is hard to standardise, there are many different technologies, and the products change almost every year. It could be a full time job just trying to keep service information and repair stock for, say, printers, where working equipment may range across line, daisy-wheel, dot-matrix, jet bubble and laser printers – all from a variety of different sources.

For most situations, there is a simple answer to any questions relating to the repair and upkeep of hardware – call in the supplier. Unless there are special circumstances, the easiest way to maintain hardware, cabling and peripherals is to take out a suitable contract either with the original manufacturer or with your equipment supplier (if he has the resources to undertake maintenance). The only decision remaining is the choice between, say, the four hour 'our engineer will guarantee to be at your site' type of contract, or the 'bring it round to the repair lab, and we will see what we can do next week' agreement. There is a dramatic variation in cost between these two types of service, and the final choice is up the client.

In parallel with this, it may be possible to take out insurance which will indemnify the company against equipment malfunction and any loss of business activity resulting. The added cost of this insurance may perhaps be traded off by using the cheaper but slower service contract.

Regardless of the strategy adopted, breakdown records should be kept to indicate the supplier, part number, type of fault, supplier service record, and frequency of occurrence. This is precisely the sort of data that will be of value the next time the company goes out for a major re-equip exercise.

One last point. If you have a maintenance agreement with a supplier or any other outside organisation, treat them with a measure of respect, since one day you may really need a favour from them in a hurry. In this light, Figure 11.3 is, perhaps, not a fully recommended code of conduct. (This set of selected items was taken from a list found on a certain departmental notice-board!)

Third-party Maintenance

One other option not discussed so far, involves the use of a third-party service organisation. For a variety of reasons, the manufacturers would generally prefer to have the maintenance carried out by their own service department. However, with a separate manufacturer agreement, it is always the other guy. If your files won't print then the software application support team blames the hardware supplier; the PC manufacturer blames the printer interface; and they all suggest that the networking link is basically the source of the problem. This sort of dispute is one reason for the growing popularity of the third-party service agreement.

There are three main areas where this option has been exercised. The first is concerned with running and maintaining the entire computer operations in the company (facilities management). This will involve bringing the third-party workforce permanently onto your site, in order to run and maintain all your equipment and systems. The second is purely related to equipment maintenance, where the hardware is serviced and maintained by someone who may come to your site temporarily, as and when the work requires it. The third case covers the area of disaster recovery management, where the service involves a complete duplication of every transaction carried out by your system. This is followed by transmission and storage at some off-site location. In the event of, for example, a fire or an explosion, all the system programs and up-to-date data can be brought back on line within hours.

☞After several days, when the machine malfunction has become a major emergency, place an URGENT call for service. Fridays are best, but any day after 4pm is OK.

☞Be sure that the lights are off in the room where the machine is to be repaired. A service engineer likes to demonstrate that he can fix it blindfolded.

☞The machine should be as dirty and greasy as possible. A mixture of oil and pencil sharpener shavings works well. If the machine has electronic components, add staples and paper clips.

☞Assign someone to supervise the repair; a person who has never seen the machine before is preferred. Halitosis is a plus.

Figure 11.3: How to help your service engineer

In these three cases, the host company will pay for outside expertise and can usually negotiate exactly the specific service that they require. At all times, if the service is not satisfactory, they can seek a better service from a competitor. Thus, they can have the advantage of one source maintaining *all* their equipment, regardless of make or version, while, at the same time, retaining full commercial control of the situation in an open and competitive market.

It is not all peaches and cream. Such agreements have to be entered into with a measure of caution and the contractual details should be studied at length. After all, you could be entrusting the entire fabric of your commercial trading capability, the operations of all your computer based systems, into the hands of perfect strangers. This is not something to be undertaken lightly. For all that, these agreements are being entered into by a growing number of companies.

Policy Maintenance

Consider once again the last report at the head of the chapter. This is the sort of situation which system managers have nightmares over, and yet it happens again and again – and not just with mergers. Changing three year plans every six to nine months, centralising control in the summer then decentralising the following winter, designing the system for mainframes, but installing it on minis – it has all been done before. To be frank, your scope for controlling or minimising the impact of these about-turns is limited, but they do occur and you should attempt to limit the damage. This might include one or more of the following options:

❏ Keep the management informed of the potential cost and staff morale impacts resulting from the latest proposed changes.

❏ Make sure that the overall costs of the last exercise in this area are well known, with a view to limiting future excursions of the same type.

❏ Offer counter proposals based on a structured evolution rather than revolution.

❏ Protect your group from the change and cover the result with suitable smoke-screens.

❏ Swim quietly with the tide, whatever its direction.

❏ When all else fails, keep your *Curriculum Vitae* up to date, well polished and ready for all eventualities!

Unstructured Maintenance

Maintenance has been considered a serious problem in software systems over the last two decades. Unfortunately, during that period, there have been no dramatic breakthroughs in any recommended treatment. The problems are largely caused by trying to apply maintenance to 'alien code'. These are assemblies, packages or modules of software statements which are currently functioning (or malfunctioning) and which more or less satisfy the criterion of the four 'no's:

No Designer: The original designer of the system and/or original code programmer will have a valuable role in explaining the philosophy that went into the particular design. By the same token, the absence of the original design team, which is far more usual, will ensure that the secrets of the original design objectives may never be deciphered.

No Methodology: If there is a clear adherence to some well established methodology for the design process (such as SADT or SSADM) the resulting documentation and system structure will materially help in determining the original objectives and the selected means to achieve them. Again, the usual absence of any structured approach means that each system is more or less uniquely assembled, the existing documentation will probably not match the current system operation, and it will be difficult to determine any underlying strategies that will affect the redesign.

No Modularity: One of the early procedures in structured system design is to carry out a top-down analysis which will break up the proposed system into manageable-sized system modules. These can then be sensibly designed and tested independent of the other modules. Such a design will allow for maintenance within a module which is more or less self contained, and restricts the scope of introduced errors and the resulting rework.

Yesterday's systems were not always designed this way, which usually means that the scope of design comprises the entire system.

No Comments: It seems a generally agreed rule that code without comments will be difficult to understood *by the programmer himself* six months after having written the lines. (For some strong words on this topic, see page 73 of reference 28.) In any case, there are virtually no acceptable excuses for not commenting on newly designed code i.e. explaining the purpose of each few lines or group of code in simple language.

This type of information is invaluable in assessing software for maintenance purposes. Equally, when it is absent, the problems of understanding the flow of the program code are magnified manyfold, if not made downright impossible.

An outline of the maintenance position with alien code is shown in Figure 11.4, and it is clear that when three or four of the 'no's are present, the evaluation of the proposed code modification will be difficult, costly, and almost certainly lacking in integrity. If we go back to Figure 11.2 for a moment, the first activity is to assess the nature and difficulty of the proposed maintenance change and to evaluate its worth to the company. Here we can see that the analysis element on the right hand side is the major sticking point. Only when such an investigation has been carried out can any real assessment be made of the difficulty and potential value to the organisation. But, from the above discussion, this investigation, itself, may turn out to be very costly to implement. What can be done?

The initial response is: not very much. If you are looking for a solution that will maintain an alien code system here and now, it is going to be a costly and time consuming business. Fully understanding the purpose of the coding and generating test routines that will provide some measure of system validation is going to take a lot of effort. Even throwing out the entire package has its drawbacks. The rework costs drop to zero and the new system can be fully structured, i.e. future maintainable. However, it may take one to two *years* to come up with this workable replacement. Throwing scarce resource into providing full documentation for a largely obsolete system also lacks any real appeal. As an alternative, providing the absolute minimum rework in recoding will allow the package to stagger on for another few months. This is not an elegant or recommended solution, but it is understandable why such an approach should ever be adopted.

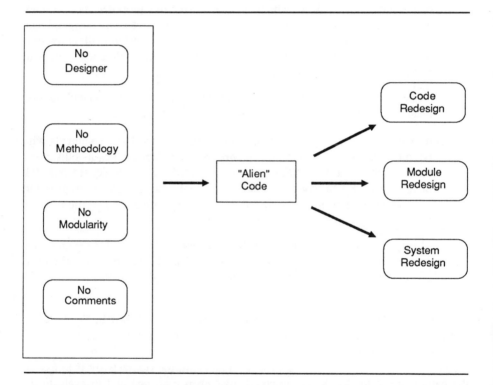

Figure 11.4: The unstructured maintenance format

This is the situation for the short term. However, when considering long term strategies, there are a number of positive steps that can be taken:

❏ A team can be set up to analyse the existing system(s) while it is still operational and to liaise with the workforce who will be familiar with it. The ultimate objective will be to provide or restore working documentation for the overall system and for this documentation to be available for the next upgrade or system iteration.

❑ All current rework programs, however unsatisfactory, can be planned to be formally documented with copies sent to the archive. This will eventually lead to a high proportion of the system having been repaired and thereby documented. Further work will then be relatively easy and reliable.

❑ All current and future system design will be fully structured (see the next section). This will limit the number of unmaintainable systems, and these will slowly be replaced with time.

❑ Analyse the older systems for the most critical elements. Prioritise your resources for reworking in just those areas.

❑ Establish a specialised 'hit-team' of experts in the language and coding used in obsolete systems.

❑ Implement a set of common procedures for analysing and recoding old systems. These can be upgraded with feedback from the staff and will become increasingly more effective as the experience of the maintenance team grows.

All these possible activities will cost effort and take expensive resource to set up. However, if there are a number of obsolete systems currently in use within the organisation, then they are going to need full on-going maintenance and all this added expense will be fully justified.

Summary

This brings to an end the review of *ad hoc* maintenance techniques applied to various hardware and software situations within current systems. We have looked at the options for hardware support and upkeep which basically involve using either the supplier and some independent third-party consultant. Then the subject of long term policy variation and change was addressed. Support and recovery positions under these circumstances are not easy, but there is some scope for possibly reducing the impact.

Finally, in the last part of this section, we have spent some time in trying to understand the problems of maintaining unstructured packages and looked for means to minimise the difficulties that this type of work can cause. There are no satisfactory or even cheap solutions in this area, but some procedures can be undertaken to tackle the long term effects.

11.4 A Strategy for Maintenance

The major step for any organisation lies in recognising that maintenance is a serious drain on the organisation's resources and will need a formal, planned approach in order to reduce the problem to manageable proportions. In providing such a strategy, it will be become clear that most of the related topics have already been discussed in other chapters. However, it is only in this section that all the various strands of the structured methodology are brought together for co-ordinated application. Thus, good maintenance practices will only become possible after formulating and applying standard procedures for design, documentation, test, change control, and configuration management. Adopting these procedures will promote the development and maintenance of information systems in accordance with a coherent and efficient plan of action.

This, at least, is a most laudable objective, even if it is not always realised (or realisable) at present. So let's start with the main criteria for designing systems with maintenance in mind.

Design

In essence, the main design objective is to avoid the generation and proliferation of alien code. Thus, the system should be analysed and modularised before any design activity begins. This is achieved by providing top-down definitions of the various blocks that go to make up the system. Then the development methodology should be selected (e.g. prototyping) and clearly defined. Conventions for the construction of Entity-Relation Diagrams and Data Flow Diagrams should be established and and adhered to. Where CASE tools cannot be applied, institute rigourous checks of the ER diagrams and Table layouts in the database for full 100% conformance between the two. Finally the coding style should be structured (no spaghetti, no GOTO statements, etc.) and fully commented. Where a CASE tool is to be employed, the workforce should be well versed in its application, and the particular version in use should be defined and copied to the archive.

Documentation

The only way to understand the system design objectives, strategies, and processes after the event is through the study of three text based groups of material, each of which should be stored and available on demand:

Specifications

The basic definitions of objectives are laid down in the requirement, test and product specifications. There may well be many other defining documents, but these represent the core material. As they are modified or upgraded for any reason, then each iteration should be added to the store of all the other previous versions along with the reason for the change. Note that the *List of Documents* document is itself an important and maintainable item in the specification set.

Project Documentation

Printed material related to the project consists of reports of various strategic presentations, progress and update meetings, test data results, interim performance assessments, user feedback comments, policy decision statements, glossaries of labels and filenames and all the other printed inputs that are used in the business of project administration. They establish where the project has been and where it is going, and how long this wondrous transformation was originally planned to take.

This treasure trove is vital material for the system archaeologist who is trying to uncover the original thrust of the project and which decisions were made and, more importantly, why.

Once again, we come to the recurring if fundamental requirement: all these project related documents should be reviewed, signed off and stored so they can be made available for study at some later date.

Code

The written program code, along with the required comments, should be copied and stored. Every new version update should also be stored with an explanatory text outlining the reasons for the latest modifications.

In addition, the operational code should be backed up onto a suitable magnetic media. Other software, such as the commercial applications coupled to the program software under design will also need to be backed up and stored in the same area. The version wanted is not the latest, but the one used when the program was being designed and tested.

These three sets of documents go a long way to defining the nature of the project and the way it evolved at the time of design. If they are all available, the subsequent change to any of the packages or modules should be easy to apply (the source code is fully documented), fast (and therefore cost-effective), and sensibly error free (i.e. reliable). That, on balance, is not a bad trade-off for the bother of having to generate and maintain documentation.

Test

Of all the activities carried out before installation, test is the most expensive. This is because it takes about 40-50% of all the applied pre-handover resource just to carry out this work (ref. 4 p. 20 and ref. 24 p. 152 Figure 9.1). However, from the management viewpoint, the main impact is simply the availability of the test specification and, later, the test performance report. The key feature, for maintenance purposes, is that the test specification satisfies three criteria:

❑ It actually gets reviewed and archived

❑ It is formulated in line with the general documentation layout and test strategy of the organisation, and

❑ It is structured to monitor and measure the specific performance and parametric values defined in the requirement specification of the system under review.

Adherence to these rules will make the documents easy to read and follow across different departments of the company and at different times. In addition, the recorded test performance will then offer a useful basis for comparison for all later modifications which will all need to be re-tested for debugging and performance purposes.

Change Control

For maintenance, the important word in this heading is 'control'. That is to say, the rigourous limiting of change only to those modifications that have been formally accepted and documented by some agreed procedures. The last thing wanted is to solve a problem by some *ad hoc* cure which was brilliant but unrecorded. At that point, the documentation and the working system have parted company and this has effectively sabotaged any further maintenance efforts on the system.

Another reason for the disciplined control of modifications to the system is the need for a thorough review of all changes and the formal testing of the relevant module after any changes have been implemented. This is to eliminate, hopefully, the phenomenon known as 'side effects', which is the unintended introduction of error as a result of making a modification to some part of the system. Some of these knock-on effects can be very subtle and a useful list of the commonly found side effects is given in reference 28, page 93. However, for the moment, a simple example involving the use of procedure calls in Pascal should illustrate the nature of the problem.

A section of structured code calls up a procedure (the Pascal equivalent of a sub-routine). That is to say, somewhere in the block of code a particular line directs the program flow from the main block to the first line of code in the procedure. Now, if the main portion of code no longer needs to apply the procedure, then this procedure can be fully deleted with no loss of program integrity. This, of course, is completely true, provided only that no other line in the rest of the main program, *or in any other procedure*, ever calls up that same now-deleted procedure. Until this has been fully and carefully checked, the exposure to a possible side effect remains. Change should generally be introduced with a great deal of caution – it tends to save money in the long run.

Another important aspect of maintenance is *priority*. Too much of the available effort and resource is expended on repairing and improving systems already in operation with the client. There has to be some way of identifying the truly critical failures that require a heavy commitment of effort, as opposed to the more trivial problem that can be left for a while. Well, there is such a way and it goes under the rather prosaic title of 'record keeping'. This is not something for immediate assistance, but will prove invaluable in the long run. Simply log, either manually or via a database table, every act of corrective maintenance that is undertaken for an existing system – the part of the system that requires attention, the nature of the apparent fault, and the scope of the change that was introduced to solve the problem. After 10 to 20 such calls to a system, a picture will begin to emerge as to the areas of weakness in the original design. This will not only offer useful clues to the probable source of the next problem to be tackled on a piece-meal basis, but it will also point to the block or blocks which should be re-appraised and possibly redesigned in their entirety.

In conclusion, it can be seen that some discipline is needed to keep working systems as fully maintainable items. This maintainability will be materially assisted by introducing or supporting a change-control mechanism to protect the integrity of the documentation, to minimise the introduction of side-effects, and to identify those areas of the system that require the major on-going repair activity.

Configuration Management

Some basic definitions and an introduction to this subject have already been given in section 5 of Chapter 8 – Communications. However, the real application and value of CM is only established when some repair or improvement of existing equipment is called for. It is at that point that the ready availability of accurate documentation (discussed a few pages back) will save weeks or months of scavenging for possibly unreliable information.

Briefly, CM will have two main objectives and one central location.

The first objective will be to store documentation about each system component. In addition it will also store the definition of every component with which it interacts at any one time. The second will be to store the actual components themselves. Thus, the documentation related, for example, to a particular version of Unix installed on a Hewlett Packard machine should be stored, *as well as* the tape of the actual working version of the operating system, *as well as* full information about the physical machine on which it was operated at the time of the design.

The location or repository of all this data will be the archive, which exists as a logical entity and as a physical address where access to the information may be sought. Note that access to this information is not free, but should be allocated and controlled by the *Archive Librarian* using physical access constraints, passwords, etc. There are two main reasons for this:

❑ The bulk of the information kept in the archive may well be historical, but is still likely to be company confidential. (Last year's financial analysis reports and strategic objective guidelines are obsolete, but could still be of enormous, if undesirable, interest outside the company.)

❏ Indiscriminate usage and careless borrowings from the archive imply that, sooner or later, documents will disappear or be misplaced. At that point, the integrity and utility of the Archive for later users will be seriously diminished.

For most practical purposes, long term maintenance for the larger installations can only be effective if there are computer based procedures for the installation and upkeep of a configuration management tool. The nature of these procedures, the actual CM package, the scope of the documentation storing and retrieval mechanisms – all these are open to selection and review for each project. However, a CM archiving procedure has to be driven by the corporate strategic aims. Once again, this type of structured and disciplined working environment has important long term advantages, but is costly to set up initially. For this reason, there has to be a top-down recognition and support from senior management of the value and need for such an investment.

We will finish this section with a short overview of one dedicated CM tool which runs on a variety of hardware platforms and under a number of operating systems including MS-DOS. Again, this is considered as a representative product, and no endorsement is implied with any of the following discussion. The product is called Software Management System or SMS from Intasoft and its main features include:

Version Control: Automatically maintains and updates different version levels for any configuration item (CI) whenever changed for any reason. Note that a *configuration item* can be any predefined software module within the total package, any document to be maintained or stored within the documentation plan, or any hardware item operating as part of the hardware platform. For text-based CIs, the differences between versions is readily available. Additional data, such as date and originating author are also stored with each version level.

Symbolic Names: Assemblies of CIs, each with its own individual version level, can be identified as a group using a symbolic name. Thus the entire system could have a symbolic name calling up nested assemblies down to basic CIs or modules. As an example, the system documentation on a given date could be given a symbolic name which identifies the various versions of all the specifications, minutes, and other reports that go to make up that particular assembly of documents.

Mod. Requests: The modification request (MR) can be used to formalise and control the change process. Every MR is stored in a specific MR database along with its status at any point i.e. *submitted*, or *accepted*, etc.

Authorisation: SMS files can be protected by ensuring that only fully authorised users will have access to the CM system.

In common with most packages today, the user can set up his required function via a series of menus, with separate help messages available as required, and with extensive report writing facilities. The master menu is illustrated in Figure 11.5 with all the main functions selected with a single key depression. This will often lead to a lower level menu with again another single key selection for the specific facility required. There are full audit facilities in that each change is automatically logged along with the date and user who made the modification.

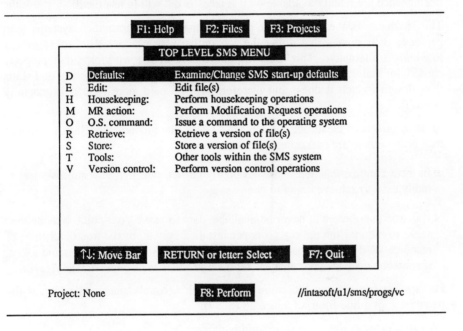

Figure 11.5: The master menu for a CM support tool

11.5 Summary

The last item to be addressed in the classic development life cycle is maintenance.

From that point of view, it is fitting that the last topic to be discussed in the book is also on the same subject. And yet, as this chapter has emphasised, the optimum time to consider maintenance is right at the beginning of the project. This is the one time when the strategies are open to analysis, the procedures are under review and the design objectives are still to be established. All these should, ideally, reflect one of the real targets of effective development – providing a working system with low post-installation maintenance costs.

The high cost of present day maintenance seems reasonably established. The GOTO spaghetti and lack of comments, the incomprehensible program labels, the alien code, the new program extensions, the management changes – they all play a part in ensuring that the repair and upkeep bills remain unreasonably high. Each new study appears to project an even worse picture that the last and the future is painted in ever bleaker shades. Does it have to be that way? Of course not! There is no great educational or cultural divide that prevents anyone from understanding the implications of archiving documents, of forming maintenance teams, of change control procedures, or of configuration management. The tools for structured maintenance are readily available – all it takes is the will to use them.

This, perhaps, is the real test for project managers in information systems – to persuade their bosses that doing the job properly is *cheaper* than any apparent low-budget alternative. This, plus the convincing of the workforce that properly carried out maintenance is more challenging and calls for more maturity and skills than design (which it does) and therefore will be paid more (which it generally doesn't).

In these efforts to clean out the Augean Stables, the modern day Hercules should take heart – there are two things in his favour:

❏ In most centres, maintenance is so poorly carried out, that any improvement is really easy to achieve – and to demonstrate.

❏ It is true that there will never be available data to prove your point. No-one ever seeks to monitor the upkeep costs per installed system, or the true percentage of resource used to keep obsolete programs running. But then, by the same token, if someone disputes your analysis *let them produce their own back-up figures.*

Perhaps we can sum up the entire chapter with a simple statement which is the paraphrase of a line from reference 28 (p. 37):

"No structured design – no structured maintenance"

Questions

1. Your computer department is so busy repairing *ad hoc* software and hardware crashes, that they have no time to set up a maintenance function.

   Provide some proposals for reducing the pressure on the department.

2. Outline some possible procedures and activities that could be set up to ensure that your organisation has a fully structured strategy for reliable Hardware utilisation.

3. You have been offered some eight year old PCs as a gift.

   Establish a response and justify your reaction as a:

   a) Start up home-based company

   b) Computer buff in the Data Processing department

   c) Finance department manager.

4. Your executive is unwilling to allocate personnel specifically to maintenance. At the same time, you know that the computer room is virtually at a standstill with respect to new projects.

> Given a three month period, what would you do to convince your management to reconsider their position?

5. The key patient data in the Newtown hospital system can be unavailable for up to 60 minutes as a result of any one system failure. After that time, it must be available and on-line to users again.

> What proposals would you make to tackle this problem?

12

Wrap up

Productivity tools cannot help jumbled databases

As things stand the majority of IT does not support organisations' business objectives, Goodair believes. He has come across companies where 90% of the software written has been unnecessary.

Computer Weekly p. 2 13.10.88

Hard truths for the software industry

If the UK software industry is not to decline further, something akin to a management revolution is needed. Otherwise, it might well suffer the same fate the UK motor industry experienced 15 years ago.

Computing p. 22 26.10.89

Steering your strategy through stormy weather

Why is it that developing IT, or any other strategy, seems to end in so little achievement and so much disappointment?

Computer Weekly p. 13 25.1.90

NHS plan on sickbed

A lynchpin of the government's health service reforms has been branded unrealistic, underfunded and hopelessly disorganised.

Called the Hospital Information and Support System, it is intended to be a complete information network for hospitals, capable of supplying data for cost analysis.

But it has been slammed for being:

Unrealistic - *The operational requirement is eight inches thick and has been dismissed as a "wish list".*

Underfunded - *The proposals for one site alone are up to £8 million more expensive than the government's estimates.*

Disorganised - *The Department of Health has yet to decide how much of what it wants is worth the money.*

Datalink p. 1 4.9.89

12.1 Introduction

There seems to be a bit of a contradiction. If we look at the quotes, we see there the sort of difficulties that are typical across the industry. On the one hand we have the warnings expressed in no uncertain terms about the clear need for more discipline and better, more reliable deliveries to the client. On the other, the repeating pattern of the client asking the wrong questions, defining the wrong product and, in effect, setting up a disaster of his own making. Remember, this is not some historical exercise - we are talking about the cost-effectiveness of information technology as a contemporary problem and one which shows no material signs of having been solved over the last two or three decades.

Requirements have grown 10 times in as many years and hardware has improved by the most amazing bounds to meet these needs. Analytical tools have been developed of the utmost precision and automation techniques have proliferated to cover every possible requirement in an efficient and reliable manner. The techniques are there and the analysts and designers have been trained to use them. And yet, for all that, the capabilities of system design in providing on-going user satisfaction does not seem to have made any significant advance over the same period.

All through the book we have shown examples of experienced, well trained and well-meaning individuals and groups making a complete hash of things. As we defined success in the first chapter, the examples at the beginning of each chapter have shown a conspicuous lack of it. This is not to say that there are no successes; or that there have been no developer and end-user teams which have generated a useful system meeting all the targets as set out at the time of the contract. What is clear, though, is that there have been a number of projects which decidedly do not make it in the success stakes and which have constituted nothing less than a catastrophe for some of the unfortunate participants. There has to be a better way. We will start this chapter by briefly going over the main lessons of the preceding chapters. Then we can get on to a review of the current situation and follow this up with some practical advice on what could possibly be done to improve on the current malaise.

That, at least, is the objective.

12.2 System Development - An Overview

This section will provide a short reminder of the main issues raised in each section of the book.

Introduction

In this part, we identified the key activities of information system development:

❏ The critical part of the life cycle is the Feasibility Study leading up to the writing, reviewing and acceptance of the Functional Requirement Specification. Mistakes made at this point will cost the most to correct at some later stage.

❏ The most expensive part of the life cycle only occurs after the system has been installed with the client. Estimates from various sources suggest that anything from 40 to 70% of the total cost will be expended at this stage.

❏ The work of system development is a multi-disciplinary exercise, and involves the complex and co-operative interworking of a number of people in different teams. This smooth interworking is vital for the project to go forward without major delays.

Background

Here the main thrust lay in exploring the tools and techniques that are used in the development process:

❏ The initial phase of any design activity lies in converting the physical model of the existing system into a logical format. For this purpose, the Data Flow Diagram and the Entity-Relationship Diagram are used to establish the way in which data is moved round the organisation and the entities that are relevant for this operation. All elements used in these diagrams are entered into the Data Dictionary, which ensures that they are formally defined, either in terms of other elements, or with a description of the simple function that is carried out.

❏ The concept of a structured design lies in the following of formal rules that are laid down as part of the project activities. Thus, the documentation will be defined in advance, written, formally reviewed and accepted as part of this process. One important tool that can be used in a structured environment is the CASE tool, which allows for screen based generation of the DF and E-R diagrams along with an automated generation and upkeep of the Data Dictionary.

❏ The last part of this section was concerned with the interaction of people involved in the project. Here the important causes of friction and low morale were reviewed along with a simple technique to assess the potential co-operation that could be expected from the various teams.

The Requirement Specification

This section was used to evaluate all the factors that should be involved in writing the specification.

❑ Before the specification can be finalised, there are a number of system features that have to be agreed by all the parties. For example, what database system is to be used, which CASE tool, and so on. In addition, system parameters related to performance have to be established. Finally some consideration has to be given to safety and security in order to design them into the system from the outset.

❑ Finally the specification, itself, can be addressed. This will involve bringing together all the imposed constraints - i.e. budget limits, schedules, resources and system complexity - into a realistic program that lies within the capabilities of the design team. At that point the specification can be written. In the same timeframe, the full documentation program is defined along with the justification for each document.

Managing the Design

There is little or no description of the actual development activity as carried out by the programmers and analysts. However, an outline of the *management* of the design and test phase is established and reviewed in this part.

❑ A general listing of the items to be developed and handed over to the client will be needed to define, in effect, the total workload associated with the project. In addition, this part discusses the possible procedures that should be introduced to ensure good project management. Finally, the interaction of the staff with the project and some of the problems that can occur were evaluated.

❑ One of the key aspects of any co-operative undertaking is ensuring that efficient communication is available. The different types of communication were covered and the pros and cons for each application were established.

❑ Another area that requires close attention is related to change. Change in the environment, requirements or workforce, will always add to the difficulties of steering the project to completion. It is only by analysing the various types of change that optimum solutions to the resulting problems can be realised.

The Post-design Phase

Once the design has been completed in the logical form and translated into a physical system, there are only two major activities outstanding in the life cycle:

❑ The installation of the new system at the client's site will often cause some initial dissatisfaction. The only way to avoid this, is thorough planning in advance and meticulous attention to detail.

❑ Finally, once the system has been installed, there will be a need for continued enhancement or improvement of the system for the rest of its operational life. It was shown that most modifications can be carried out effectively, providing that the original design was implemented in a structured way. This implies full design reviews, storage of documentation and formal reporting of all decisions made.

12.3 The Current Reality

The last section has outlined a system development plan based on the premise that existing projects tend not to be successful and that maintenance is the most important cost factor of the entire development program. The problem is that this cannot be easily proven or substantiated. There are some examples that support this view and there are some authorities that tend to offer a similar sort of message. But that is not proof. There may be many systems that are currently installed successfully. There could be 80%, or 30%, or some other percentage of all systems that meet the original requirements and are delivered reasonably near to the target date for about the budgeted figure. It is possible that maintenance for most systems is not as serious a problem as it has been painted. Or it could be worse.

The reality is that there is no statistical accumulation of data to indicate a probability of success. There have been some well reported, very large system exercises for military and space purposes, but for the majority of medium and small-scale system development programs, there are just no figures available. If you look at the physical factors involved, the complexity of the environment, the tools, the learning curve, and the variability of the delivered objectives, then perhaps this lack of definitive support information is not so surprising. What is the potential effect for system design of changing the database type, operating system, or networking software? Not clear. Now, on top of this, estimate the potential range of the various human factors in the design and use of information systems. The uncertainty expands again. We may reasonably conclude that there is no likelihood of generic data being available in the near future.

No matter. If you really want to establish the truth about these assumptions on system development, remember that you are close to the most important source there is - your own departmental performance figures. Of course, the data does not yet exist in any useable form. But it does exist, and it may well be of value if you have the cunning and perseverance to extract it. (Keep in mind that any resulting information may be of explosive value. If, for example, you go round suggesting that your internal MIS department has a 28% success rate for installed systems, there is likely to be a strong political backlash.)

However, in the first place, let's establish the need for this data. The argument goes like this: the conventional expert wisdom holds that maintenance is the most important cost factor in any design program. Furthermore, of all the pre-handover activities, the same conventional wisdom holds that test is the most expensive. Sociologists might even suggest that *the* most critical dependency for the entire system implementation exercise is the workforce and their morale.

Now, in spite of all this, everyday system managers take the position that design is the only significant activity of the whole life cycle.

This last statement can be readily supported by looking at the general demand for the different parts of System Development. This demand can be indirectly monitored by assessing the availability of material on the open market, assuming that the more the demand grows the more the market will provide material to satisfy that demand. On that basis, you can analyse the availability by book titles (bookshop or library), convention and symposium subjects (professional magazines), and recruitment requirements (advertising sources). In the field of System Development, design is the one topic that outstrips all the rest.

Here is the real contradiction. The experts, consultants and educationalists offer one view of priorities, while the end-user in the shape of line managers and forward planners are creating a demand for something completely different. It could be argued that the current management position is perfectly correct, but the inescapable fact remains that a lot of system development programs up to the present time appear to have been properly managed and yet have been woefully inadequate in meeting their objectives.

Let's summarise the current position. There is a large trained and motivated workforce ready to design and install systems. There are the corresponding end-users who are eager to use the new systems. The hardware, application programs and support tools are available and more or less adequate for the task. The only remaining thing open to review is the management direction and priorities. And there a conflict appears to exist with no means to resolve it as there is no data to substantiate either point of view.

12.4 System Design Effectiveness

So how are we to get this data? What are the standard metrics for measuring the overall utility of a systems design team over a number of years? How can the investment in a software Quality Assurance group be justified? Where is the proven pay-off in budgeting for a full documentation set, its production, review and storage?

These are valuable questions. It is, perhaps, unfortunate that for most sites they cannot be answered at this stage, because up to now there have been virtually no records kept. This makes it relatively difficult for any rational assessment or logical decision-making to occur.

Are there any indirect methods of getting this data? Let's simplify the problem: is there any way to estimate the ratio of design to the sum of other activities in the total work carried out by any system design group? The answer is a qualified 'yes'. It is qualified for three reasons. In the first place, the data will be of the indirect type, and the inferred connection may not in fact exist. Secondly, the information may have to be 'snooped' for, and that may rapidly reach the level where the situation and objectives become unethical. Finally you may not have the time required to carry out the analysis. For all that, let's look at some possible sources of data:

❏ Time cards may hold the secret, assuming that you are allowed access to the records over the last few years. The time-cards in question will belong to the members of the design group. If these cards exist, then it is likely that each project will be referenced by a different number. By analysing all the hours against the projects some overall picture of the group activities will begin to emerge.

❏ Project estimates could prove of interest, if they were ever kept. The original estimates can be compared to the eventual accounting figures (again, if they are available) which establish the true overall cost of the particular project. The difference will relate to the initial lack of recognition of difficulty or the amount of time taken up in maintaining previous projects.

❏ Regular Schedule information, if available, will chart the slippages throughout the development program and will usually indicate the reason. This may directly provide the required data.

❏ End-user recollections might be politically slanted, but they should know how often their system has needed correction or added work to enable it to work properly.

❏ In the event that there is a configuration management facility (and you have permission to browse through it) then the dates and authors will be held for all modifications of current and past projects. With the names and period for the present project, you can scan the changes introduced to all other systems. Any changes produced this way constitute the current maintenance work.

It has to be said that these methods will not necessarily guarantee results in any useful form. On the other hand, they might provide exactly the data you need to justify a change of emphasis.

Certainly answers are needed. If you have the patience, the most reliable way to generate this sort of information is to set up a direct reporting mechanism whereby the group or individuals identify what amount of work is carried out each week and on what activity. After three to six months of such reports, you should have a clear idea of just how effectively the department is operating - and where the faults lie.

12.5 The Way Forward

So far in this chapter we have discussed the mechanics of running a system design project. Apply this tool, write that document, and so on. But, as we suggested in the first chapter, this is simply not enough. This is what all those consultants, specialists, bank departments, local government DP groups, software houses, retail chains and international companies are all doing. And the results are not always satisfactory.

As shown above, I cannot *prove* that this new approach is valid. Nevertheless, looking at all the indirect evidence, I am confident that a change of outlook is required and that new lessons need to be learnt. On this basis, there are three lessons that can be drawn from this book.

In the first place, the project philosophy has to change. Currently, the resource and funding is concentrated on design. Very commendable, but it will have to be altered. A project should be structured from the outset to ensure that the maintenance is the crucial property of any system development program. This will require a formally organised development with formal reviews, documentation and communication. The details are not too important, but the existence of a framework is crucial. In passing, this structured approach will eventually *reduce* the work required from the design team. The schedule to completion will be longer, *but it will be reached first time*. No extensions, no rework, no excuses.

In the second place, it could be time to re-emphasise that system development is primarily about people. It concerns the worries of the clerical workforce; it involves the care and attention of the designers; the uncertainties of the client - in fact it takes in everyone who is associated with the project. A good project is one where the people work together and respect one another. This concept is not derived from some inner spiritual need, but as a bottom-line comment that co-operation is cost-effective. Ask the Japanese.

Finally, it may be worth noting that the manager turns out to be the key to the whole operation. It is he or she who has to set out the philosophy, drive the project forward, hold it together on a daily basis and keep the motivation high. Project success is not just about technical competence – it is about the manager who has project competence, and that could be a vastly different and more important quality.

Answers

In general, the questions reflect the sort of management problems that can occur in real life. As such, most of these questions could be satisfied with a number of possible answers; while for a few of them, much like some of the problems in life itself, there are no successful responses, only damage limitation. Virtually all the answers given here provide one possible approach to these management problems. Yours could be different but just as good – or better. One way to assess your answer is to try it out on someone else – and if you can't convince them, then it probably wasn't the right response.

Note that the bulk of the replies would normally be fashioned in the form of in-depth reports, extended advice notes, or multi-part drawings. For brevity, the responses given here can only be approximate, highlighting the main headings or giving outlines only of the topics involved.

Chapter 2

1. Mending a puncture

One view of the operation is given by the data flow diagram:

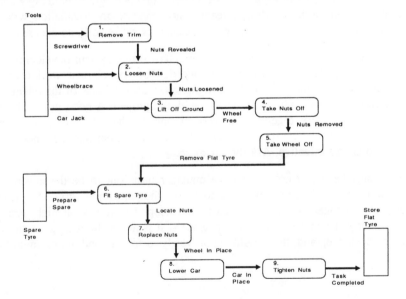

2. The tyre transaction

The (much simplified) means of handling this activity could be:

CONTEXT DIAGRAM

FIRST LEVEL DFD

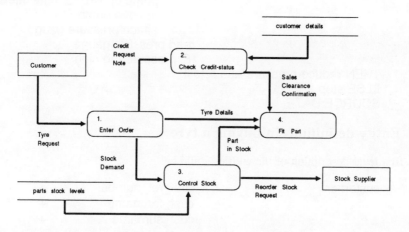

SECOND LEVEL DFD (Block 3. only)

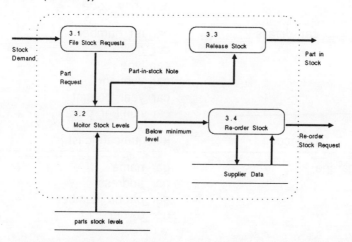

3. The mini-spec for pumping up a tyre

The model will be of the form:

PROCESS	:	pump_tyre
PROCESS NUMBER	:	4.6.2 (or whatever)
DESCRIPTION	:	Check if puncture mended

                                    IF not mended
                                    THEN send to garage
   ELSE continue
   WHILE NOT up to correct pressure
         attach pump to tyre
         pump up tyre for time interval
         remove pump
         attach pressure gauge
  read pressure gauge
  IF pressure too high

THEN reduce pressure and retest
ELSE stop
SOURCE:DATE:

4. Entity definitions in buying a tyre

A first level description of the entities could be:

customer	=	cust_ref_number	+
		cust_forename	+
		cust_surname	+
		cust_address	+
		cust_phone_number	+
		cust_car_details	+
		cust_pay_code	
car_details	=	car_ref_number	+
		car_make	+
		car_type	+
		car_version	+
		car_year_bought	+
		car_number_plate	+
pay_code	=	[cheque|card|cash]	
garage	=	gar_name	+
		gar_address	+
		gar_phone_number	+
		gar_owner	+

		gar_service_manager	+
tyre	=	tyr_stock_details	+
		tyr_supplier_name	+
		tyr_type_number	+
		tyr_dimensions	+
		tyr_description	+
		tyr_price	+
	stock_details	= sto_reference	+
		sto_location	+
		sto_number_parts	+
		sto_supp_details	
	description	= [normal|high performance]	

(Notice that 'sto_supp_details' given above (i.e. the data concerning the supplier of the given part) would itself be subject to definition in terms of its proper attributes)

5. The E-R Diagram for buying a tyre

The entities could be represented with the following diagram:

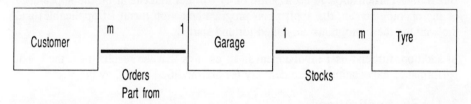

Chapter 3

1. Home Office

a) **Feasibility:** Establish needs from the user (software packages, possible hardware platforms, memory requirements, cost and time scales).

b) **Design:** Define (and document) the complete planned package of software and hardware items along with relevant costs.

c) **Coding:** Customise the system to meet the objectives of the users (e.g. set up the MS-DOS screen and keyboard interface files – the 'autoexec.bat' and 'config.sys' files; add menus; set up the printer interface of the wordprocessor).

d) **Test:** Assemble the whole package at some convenient location. First test the working of all the elements involved, and then test the overall system linked up in the intended configuration.

e) **Install:**   Inspect the proposed location and generate a site lay-out plan for installation purposes, e.g. table, chair, peripheral items (multiple mains sockets, back-up site, wiring runs, etc. Following agreement on layout and date of handover, install the system.

f) **Maintenance:** 'Fine tuning' of system (say, including certain application programs into the PATH statement of the start-up batch file); upgrading existing programs to latest versions; changing *this* graphic interface to *that* interface.

2. Prototyping

This could be an ideal project for prototyping since:

❏ Environment subject to rapid change of perceived need.

❏ Gets the inexperienced user accustomed to the equipment.

❏ Provides good interface with user for modifying the system.

❏ Fast turn round of first proposals.

The user is always involved in a) and b) covered in question 1 above.

But further participation in each phase of c) will get agreement on the appearance of the opening screen, the application program selection menu (if applicable) and the way the these programs are called for and started.

In addition, full end-user involvement in d) ensures that the results meet the client performance expectation before delivery (or are modified until they do).

3. CASE Application

At first glance, this is a trick question since, for the problem posed in question 1, any advantages of using CASE appear to be totally outweighed by the disadvantages i.e. formal rigid structure, slow development timescale, lack of user participation, high initial cost (and limited development budget), and long training curve. However, CASE could be applicable if:

❏ A CASE tool was already in use for other applications

❏ The project environment would not change over a reasonable period of time and

❏ The client specifically requested the formalism that is only obtainable from such a development tool.

4. Large organisation project

Here the general decisions related to the above two questions would tend to be reversed for the following reasons:

❏ Multiple application of the same pattern of deliverables warrants a more formal approach. (Large organisations will need more reviews, documentation and test plans).

❏ Large volume system application would minimise the cost penalties of using CASE products which will ensure full conformance to the agreed overall plan. In turn, the impact of making an error using prototyping will be costly for a high volume user.

❏ More disciplined design tools (DFDs and ERDs) will be naturally required by such a large organisation. (These tools are an important part of the CASE methodology.)

❏ Prototyping is not amenable to controlled planning due to the repeated interaction with the user until satisfaction is obtained.

Chapter 4

1.(c) Job descriptions

Descriptive Working knowledge of (*named hardware*), (*named operating systems*) and (*named application packages*) required.

Previous administrative experience ('n' years) in higher education, or research, systems support and operations.

Qualifications and/or professional membership requirements.

Qualities wanted: (*say*) problem solving flair, good man-management, self-motivation (and good sense of humour).

Number of staff working on site (x), main projects currently under development (y and z), primary functions to be fulfilled (a, b and c).

Vague Requires an experienced adaptable person to play a key managerial role, while co-ordinating support staff activities.

Responsible for initiating and implementing I.T. service policies to meet a wide range of teaching, research and administrative needs.

Will establish and implement a forward looking strategy to maintain the University in the van of I.T. usage in a cost-effective environment.

(One could go on, but by now the differences should be clear.)

2. Change of job style

Environment: Completely different type of job role (Test Manager) from that of advertising. May well be difficult to adjust to.

Function: Again, the main work is concerned with the production of standards, and this could be a far cry from the cut and thrust of media work.

Location: Working at home will be a) difficult as the children will be a disruptive influence and b) uninteresting as the social interaction with co-workers is missing.

3. Style plots

One view of how these organisations might develop is given below.

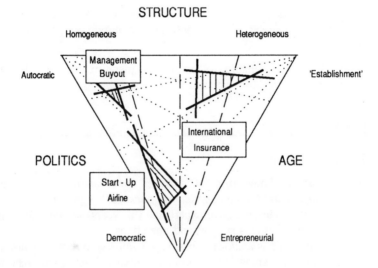

4. Collaboration assessment

Possible estimates of style are given in the diagram.

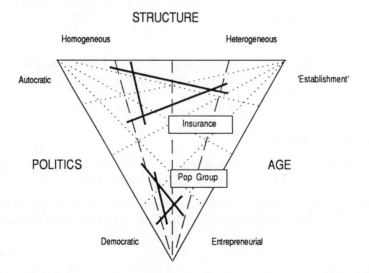

Chapter 5

1. Inexperienced staff

Ops. Manager: May not allocate enough facilities (e.g. memory)for the system requirements.

May not optimise the operating conditions for best performance of the system.

May not maintain the equipment to minimise computer 'down-time'.

May not plan for effective equipment upgrades.

Designer: May not be experienced in proposed programming language, external application programs, operating system interfaces, communication techniques and packages.

May not plan for adequate test and documentation requirements (time and staff).

May not generate a structured environment for the design process. (Will lead to maintenance problems.)

DBA: May not optimise the database system for best performance (indexing fields and clustering).

May not optimise the space requirements of the system.

May not run or maintain an effective security strategy for entry to the system.

May not carry out effective upgrades for new versions of the database management system.

Options: Short Term – take on temporary contract staff of the right calibre; borrow suitable staff from other departments; temporarily block all changes and innovations (they will probably degrade the system); allow changes but rigorously define and document them for subsequent corrective action.

Long Term – institute a program of improving the quality of management – recruit permanent staff or train up existing staff; establish a requirement for management support tools (standards, procedures, etc.) and plan activities to satisfy that requirement.

2. Lack of documentation

Environment: The various specifications will outline the hardware, application programs, operating systems (and the versions) on which the design was based.

Objectives: The documentation will identify the end goals of the design phase. Without it, there will be no formal definition of what should be expected of the maintained product.

Performance: The test specification and results will define the targetted and realised capabilities of the system. Good maintenance will need this data for comparison purposes.

Coding: The original programming code (along with the crucial explanatory remarks) will reveal how the original system was implemented.

Upgrades: The only way that the current model can be defined is by studying the original documentation and taking into account all the upgrades that have subsequently occurred. (Without the upgrade information there can only only be limited correlation between the system today and the initial specifications. And that is not enough.)

3. Security

Definition: Provide frame of reference: access and control of data only by owners of data.

Climate: Current situation in the industry. (For example, see third quote at head of chapter.)

Problem Areas: Physical access, Unlicensed copying, Fraud, Virus, Hacking, Confidentiality, Legal obligations.

Change: Advantages of improved security. (If *you* can't find compelling reasons, don't try to sell the idea onward!)

Proposals: Corporate involvement, Controlled entry, Declared policy on copying, Regular audits and checks for infections, password implementation with regular changes, and adherence to the current law.

4. Possible student system attendees

(It is assumed that the University MIS (design group) and the University administration (client management) will comprise the main development parties.)

❑ Student clearing body (in the UK: UCCA) for compatibility of data format, types and presentation.

❑ Student representatives (in the UK: National Union of Students) to address questions of privacy and data need.

❑ University clerical staff representative (end user) for conformance with existing systems, health requirements, and general involvement from the start of the project.

❑ Staff representative. The lecturers and tutors may need to use (or at least be acquainted with) the system and how it is applied.

❑ Operations. The University computer manager will need to keep in touch with the planned implementation and operational requirements of the new system.

5. Physical access

Single Room Card (or key controlled) entry door.
Access can involve signing a registry (and registering the local employee who will be responsible for the visitor.)
No visitor unaccompanied or left alone.

Distributed Only access to the site is via the main reception area. (All other doors, including fire exits, one way only and carrying alarms.)
All visitors checked for identity.
All visitors must be visiting someone who is a current member of staff. That someone will take responsibility for the visitor.
All visitors accompanied at all times.
Confidential data only available on a limited number of machines located in a secure area.
Generous use of remote video cameras linked to reception or the guardhouse.

Chapter 6

1. Interviews

a) **Analyst:** Pro – Knows systems/start-up data needs.
Con – No 'feel' for hospital or personnel.

b) **Medic:** Pro – Knows hospital staff requirements.
Con – Probably no training in systems or non-medical interviewing.

c) **Sister:** Pro – Full end-user perceptions.
Con - Intimidating to junior staff; no time for repeated evaluations.

2. Blocked project

a) **Fight on:** Talk over possible strategy with boss.
Discuss status with user group for support.
Establish reasons why review body rejected proposals, either by meeting or report.
Request new review, based on revised proposals.

b) **Give up:** Stand down design and project team(s).
Liaise with old client for workrounds or new requirements.
Assemble a 'why did we fail?' review board.
Set up planning team for new projects, tasks, and possible schedules.

c) **Do both:** Defers decision to later date.
Requires added resource (and budget).

3. Project administration personnel

Overload: The senior surgeon and the sister will probably not be available for regular meetings.

Experience: Apart from the MIS member, all other parties will probably not have any expertise in system based development projects (or their administration).

Low Priority: Head of MIS will have many more stressing problems on a day-to-day basis.

Distance: The FPC representative will be off-site, i.e. not readily contactable for instant decision making.

Delegation: Assign more junior staff who will have the time to attend meetings.

Training: Add courses on system development topics.

Decisions: Set up decision making process where, say, only two or three members needed to address daily problems.

Reporting: Ensure that regular status reports are sent 'upwards' for review and possible veto.

Proposal: Appoint a suitable staff nurse, junior surgeon, and analyst from the MIS department to participate in the group with a defined set of objectives and procedures. FPC rep. to be kept informed of all developments and will attend as and when possible.

4. Uses of Data Definition

Design: Data matching and code integrity.

User: Conformance to existing system definition and current data flow/ entity diagrams.

Debugging: Processing error messages. Checking data type compatibility and field name duplication.

Test: Programs can only test fully defined data objects.

Operations: The memory allocation for new system and stored data will relate to field types and their sizes.

Maintenance: Revealing the nature of old version. Ensuring upgrades are equivalent to it and providing list of *all* known uses of given item. Configuration management will need to maintain listings of definitions and their evolution.

Virtually all technical functions, as shown above, will find the document of value.

5. Archive need

Security: Second location reduces risk of loss of project documents and system deliverables due to accident or sabotage.

Mobility: As people relocate, there is always one guaranteed source of documents, etc. for the next generation.

Maintenance: Permanence. Independent of 'clear-ups' or item replacement by later versions, a copy of data related to the working system at the time of development (or test, or installation, etc.) will be available for the life of the system.

Decisions: A store of project related documents will retain information on the tactical and strategic reasons for the way the project evolved.

Strategy: Effective future planning will depend on analysis and results of previous activities. Learning from past projects requires that complete and reliable data about them is available for review.

Chapter 7

1. Deliverables

DELIVERABLES	PROJECT
Test Equipment	Salary Slips
Air Conditioning *	Installation *
MTBF figures	Resource Planning

* This could be in both columns

2. VDU screen radiation fears

❏ Provide the latest information on the subject to the workforce (liaise with the Union representative).

❏ Review the possible purchase of low-radiation VDUs

❏ Negotiate a policy of no more than 'x' hours a day in front of the screen. (Or one week on, one week off, etc.)

❏ For the case in question, it will probably not be possible to provide reassurance. Alternative work should be discussed (perhaps on a temporary basis).

(There is, at best, only marginal evidence that there is any measurable effect on health. However, like most people, the staff can be strongly influenced by popular views, and it is their opinions and fears that are of crucial importance here.)

3. Project status

Direct: Ask the present designers/project managers/end-users for verbal inputs on their difficulties.

Status: Request reports on the current project position from the related project managers. Further, obtain copies of the intitial schedule plans along with the progress reports of one month ago.

Documentation: Obtain copies of all related standards and specifications.

Delegation: Appoint some suitable audit authority to carry out the above activity and provide a list of recommendations within a defined timescale.

4. Revised schedules

Resource: Reduced time scales can be partly offset by increases in personnel. Added contract staff may help to minimise the problem.

Functionality: With less time, you can propose a reduction in performance or user friendliness. (In particular, the user interface module could be a good candidate for reduced effort.)

Multi-stage: Offer to provide a more basic system in the required timescale, and then upgrade over the longer term.

Quality: Reduced effort in documentation and test will give immediate results in schedule plans. Not professional, but the customer is always right.

Review: Seek to get the client to change their minds.

5. End-User at the Developer's progress meetings

Privacy: When things are going wrong, who needs strangers?

Disruption: Explaining all the different activities to untrained personnel will take extra time and reduce throughput at the meetings.

Honesty: There will be a reluctance to discuss sensitive issues (say, the client's petty-minded attitude).

Misconception: The user may jump to the wrong conclusions from what he hears and sees.

These problem areas can be largely resolved or minimised if there is a) regular communication and rapport with the user representative; and b) where privacy is needed – ask for it.

Chapter 8

1. The 'un-boring' presentation

Environment: Fresh air, low ambient noise, coffee, good lighting, good seating, query notepad (for involvement), breaks every two hours.
Preparation: Considerable
Delivery: Can be heard at the back of the room, varied cadence, plenty of silence for contrast.

Material: Major points only (supported by distributed – but not discussed – appendices).

Style: Mixed media (slides and paper); mixed data (text and colour graphics)

Participants: Invitation based on direct interest in subject.

Back-up: Support by local experts to break up the pattern.

2. Reporting structures for Newtown General

This will vary from hospital to hospital, but will be of the form:

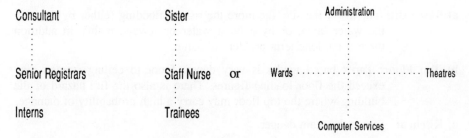

3. Requirements discussion

a) Walkthrough: Largely unstructured. Requires subject competence, self control and peer respect to work effectively. Will depend very much on the attitude of the participants. If the attendees are not well known (to you and each other), then the chances of overall disagreement or mutual antagonism could be high.

b) Presentation: Could be a useful first approach to getting the main message across (to be followed up by supplementary discussions at some later date). However, it is very possible that the participants will want to comment at each stage thus breaking up the flow of communication.

c) Meeting: Has the advantage of permitting all parties to discuss the matter in a controlled manner (i.e. through the chair). In addition, the agenda can be circulated in advance allowing to attendees to review their position on each topic.

Note: where a number of meetings occur between the same attendees over a period of time (such as in this example) then structure the meetings in line with group experience. The first assembly could be a meeting (or meetings); then, when the first prepared documents are available, presentations could be held; and final acceptance could use a walkthrough technique.

4. Some advantages of an early User Group formation

Objectives: An effective channel for a knowledgeable 'wish list' driven by experience of the current product.

Communication: A reliable route for keeping all potential users informed about the progress of the project.

Involvement: On-going links with the new product provide the interest and motivation to use it.

Familiarity: The training program and introduction of the new product will be made easier for the end-user.

Rapport: Working together with the design team makes for good co-operation and interworking at the crucial handover stage.

5. Risk to data

a) **Basement**: The lower the site, the more the risk of flooding (either by a rise in the water table, or by a burst water or sewage main). In addition there is the long term problem of damp.

b) **Top Floor**: Paper based media is very dense. Floor to ceiling storage may exceed the floor loading figures. There is also the fire hazard of the building where the top floor may carry a high probability of damage.

c) **Kitchen**: Fire is the main danger.

d) **Airport**: Two main problems. One is the possible damage due to sabotage attempts in the vicinity of the airport, or to an aircraft crashing into the building. The other is the possible degradation of data carried through internal and external communication buses and cables due to the continued presence of high radiation from radar .

Chapter 9

1. Group departure

Analysis: Why the move: Money/Treatment/Challenge?
Can it/should it be matched with a counter offer?
Any long-term recommendations back to Personnel?

Status: Collect and file all related collective and individual objectives; current progress; schedule statuses; specifications; reports; external articles, books and comments; forward plans; coding; along with all external interfaces and letters.

Training: Place existing team on standby to prepare (and possibly implement) training program for next team to take up the project.

Strategy: Modify corporate cost data and reconsider possible project options: drop; radically reformulate; or continue.

Regroup: Establish new team – reassign existing staff; or take on new staff; or take on contract staff just to see the project finished.

Reschedule: Add a generous schedule slippage to take the disruption into account.

2. Single processor damage limitation exercise

Duplication: Add a fully operational processor in parallel with the existing one.
Pro – Full security/extra capacity if required.
Con – High cost for extra equipment/extra space and services also required.

Replacement: Use alternative models such as networked PCs or Work Station islands with, say, up to 10 PC users networked to each of them.
Pro – Flexibility/reliability
Con – High cost of changeover/possible performance limitations/ possible staff training needed.

Enhancement: Upgrade existing hardware with high reliability modules.
Pro – Low cost/reduced failure probability
Con – Still sensitive to a single-point failure.

Environment: Again reduce the probability of machine failure with: secure access to machine room; fire/flood damage limitation; high grade cabling and interconnections; uninterruptible power supplies.
Pro – Good practice for relatively low cost.
Con – A mains transformer failure can still stop operations.

Insurance: Enter contracts with disaster recovery teams to bring duplicate equipment on site and on-line within x hours of a phone call.
Set up a crisis task force to handle the problem.
Pro – Good crisis management
Con – Lack of confidence until tested under fire.

3. The single entry Mac

Any Change Control Board will generally refuse such a request on the grounds of standardisation:

❏ No simple data interface or transfer capability will exist between the new machine and the rest of the hardware. Graphs produced on the new machine may not be capable of being incorporated into the presentation material produced by the PCs.

❏ No current operational experience available in the department. (Apart from the one user who requested it in the first place. When he is away for any reason, the machine is *de facto* unusable).

❏ No maintenance capability currently available without additional training. Equally, no spares or replacements currently stocked (and orders placed for just one machine are not particularly cost-effective).

❑ No application software experience available for the new machine (outside of the one user). Thus if all documents are finalised by using a PC desktop publishing program which converts the output from a number of PC word processors, how will the material from the new machine be handled?

Note: the relative merits of the different machines is not under discussion, and, in fact, is not of interest. The only question in this context is: will the added performance or convenience of making some change outweigh the disadvantage that comes as a result of that change.)

4. Buying obsolete software

Pro: Very low cost; readily available; plentiful supply of books and backup information; fully debugged; and good application experience available in the marketplace;

Con: No longer supported by supplier (or only limited support); 'bells and whistles' features not available; user not gaining experience in latest techniques; potential loss of compatibility with version of the same product at work; and interfaces with contemporary software may be inadequate or restricted.

5. The 'No Progress' project

Pointers: Progress reports. Evidence of the 'constant-time-to-complete' syndrome. If the delivery date is slipping at the rate of one week/week (or worse) over a reasonable period, it is time to put the ferrets in.

Smokescreens – Where the number of activities required to meet the same objective is growing like Topsy, take a hard look at the overall planning and review how realistic it is.

Morale – When the turnover of managers and staff in the department moves above the corporate average, look for a serious schedule impact.

Evaluation: Implement a full-scale project review. Organise an independent assessment of the original objectives, the technical problems; the competence of the workforce; and any administrative or morale problems outstanding. Identify the key issues involved.

Re-evaluate the need for the original function. Can it be supplied in a simpler form, (or removed altogether)? Will a different design tool help the development program?

Will more money help (i.e. will more people or more time be needed to solve the problem)? If so, how much and with what impact?

Will different personnel, or a different project organisation prove effective?

Chapter 10

1. Users and designers both present in Co-ordinating group

Communication: With all parties having a representative on the installation committee, they will all be kept up to date on latest status and problem areas. There can be no surprises.

Responsibility: All decisions are taken together and all parties thus share the credit or blame for the results that ensue. There can be no recriminations.

Checking: Each group can act to cover the 'blind-spot' areas of the other group.

Local Factor: Each group can bring its special priorities or problems to the committee for resolution.

2. The fire officer

a) Prevention: Smoke detector installation.
  Proper fire fighting equipment installed.
  Use only non-flammable material on site i.e. carpets, wall coverings, furnishings, and fabrics.
  Minimise sparks with non-static flooring.
  Cables ducted in non-flammable material.
  Video cameras scanning stores and remote areas.

b) Procedures: All staff trained to respond correctly to alarm.
  Fire simulations planned (and carried out).
  Fire officers assigned per section.

c) Site Rules: No smoking outside designated rest areas.
  Fire exits properly signposted for each area.
  Marshalling areas drawn up and clearly marked.

3. Corrective action on ceiling tiles

This is a no-win situation. But you still have to do something.
  Report the situation upward (senior management) and outward (all prime and secondary users).
  Prepare new budgets and schedules on the basis that the tiles will be replaced.
  Investigate possible legal or insurance redress from the suppliers.
  Propose short-term waiver from site manager with defined long term program for tile replacement.

4. MS-DOS replacement

a) Impact of change – probably catastrophic!

> Application program/Communication software usually specific to just one operating system.
> Personnel either trained or experienced in the planned O.S. Changing to a new one is a major exercise.
> Peripherals (disk drives and printers) usually interface-specific to one O.S.
> External interfaces (other system users) almost certainly compatible with planned O.S. (and almost certainly not compatible with any new one).

b) New proposals

❑ Reject the offer (probably the better decision)

> Find another supplier who can still deliver 286s in the timeframe and who can satisfy your Quality and Maintenance requirements.
> Recover any deposits made to the old supplier.

❑ Accept the enhanced package (i.e. move up to Unix)

> Start up a Unix training program for the staff
> Set up a program to replace the application software that is MS-DOS specific.
> Establish the communications requirements under Unix.
> Sort out the new interfaces needed to the peripherals and external users.

5. Increased users

a) Work impact: Purchase and installation of extra terminals, tables, chairs and telephones, etc.

> Potential preparation of workspace to accommodate the extra users (including added central heating and/or air conditioning)
> Installation of power and data cabling with the related sockets.

b) Problems: Added training and user documentation required.

> Degraded performance as more users address the same communication network and processors.
> Insufficient memory as more users take up memory space.

Chapter 11

1. Proposals for reducing pressure on DP department

HW: Take out Maintenance contract with external body.

SW: Take out Facilities Management contract with third-party organisation.

System Change Control Board: Reduce work load by rigorous control of changes (upgrades/repairs) to be carried out by DP.
Replacement – Replace 'difficult' or poorly performing systems with new bought-in packages.

Personnel: Introduce added staff from the user departments to carry out some functions related to their own systems (but, please, call it 'on-line training').
Take on contract staff for a defined short term (say three months) to clear existing work overload.

2. HW maintenance proposals

Documentation: All incoming documents stored in archive
(Applicable for troubleshooting)

Test Results: All incoming hardware tested before acceptance.
Store the test plan and results in archive.
(Troubleshooting and replacement benchmark)

Buy Policy: Standardise on single type purchases i.e. only one supplier and only type of fax or laser printer.
Simplifies repair problems.

Maintenance: Enter into a maintenance contract (internal or external organisation) which will include regular checkups.

Redundancy: Analyse the criticality of all the hardware elements – i.e. how painful is it when it stops working. Where warranted, double up on parts in house.

Insurance: Theft/Breakdown repairs/Loss of use

3. Usage of old equipment

a) Take them with thanks
Up front costs are critical in start up stage. (Maintenance is less critical – if they subsequently fail just throw them away).

b) Take them with thanks
Expertise exists in-house to maintain and upgrade the machines on a hobby or lunch-time basis.

c) Reject with regrets
They will not be compatible with existing equipment. As a result, i) with old equipment, the repair components will not be readily available and will be expensive; ii) maintenance and upkeep will be non-standard and corresponding labour costs will be uneconomic.

4. Justify a maintenance role

Current Work: Assess progress (with suitable agreement from all project managers) on all current projects over given period.
Compare with potential progress (estimated) if all team members working full time on development activity.

Past Systems: Set up 'time-card' reporting to indicate:
System being worked on
Which life-cycle function (Test/Upgrade/etc.)
Which system part (HW/SW/performance/etc.)
Status of available documents (good/poor)
Time spent

External Data: Prepare reports from magazines, books, symposia etc. to provide an information package for management to assess how other organisations tackle the problem.

Tools: Provide another information package on how current tools could be applied to assist in the maintenance function:
Structured design
Data Archive
Change control
Configuration Management

5. Reliable operation

Failure: Power: –
Add UPS (Uninterruptible Power Unit)
Diesel Power Generator (long term)
Battery operated equipment
Cabling:-
Standalone PC data system
Multi-path cabling
Printer – Standardise on peripherals, and keep main replacements.
Minis – Run redundant processors on shared or hot-stand-by basis.

SW Failure: Back-Up Hourly/daily/weekly copies made (both on and off site).
Masters – Copies of all application software available for re-installation if necessary.

System: Maintenance – set up regular check-ups
Islands – Existing PCs (say, the secretary's word processing machine) fully equipped to take over system function if so required.
Crisis – Regular simulation (say, annually) of equipment failure to check out the strategy.

Personnel: Stand by External resource agreements in place to obtain assistance on demand.

Glossary of Terms

ARCHIVE: The store for historical documents or code which have been used at some point in the development or application of the system. Such a store can be for hard copy or can be software based (i.e. ASCII or word processed files stored on magnetic media).

ATTRIBUTE: An item which is one characteristic part of an entity. Thus, the entity 'car' could have attributes such as Price, Date_of_Manufacture, Colour, and so on. The equivalent object in the logical model is the 'column_heading' associated with a particular table in a database.

AUDIT: A set of independent inspections or investigations to establish the true status of an item under review, and its conformance to some pre-determined requirements. The 'item' could be a sub-element of a system, or the entire system itself.

BALANCE: The measure of agreement that exists between two or more partners involved in following a strategic decision or philosophy related to the system design or some part of the overall project management.

CONFIGURATION MANAGEMENT: The definition, control and storage of all the various iterations and versions for any document, code segment, or subsystem used at some time during the development cycle or in operation with the end-user. In addition, the version or iteration number of all the related elements that worked or interacted with each version of the one under review will also be stored.

DATA: A fact or assembly of facts, which can be collected, processed and reported in some convenient medium. For the purposes of this book, the medium of interest is taken to be computer based equipment.

DATA FLOW: This is a line linking one source or process, to another process or sink, as appropriate. Each line is characterised by an arrow (to indicate the direction of flow) and a name which describes the nature of the data being handled.

DP: Data Processing. This is conventionally the department or group where new system designs for the organisation are implemented, installed, upgraded and maintained.

ENTITY: An object which exists in the real world, and which can be fully described by means of a group of some inherent characteristics (or attributes). It is represented in the logical model by a 'table' resident in a database.

HACKER: Usually represented as a computer operator who seeks to illegally enter someone else's computer system for reasons ranging from the frivolous to commercial crime and up to international espionage.

HCI: Acronym for Human Computer Interface, and generally used to indicate the ergonomic requirements that a computer system should satisfy in order to allow an operator to use the equipment with safety and comfort.

INFORMATION SYSTEM: An assembly of dedicated software packages, operating on specified hardware units. It will allow data relating to the organisation to be added from various sources, processed in a predetermined manner, stored and reported as outputs to accredited users of the system

INTEGRITY: Features designed into an information system that inhibit or minimise the introduction of inconsistencies during the design phase, and which act to reject the input and application of faulty data during the operational phase.

LAN: Local Area Network. A high speed data link between a number of computer related equipments, frequently based on PCs or workstations, in close physical proximity to each other i.e. operating up to a maximum distance of a few kilometers.

LIFE CYCLE: The identification of all the project related processes that have to be sequentially carried out when creating a new information system. The first process, for example, is usually defined as 'Feasibility Study'.

LOGICAL MODEL: The representation of the system at the abstract level. It will contain all the external sources and sinks of data, all the internal processes that act to change the way the data is handled, and all the data flows that connect these elements.

MAINTENANCE - HARDWARE: The upkeep of all physical computer-based equipment delivered to the end-user such that the performance will match that of the equipment when new.

MAINTENANCE - SOFTWARE: The activity that will lead to error correction, modification or enhancement of software or software modules which have already been delivered as working objects to the end-user.

METRIC: A generic term for a quantitative measurement technique. Usually applied to Quality functions such as 'program complexity'. In this case, the complexity metrics will determine that the program structure under test lies within some acceptable preset limits.

MIS: Management Information Services. The department that provides administrative and strategic support to senior management in defining the future role and application of information technology within the organisation.

PERFORMANCE: In general terms, the way the system behaves in operational use. More often applied as a quantitative measure of being compared with other like systems in a particular benchmark test.

PHYSICAL MODEL: The practical elements that will be used to implement the design based on the logical model. Thus, hardware will be identified, the relevant departments indicated, the layout of documents will be specified, and so on.

PROCESS: An element of the data model, internal to the system, where an incoming data flow is modified in form or in the structural assembly (i.e. used as a package with other data elements) such as to provide an output data flow to other processes or sinks.

PROGRAM: An assembly of coded instructions to be implemented by the computer. These instructions are initially formulated in accordance with the rules of some high level programming language (source code) which is then converted into a binary data format acceptable to the processor (object code).

PROGRAMME: A planned sequence of activities undertaken by some section or team within the organisation, with a defined set of end-results (or 'deliverables').

PROTOTYPING: A method of building up the final logical model of the system by means of repeated testing by the end-user of a practical working model of a sub-element. This continues until he or she is satisfied with the 'look and feel' of that unit, when the next sub-element will be tested.

ROLE: A collection of interfaces and some personal characteristics which are used in the maintaining of those interfaces. For example, a salesman will liaise with his internal marketing people and external clients, and will have an extensive user-based knowledge of the company's products. He will also be expected to enjoy contact with a wide circle of acquaintances.

SINK: An element, external to the system under consideration, which is structured to receive some specified data generated within the system. Examples could be an external user or external data base.

SOURCE: An element, external to the system under consideration, which is structured to generate some specified data for use within the system. An example could be an external database.

SPAGHETTI (CODING): The generic term for poorly designed or unstructured programming code sourced from an older language such as Fortran, Basic or Cobol. It will tend to contain a large number of GOTO statements (which move the program cursor to any arbitrarily defined new location) and will often lack accompanying documentation.

STRESS: Stress occurs when there are pressures applied to the individual which are beyond his or her abilities to cope with in a normal manner. It can also be present at a group level, for example, where a group of miners are collectively threatened with either a pit explosion or, in a different way, pit closure.

STRUCTURED DESIGN: A means of carrying out the design process for information systems which involves the rigourous use of defined methods and tools and the delivery of specified documents and test procedures.

STYLE: Each organisation has a characteristic and unique way of operating, in terms of strategic decision making and management approach. This way of operating, or style, is based on some set of collective beliefs and values.

TEAM: A relatively small number of people formed, by some external or internal agency, into a group with clearly defined interfaces, methods of working, and commercial purpose. Such a group will always be subject to possible modification by the initiating authority.

VIRUS: A piece of code which has been designed to attach itself to other programs resident in a non-volatile memory, say, the hard disk. At some later date it can copy itself for transfer to other systems, occupy the available memory - either at one time or progressively, and can potentially sabotage existing data.

WALKTHROUGH: An unstructured meeting, between equals, where a topic of interest is reviewed for acceptability or conformance to some existing standard or specification.

WORKROUND: A possible solution to some existing problem that was not anticipated in the initial project planning.

Bibliography

General

1. Brookes, C.H.P *et al, Information System Design,* 1982, Prentice Hall of Australia: Comprehensive coverage of the general engineering aspects.

2. Berleur, J., Clement, A., *et al, The Information Society: Evolving Landscapes,* 1990, Springer-Verlag: A set of essays reviewing the overall impact of informatio technology on individuals, society and organisations.

3. Pressman, Roger S, *Software Engineering : A Practitioner's Approach,* 1984, McGraw-Hill International: A practical orientation to software development with valuable sections on Software Reliability and Maintenance.

4. Brooks Jr, Frederick P, *The Mythical Man-month,* 1982, Addison-Wesley: Some very crisp home truths about managing software projects. Prepared in the 70s but still applicable.

Subject Related

Chapter 2: Design Tools

5. DeMarco, Tom, *Structured Analysis and System Specification,* 1979, Yourdon Press: *The* introduction to the techniques of Data Flow Diagrams. And throw in bonus points for the sheer style of writing.

Chapter 3: Development Strategies

6. Cutts, Geoff, *Structured Systems Analysis and Design Methodology (Second Edition),* 1991, Paradigm: A full treatment of one popular structured design method (SSADM) with emphasis on the mechanics of the process.

7. Boar, Bernard H, *Application Prototyping,* 1984, John Wiley and Sons: A very enthusiastic account of prototyping. Should be read – if only to establish the down side of structured design!

8. Tozer, Jane E, Prototyping as a System Development Methodology, *Information and Software Technology,* June 1987, p. 265: A practical look at the application of prototyping.

9. Luqi, , Software Evolution Through Rapid Prototyping, *Computer,* May 89, Vol. 22 No. 5 (published by IEEE): Current status of prototyping using a dedicated tool set.

10. Dennis, A.R, Burns, R.N, Gallupe, R.B, Phased Design: A Mixed Methodology for Application System Development, *Database,* Summer 1987,

(SIGBDP in ACM) Vol. 18 No. 4, p. 31: An interesting meld of the two opposed styles of structured design and prototyping.

11. Steenis, Hein van, *How to Plan, Develop and Use Information Systems,* 1990, Dorset House: A provoking view of the design phase with the emphasis placed firmly on establishing the human interfaces to the system.

12. Fisher, Alan S, *CASE Using Software Development Tools,* 1988, John Wiley and Sons: Good coverage of the scope and application of CASE tools along with an outline of some of the more popular products.

Chapter 4: Personnel

13. Baron, Robert A, *Behaviour in Organisations,* 1986, Allyn and Bacon: A comprehensive review for the non-specialist, with good spreads on individual, group, and organisational processes.

14. Lee, Robert, Lawrence, Peter, *Organisational Behaviuor: Politics at Work,* 1987: A good discussion on the interaction of people within an organisational framework. The role of the manager in this context is well covered.

15. Cooper, C.L and Marshall, J (Editors), *White Collar and Professional Stress,* 1980, John Wiley: A survey of the impact of stress to professional personnel. In particular includes a section on engineers and research workers.

16. Handy, Charles, *Gods of Management,* 1985, Pan Books: A racy description of why different 'roles' within an organisation can sometimes interact so destructively.

Chapter 5: The Systems Environment

17. Archer Osborne, R, *The Practical Guide to Local Area Networks,* 1986, McGraw-Hill: A good coverage of the current position with part I discussing the theory and part II the commercial products.

18. Green, Danny, *Business Guide to Communications Systems,* 1987, Pitman: A chatty but competent introduction to the main concepts and products that will be applied in both today's and tomorrow's telecommunications environment.

19. Security, *Byte,* June 1989 p. 254: A collection of articles which outline the current ideas on the subject. In addition there is a listing of a number of commercial products that are available in the US.

Chapter 6: The Base-Line for Design

20. Ceri, Stefano, Requirements Collection and Analysis in Information Systems Design, *Information Processing 86,* 1986, H.J. Kugler (Ed) p. 205, Elsevier Science Publishers B.V. (North Holland): An honest (and sometimes wry) account of the problems of obtaining information about the existing and proposed future system operation.

21. Gutierrez, Oscar, Experimental Techniques for Information Requirements Analysis, *Information and Management*, 1989, Vol. 16, No. 1 Jan, p. 31: A modern review of techniques to obtain accurate information transfer between the user and the analyst.

22. Windsor, Phil, *Introducing Körner*, 1986, BJHC Books: A straightforward breakdown of the main recommendations of the Körner Committee for future UK Hospital IT strategy.

23. *Rules and Regulations – Part 15 – Radio Frequency Devices*, Federal Communications Commission, 1981: The basic US requirement to be met (subpart J) for electronic noise emitted from equipment using digital systems.

Chapter 7: Project Administration

24. Keen, Jeffrey, *Managing Systems Development*, 1981, John Wiley and Sons: Good coverage of the formal aspects of running a project, e.g. budgeting and estimating.

25. Cambell, Duncan, VODS up, Doc? *Personal Computer World*, December 1989, p. 144: A refreshing debunking of some of the myths surrounding the apparent radiation danger from VDUs.

26. Wood, Lamont, The Promise of Project Management, *Byte*, November 1988, p. 180: A review of some of the PC-based Project Management application software.

Chapter 9: Change Control

27. Mankin, D, Bikson, T, Gutek, B and Statz, C, Managing Technological Change: The Process is Key, *Datamation*, September 15 1988, p. 69: A number of concrete examples of both good and bad corporate approaches to change control. And the results!

Chapter 11: Maintenance

28. Parikh, Garish, *Techniques of Program and System Maintenance*, 1988, QED Information Sciences: Sound coverage and review of published material on this subject by one of the specialists in the field.

29. Versley, Eric, Admitting Your Maintenance Problem, *Software Management Magazine*, July 1989, p. 22: A review of the current problem areas in DP organisations, and why maintenance spending should be the no. 1 priority.

30. Gudgion, Geoffrey, Management of Change, *Systems International*, May 1988, p. 83: A short, general review of Configuration Management as a tool of growing importance in system development.

Software Source List

A number of software packages have been mentioned in the main body of the text. The items were selected as being representative of their group and it is quite possible that other items would be a better choice for a particular application. However, for those who would seek further information about the quoted packages, the following information is valid at the time of writing.

Name	Function	Supplier	UK /US Phone numbers
ASA-PG	Test Generator	Verilog	081 940 2212 *(214) 241 6595*
dBase IV	Database	Ashton Tate	0628 33123 *(213)329 8000*
Excel	Spreadsheet	Microsoft	0734 391 123 *(206) 882 8080*
Excelerator	CASE tool	Intersolve	0442 232 345 *(617) 494 8200*
Harvard Proj. Manager	Project Management	Software Publishing	0344 867 100 *(415) 962 9564*
LDRA Testbed	SoftwareValidation	Program Analysers	0635 528 828 *(contact UK)*
MS-DOS	Operating System	Microsoft	0734 391 123 *(206) 882 8080*
Netware 386	Networking	Novell	0344 860 400 *(415) 506 7000*
Oracle	Database (Relational)	Oracle	0932 872 020 *(801) 429 7000*
SMS	Configuration Man.	Intasoft	0392 217 670 *(contact UK)*
SSADM	System Methodology	LBMS	071 636 4213 *(713) 623 0414*
Word	Word Processor	Microsoft	0734 391 123 *(206) 882 8080*
WordPerfect	Word Processor	WordPerfect	0932 850 500 *(801) 225 5000*
YSM	System Methodology	Yourdon	081 643 4443 *(919) 847 9508*

INDEX